Focus on Assessment

Focus on Assessment

Eunice Eunhee Jang

OXFORD
UNIVERSITY PRESS

OXFORD
UNIVERSITY PRESS

Great Clarendon Street, Oxford, OX2 6DP,
United Kingdom

Oxford University Press is a department of the University of Oxford. It furthers the University's objective of excellence in research, scholarship, and education by publishing worldwide. Oxford is a registered trade mark of Oxford University Press in the UK and in certain other countries

Photocopying

ISBN: 978 0 19 400083 3

Printed in China

This book is printed on paper from certified and well-managed sources

ACKNOWLEDGEMENTS

The authors and publisher are grateful to those who have given permission to reproduce the following extracts and adaptations of copyright material: p.6 Extract from 'Book review: Penny McKay (2006) Assessing young language learners, Cambridge University Press' by Constant Leung, *Language Testing* Vol. 26 (1) pp.145–149. Copyright © 2009 by SAGE Publications. Reproduced by permission of SAGE; pp.24–6 Extracts from 'How to Assess Language in the Social Studies Classroom' by Rod Case and Kathryn M. Obenchain, *The Social Studies* Vol. 97 (1), Taylor & Francis, 2006. Reprinted by permission of the publisher (Taylor & Francis Ltd, http://www.tandf.co.uk/journals); pp29–30, 43 Extracts from *2011 Field Research on Steps to English Proficiency* by Jang, E. E., Cummins, J., Wagner, M. Stille, S., Dunlop, M. and Starkey, J.. © Queen's Printers for Ontario, 2011. Reproduced by permission of Eunice Jang, Jim Cummins and Ontario Ministry of Education; pp.36–7 Adapted from Table 11.1 from *Program Evaluation in Language Education* by Richard Kiely and Pauline Rea-Dickins, Palgrave Macmillan, 2005.

Reproduced by permission of Palgrave Macmillan; p.40 Extract from 'Teacher practices and perspectives for developing academic language' by Jeff Zwiers, *International Journal of Applied Linguistics* Vol. 17 (1), 2007. © John Wiley and Sons. Reproduced by permission of John Wiley and Sons, Inc.; pp.41–2 Extract from 'Language, Literacy, Content, and (Pop) Culture: Challenges for ESL Students in Mainstream Courses' by Patricia A Duff, *Canadian Modern Language Review* Vol. 58 (1), 2001. Reproduced by permission of University of Toronto Press; p46 Extract from *Steps to English Proficiency (STEP): Validation Study* by Cummins, J., Jang, E. E., Wagner, M. Stille, S., Byrd Clark, J. and Trahey, M.. © Queens Printer for Ontario, 2009. Reproduced by permission of Eunice Jang, Jim Cummins and Ontario Ministry of Education; p.56 Extract from 'Sensitivity of narrative organization measures using narrative retells produced by young school-age children' by John Heilmann, Jon F. Miller and Ann Nockerts, *Language Testing* Vol. 27 (4) pp.603–626. Copyright © 2010 by SAGE Publications. Reproduced by permission of SAGE; pp.62–4 Extracts and figures from 'Elementary School ELLs' Reading Skill Profiles Using Cognitive Diagnosis Modeling: Roles of Length of Residence and Home Language Environment' by Eunice Eunhee Jang, Maggie Dunlop, Maryam Wagner, Youn-Hee Kim and Zhimei Gu, *Language Learning* Vol. 63 (3), 2013 © Language Learning Research Club, University of Michigan. Reproduced by permission of John Wiley and Sons, Inc; p.70 Extract from 'Defining Identities Through Multiliteracies: EL Teens Narrate Their Immigration Experiences as Graphic Stories' by Robin L. Danzak, *Journal of Adolescent & Adult Literacy* Vol. 55 (3), 2011 © International Reading Association. Reproduced by permission of John Wiley and Sons, Inc; p.88 Extract from 'The Receptive Vocabulary of English Foreign Language Young Learners' by Rosa María Jiménez Catalán & Melania Terrazas Gallego, *Journal of English Studies* Vol. 5 pp.173–91, 2008. Reproduced by permission of Rosa María Jiménez Catalán & Melania Terrazas Gallego; p.104 Extract from 'The effects of self-assessment among young learners of English' by Yuko Goto Butler and Jiyoon Lee, *Language Testing* Vol. 27 (1). Copyright © 2010 by SAGE Publications. Reproduced by permission of SAGE; pp.108–9 Extract from Messick, S. (1998). Consequences of Test Interpretation and Use: The Fusion of Validity and Values in Psychological Assessment. *ETS Research Report-98-48*. Educational Testing Service (ETS). Reproduced by permission; pp.115–16 Extract from 'Portfolios, Power, and Ethics' by Brian Lynch and Peter Shaw, *TESOL Quarterly* Vol. 39 (2), 2005. © TESOL International Association. Reproduced by permission of John Wiley and Sons, Inc.; pp.122–3 Extracts from 'Interaction in group oral assessment: A case study of higher- and lower-scoring students' by Zhengdong Gan, *Language Testing* Vol. 27 (4) pp.585–602. Copright © 2010 by SAGE Publications. Reproduced by permission of SAGE; p.124 Extract from 'The effects of group members' personalities on a test taker's L2 group oral discussion test scores' by Gary J. Ockey, *Language Testing* Vol. 26 (2) pp.161–86. Copyright © 2009 by SAGE Publications. Reproduced by permission of SAGE; pp.138–9 Extracts from 'The contradictory culture of teacher-based assessment: ESL teacher assessment practices in Australian and Hong Kong secondary schools' by Chris Davison, *Language Testing* Vol. 21 (3) pp.305–334. Copyright © 2004 by SAGE Publications. Reproduced by permission; pp.141–2 Extract from 'Why the 'Monkeys Passage' bombed: tests, genres and teaching' by Norton, B. & Stein, P., *Harvard Educational Review* Vol. 65 (1) pp.50–65. Copyright © President and Fellows of Harvard College. Excerpted with permission; p.144 Extract from 'Did we take the same test? Differing accounts of the Ontario Secondary School Literacy Test by first and second language test-takers' by Janna Fox and Liying Cheng, *Assessment in Education: Principles, Policy & Practice* Vol. 14 (1), Taylor & Francis, 2007. Reprinted by permission of the publisher (Taylor & Francis Ltd, http://www.tandf.co.uk/journals); p.148 Extract from Chapter 6 'Electronic feedback and second language writing' by Mark Warschauer and Paige D. Ware of *Feedback and Second Language Writing: Contexts and Issues* by K. Hyland and F. Hyland. © Cambridge University Press 2006. Reproduced by permission; pp.170–1 CEFR self-assessment grid from *A Common European Framework of Reference for Languages: Learning, Teaching, Assessment* by Council of Europe. © Council of Europe. Reproduced by permission; p.95 Extract from 'International Language Test Taking Among Young Learners: A Hong Kong Case Study' by Alice Chik and Sharon Besser, *Language Assessment Quarterly* Vol. 8 (1), Taylor & Francis, 2011. Reprinted by permission of the publisher (Taylor & Francis Ltd, http://www.tandf.co.uk/journals).

Sources: *Response To Student Writing: Implications for Second Language Students* by Dana R. Ferris (2003).

Contents

Contents

Acknowledgments

I am grateful to many people without whom this book would not have been possible. Heartfelt thanks to my daughter Jayun, my biggest fan and harshest critic, who had to share two years of her mother's attention with this book. I would also like to thank Maryam Wagner, who was there for every step of the journey. I want to thank my series editors, Nina Spada and Patsy Lightbown for inviting me to contribute to this OUP series for teacher development. I appreciate their timely feedback and encouragement throughout the book project. Finally, I thank the many teachers and students who shared their experiences, beliefs, and visions about assessments by participating in various research activities presented in this book.

Series Editors' Preface

The Oxford Key Concepts for the Language Classroom series is designed to provide accessible information about research on topics that are important to second language teachers. Each volume focuses on a particular area of second/foreign-language learning and teaching, covering both background research and classroom-based studies. The emphasis is on how knowing about this research can guide teachers in their instructional planning, pedagogical activities, and assessment of learners' progress.

The idea for the series was inspired by the book *How Languages are Learned*. Many colleagues have told us that they appreciate the way that book can be used either as part of a university teacher education program or in a professional development course for experienced teachers. They have commented on the value of publications that show teachers and future teachers how knowing about research on language learning and teaching can help them think about their own teaching principles and practices.

This series is oriented to the educational needs and abilities of school-aged children (5–18 years old) with distinct chapters focusing on research that is specific to primary- and secondary-level learners. The volumes are written for second language teachers, whether their students are minority language speakers learning the majority language or students learning a foreign language in a classroom far from the communities where the language is spoken. Some of the volumes will be useful to 'mainstream' teachers who have second language learners among their students, but have limited training in second/foreign language teaching. Some of the volumes will also be primarily for teachers of English, whereas others will be of interest to teachers of other languages as well.

The series includes volumes on topics that are key for second language teachers of school-age children and each volume is written by authors whose research and teaching experience have focused on learners and teachers in this age group. While much has been written about some of these topics, most publications are either 'how to' methodology texts with no explicit link to research, or academic works that are designed for researchers and postgraduate students who require a thorough scholarly treatment of the research, rather than an overview and interpretation for classroom practice. Instructors in programs for teachers often find that the methodology texts lack the academic background appropriate for a university course and that the scholarly works are too long, too difficult, or not sufficiently classroom oriented for the needs of teachers and future teachers. The volumes in this series are intended to bridge that gap.

The books are enriched by the inclusion of *Spotlight Studies* that represent important research and *Classroom Snapshots* that provide concrete examples of teaching/learning events in the second language classroom. In addition, through a variety of activities, readers will be able to integrate this information with their own experiences of learning and teaching.

Introduction

This book centers on teachers' *use* of language assessment to guide students' language proficiency development and academic achievement. It takes a use-focused approach to assessment in order to engage teachers in discussions about the positive benefits of assessment for guiding teaching and learning; the conflicting roles of teachers in the use of assessments that serve different purposes; and the practical challenges teachers experience when designing, using, and evaluating specific assessments.

Through these discussions, I hope that the book will help teachers to develop the competence and confidence required to make informed judgments about their assessment practices and to justify their decision-making processes. When we take this use-focused approach, teachers and students become 'major league players' in assessment, and their experience with and actual use of assessment in a particular context become key evidence for judging the quality of assessment.

Assessment practices are more important than ever in today's Kindergarten to Grade 12 (K–12) classrooms given the unprecedented diversity of students, in terms of their linguistic, socio-economic, and cultural backgrounds. For these students, the instructional language is neither what they hear and speak at home nor the language with which they feel most competent and comfortable. These school-aged learners must catch up to 'a moving target' (Coelho, 2003). They are expected to develop social and **academic language proficiency** to meet language demands in schoolwork, while simultaneously learning academic content. Assessing their language learning needs and providing the necessary support have become not just second or foreign language teachers', but every teacher's responsibility. Most teachers and language educators have some knowledge and experience with educating language learners in classrooms. However, their assessment competence is relatively less developed partly because little attention is given to assessment issues and approaches concerning language learners in professional development for pre- and in-service teachers.

In some contexts, students learn a foreign language as part of curricular requirements or because they seek admission to higher education programs. Taken together, these students are referred to as language learners in this book. Because education systems vary widely across countries, I will consider children whose age ranges from 6–9 as young language learners. Early adolescent language learners will refer to students whose age ranges from 10–13, while adolescent language learners will refer to secondary school students aged 14–18 (14–17 in the UK and certain other countries).

This book has five chapters. Chapter 1 lays the groundwork for the readers by introducing language learners, identifying multiple roles that teachers play in assessments that serve various purposes, and introducing some key concepts of assessment. Subsequently, we look into the use of assessment in the form of feedback in classrooms and survey other uses of assessments in large-scale settings around the world.

Chapter 2 discusses the key features of academic language proficiency that school-aged students are expected to develop and examines research evidence to explore assessments of their language development in content-based instruction.

In Chapter 3, we will take into account some of the principles for assessing young language learners and discuss various assessment approaches and issues associated with them according to the purpose and degree of standardization of assessment.

In Chapter 4, we will continue to discuss assessment principles for adolescent language learners based on an ecological assessment systems framework.

Chapter 5 invites you to reflect on your views about the key issues discussed in the book and provides a summary of the main points raised in the earlier chapters.

Each chapter engages the reader through the use of Classroom Snapshots, Activities, and Spotlight Studies. Classroom Snapshots take you through authentic classroom situations and illustrate interactions between teachers and students or between students and their peers, as they engage in learning and assessment activities. Each chapter also contains a number of Activities to facilitate your inquiry-based reflection and discussion about specific issues arising from assessing language learners. Spotlight Studies will further inform your critical reflection and discussion, offering not only empirical evidence which will help answer questions but also an introduction to the different inquiry approaches taken, to seek evidence in particular assessment contexts.

The book concludes with Suggestions for Further Reading, along with brief annotations. This annotated list will introduce you to some excellent sources that will help continue your professional development and learning about language assessment. A Glossary at the end of the book provides brief definitions of some terms with which some readers may be unfamiliar. The terms included in the Glossary will appear in bold print the first time they are used in the text.

Throughout the book, the terms 'test' and 'assessment' are used interchangeably. In some cases, I use the term 'assessment' to refer to general assessment practice, not to a specific method. Assessment tasks refer to activities used in **performance assessments**. The test item refers to an individual question used for a **selected-response test**. The contexts of assessment which I consider in this book are ones in which English is learned as well as other languages. Students learning any additional language will be referred to as 'language learners.' Students learning English as a foreign (EFL) or a second language (ESL) will be referred to as English language learners (ELLs).

1
Uses of Language Assessment

Preview

Language assessment is a purposeful activity that gathers information about students' language development. It is a means to a wide range of educational ends and is fundamental to all educational pursuits. It is a practice that involves multiple people in specific socio-cultural contexts. Assessment is not a tool whose value is judged technically nor is it a panacea that can solve all educational and social problems. It is an activity whose primary purpose is pedagogical, that is, to help teachers plan instruction and guide student learning. If assessment results are not used to inform instruction and improve student learning, they are of little use. This disconnect between assessment and instruction happens in some contexts where educational reforms are driven by mass testing and where testing becomes the end in itself. If assessment is purposefully used, it has effects on people and their surroundings, even though not all effects will be positive, intended, or clear.

In this book, I take a use-focused approach to assessment based on my belief that the quality of assessment should be evaluated in terms of its usefulness for students and teachers. Assessment is about and for students and teachers, the main **stakeholders** in the assessment activities that are the focus of this book. They should not be viewed as passive recipients of test information, but key players in assessment development and evaluation. Let us first examine some of the characteristics of learners and teachers in today's classrooms before delving into the various uses of assessment in and outside of classrooms.

Language Learners in Today's Classrooms

Today's classrooms reflect shifts in demographics, culture, and languages as a result of unprecedented rates of migration. Given the increasing linguistic and cultural diversity of our students, many of whom are completing their education in a second or third language, assessing **language proficiency** has become a pedagogical necessity for all teachers. Labels such as ESL and EFL have become too simplistic to represent the diversity of language learners' backgrounds and learning opportunities. In many parts of the world, children begin to learn additional languages at increasingly earlier ages because of the perceived benefits of early language learning. As Leung (2009) sees it:

> ... increasing numbers of young people in primary or elementary schools around the world are learning a second/additional language (L2 from now on) for a variety of economic, educational, political, and social reasons. In a large number of countries young people are expected to learn an L2 because a non-native (often ex-colonial) language such as English or French has been adopted as an official language; Singapore and India are obvious examples. For countries where international trade is a vital economic activity, foreign language learning is regarded as part of a basic curriculum. In addition there are countless international schools located in different parts of the world which provide second/foreign language medium education. This widespread learning and use of L2 is accompanied by an increasing need to better understand and define what counts as L2 proficiency for young language learners and how to assess it in diverse circumstances. (p. 145)

In Canada, the USA, and many other developed countries, a large proportion of students in urban schools are new immigrants and children living in multi-generation immigrant families. Some may be raised in families or communities in which languages other than English are primarily spoken. These students' prior exposure to L2 or L3 varies greatly, and consequently they may show distinctly different language profiles. Others may have had limited or inconsistent access to schooling and may have migrated following a crisis in their home country. Some students may have experienced traumatic difficulty and may not have support from parents at home. Still others may be international or visa students who have paid fees to attend schools; these students often live away from their parents. Language learners also include Aboriginal students who speak indigenous languages at home. They may mix languages extensively with seemingly fluent conversational language proficiency, but often enter school with limited literacy proficiency in the school's language of instruction.

Regardless of whether they are domestic or foreign, a large number of students in Kindergarten to Grade 12 schools are learning an additional language or multiple languages. Various terms are used to refer to these language learners, such as limited English proficiency (LEP), English as an additional language (EAL), or English language learner (ELL). In some jurisdictions, the term English literacy development (ELD) is used to refer to those who have limited or interrupted schooling, resulting in underdeveloped literacy skills in their **first language** (L1).

Multiple Roles Teachers Play in Language Assessment

Effective teachers do not view assessment as an add-on to their teaching responsibilities, but as an integral component of their teaching. Assessment provides teachers with the information they need in order to understand individual students' unique qualities and areas that need improvement. They use assessment information to design and refine instructional activities and strengthen their professional bases to communicate about their students with parents and colleagues in and outside of school. They understand that assessment is not a 'one size fits all' approach. As Clarke (1998) says, assessment 'manifests itself as a wealth of different strategies and products' (p. 5). Of course, competent teachers know how to use a range of assessment methods including tests, **portfolios**, and observations of students' performance on language tasks.

Teachers' involvement in assessment is not limited to their classrooms. Increasingly, teachers are called upon to participate in school-wide 'reculturing' initiatives (aimed at changing school culture) through the introduction of new assessment approaches, such as **assessment *for* learning** and **assessment *as* learning** (Assessment Reform Group, 2002; Black & Wiliam, 1998; Hargreaves, 1997). Such school 'reculturing' initiatives make demands on teachers to draw upon their professional knowledge to make curricular and programming decisions in their students' interest.

On the other hand, when school reforms are based mainly on students' academic outcomes (which are measured by mass testing), teachers in urban schools with a high number of language learners are challenged by their achievement gaps. Such mass testing-driven educational reform policies appear to overlook the fact that it takes time for language learners to develop the language proficiency necessary for mastering curriculum content. Inevitably, teachers often find themselves playing contradictory roles, one in using assessment *for* learning and the other in dealing with demands to evaluate learning outcomes summatively (Bailey, 1998; Rea-Dickens, 2004). These conflicting roles and purposes of assessment place a great burden on teachers. Classroom Snapshot 1.1 illustrates the challenge faced by an ESL teacher.

Classroom Snapshot 1.1

Consider the following questions while reading the Classroom Snapshot:

- What do you think of the assessment policy?
- What is Ms Smith's dilemma?
- What is at stake in this assessment practice?
- If you were Ms Smith in this classroom, what would you do?

The following observation is based on classroom research that took place in 2003.

I met Issam (pseudonym), a Grade 3 Palestinian boy in an ESL program, at a multicultural local school in the USA. Approximately 26 percent of the students at this school were ELLs, 43 percent were African American, and 30 percent were White American. The school was known to be an exemplary multicultural school in which parent volunteers offered students first-language instruction in over 20 different languages. Since the implementation of the No Child Left Behind (NCLB) Act of 2001, the school has had to participate in two state-mandated tests: ISAT (International Student Admissions Test) for all third graders and IMAGE (Illinois Measure of Annual Growth in English) for eligible ELLs. Both tests were scheduled in the first week of April. Issam looked lost during test preparation. Clearly he could not follow his teacher's instructions. He could not read questions on the practice test. He looked sad and frustrated. He often looked around to see what other kids were doing, but mostly stared at the test paper on the desk.

I interviewed his teacher, Ms Mary Smith (pseudonym) after class.

Eunice: What about the boy, Mary? I mean, during the class today, he couldn't read the questions. Does he have to take the test even though he can't read English?

Ms Smith: Well, it's Issam. He's originally from Palestine. He was in fact here in kindergarten and went back to his home country. But he wasn't in school because soldiers wouldn't allow teachers to teach kids. So he came back this year, and he is technically eligible to take the test (based on the testing policy that considers only the duration of residence). I feel sorry for him. We will have to make special accommodations, like he will get additional time.

Eunice: Can't we exempt him from the test?

Ms Smith: We can't. He has to take it because he has been here more than six months. I heard some teachers saying that some kids were in tears during test preparation classes. It's just so hard. A lot of these kids take education so seriously. When they can't do well, they take it personally. I tell them, it's OK and it doesn't have anything to do with you.

(Jang, 2004) ■

Despite Ms Smith's extensive teaching experience, the new testing policy made her feel as though she was unable to act as an advocate for her own students. Many teachers can relate to her in that they fear they have little control over external government-mandated tests. Situations like this one can be even more challenging for new, less experienced teachers.

Classroom Snapshot 1.1 illustrates the tensions arising from assessments that are being used for multiple conflicting purposes. For example, teachers and school administrators are expected to employ externally mandated tests with their students and use test data to monitor and evaluate the effectiveness of language programs, and to determine how to allocate resources (O'Malley & Valdez Pierce, 1996). On the other hand, teachers use classroom-based **formative assessment** to offer assistance and provide multiple opportunities for students to demonstrate their proficiency. This role as a facilitator is at odds with a teacher's role as a test administrator in external testing (Haertel, 1999; Rea-Dickens, 2004). When teachers experience such tension along with changes in national assessment policies, they feel confused and resistant to changing their practice, even if they receive substantial training (Cheng, Watanabe, & Curtis, 2004).

Unfortunately, many teachers enter the teaching profession without sufficient formal training in student assessment (Stiggins, 1995). Furthermore, there are not many high-quality language assessment tools available for classroom use. Nor are there clear guidelines for judging the 'goodness' or appropriateness of assessments for the students they teach. In-service professional development in assessment is not often accessible to all teachers. As a result, some teachers repeat the same testing methods they experienced as learners many years previously. Teachers also have to deal with culturally different experiences and expectations of assessment that language learners bring with them to the classroom.

Activity 1.1 includes some statements that describe general perceptions about language assessment that pre- and in-service teachers may have. As you read further in this book, I encourage you to return to these statements and consider whether your initial opinions have changed. You can also use the questionnaire to engage your students and colleagues in discussions about assessment in your classroom and school.

Activity 1.1

Read each statement and indicate your opinion by putting a check mark/tick in one of the columns. How many statements do you strongly disagree or agree with? How many do you feel uncertain or unfamiliar with? We will revisit these statements in Chapter 5.

SD = Strongly Disagree; D = Disagree; A = Agree; SA = Strongly Agree; UN = Uncertain/Unfamiliar

Statement	Your response				
1 Students develop language skills at a fairly even rate among oral, reading, and writing skills.	SD	D	A	SA	UN
2 Students' oral fluency is a good indicator of their academic language proficiency.					
3 Students are not capable of assessing their own ability.					
4 Teachers' assessments are too subjective.					
5 Students should know how their marks compare with their peers'.					
6 Frequent testing is an effective way to motivate students to study harder.					
7 Students care only about marks. They rarely pay attention to feedback.					
8 Formative and summative assessments are different types of tests, so they should not be mixed.					
9 Standards-based assessment allows teachers to assess students' academic achievement relative to curricular goals.					
10 Introducing a new test is an effective way to leverage curriculum change.					
11 Most teachers know how to assess students' language proficiency in other subject-matter classes.					
12 Providing accommodations for some students is unfair to other students.					
13 Teachers should treat all students equally by using the same assessment methods for everyone.					
14 Reliability in assessment is the most important factor for high-quality language assessment.					
15 A test is valid as long as it measures what it was intended to measure.					

Purposes of Language Assessment

Assessment serves various educational purposes in schools and society at large. Its use has consequences, favorable or unfavorable, like a double-edged sword. Use takes place in real contexts involving multiple people, and it is influenced by contextual factors.

Thus, original purposes intended by assessment makers should not be the absolute rationale for justifying all actual uses. Before we further explore this relationship between the purpose and use of assessment, let us reflect on assessment practices that take place in your classroom and school in Activity 1.2.

Activity 1.2

Pick three frequently used assessments that you administer in your classrooms and school. Use the table below to categorize them according to a few key features. In some cases, you may find multiple purposes associated with a single assessment. Some purposes will be obvious or overt while others may be covert or secondary.

	Assessment 1	Assessment 2	Assessment 3
1 What is the context of the assessment?			
2 Who are you assessing? What's their linguistic and cultural background?			
3 What is the primary (and secondary, if any) purpose of the assessment?			
4 Do your students know the assessment's purpose?			
5 How do you use the assessment?			
6 Is its actual use congruent with the intended purpose?			
7 How do you communicate the assessment results and with whom?			
8 Are you aware of any (potential) conflict arising from the assessment?			

Photocopiable © Oxford University Press

Among the assessments you identified above, do you have any example of assessments used for formative and/or summative purposes? Scriven (1967) conceptualized formative and **summative assessment** in his work in the field of program evaluation, which Bloom (1969) then applied to education. In general, formative assessment is used to provide feedback at various stages of the learning process while summative assessment is used to evaluate what the learner has achieved at a particular instructional time (typically at the end of the school year). Many language teachers use a variety of different tasks for a formative purpose to provide ongoing support for student learning (Black & Wiliam, 1998). Teachers are also expected to provide summative judgments about what students have attained over a specific instructional term.

You may notice that despite the popularity of the terms 'formative' and 'summative' assessments, they are not clearly distinguishable in classroom contexts. Summative assessment at the end of an instructional term may actually be used for determining learning goals for the next term and for planning instruction to help students to meet those goals. Therefore, distinguishing formative from summative assessment based on the instructional cycle and frequency of assessment is not useful for many teachers (Bennett, 2011). Nonetheless, any assessment in classroom contexts should provide information about what learners can and cannot do and inform educators about how to support their future learning.

Do you have any examples of assessments used for placing students into language programs or courses? Language placement tests are fairly widely used in higher education as a tool to assist educators in placing language learners into courses appropriate for their current proficiency levels. Placement tests are also popular in private language programs in EFL contexts. Because the purpose of placement tests is to determine which program or course is appropriate for students, it is imperative that the tests be well aligned with program goals and course materials.

Some institutions and programs prefer **standardized** language placement tests to locally developed placement measures. Such tests assess students' **general language proficiency** and may not be directly aligned with language courses. General language proficiency tests are mainly intended to assess students' overall language ability (based on a unitary view of language ability, which will be discussed in detail in Chapter 2). Such tests are taken by students who seek admission either to domestic educational programs (for example, foreign language high schools in South Korea) or to study abroad. On the other hand, there are many placement tests developed specifically for local programs. In using tests for placement purposes, teachers are acknowledging the importance of gathering diagnostic information about students' language learning needs to guide subsequent instructional activities. In such instances, teachers may not provide numerical marks to students. Rather, they may arrange conferences with them to discuss their learning needs.

Teachers may be more familiar with achievement tests than with proficiency tests. Achievement tests are more directly related to a specific learning context where achievement goals are established (for example, how much learners have achieved within a specific curriculum). For example, language learners' academic achievement has become a concern for educators and policy makers. As a result, there is pressure to use **standards-based assessments** to track the academic progress of all students, regardless of their backgrounds, with reference to common benchmarks of achievement. We will review such standards-based assessment practices in more detail later in this chapter.

Are any of the assessments you looked at in Activity 1.2 used to provide diagnostic information about language knowledge and skills that students have or have not mastered? The purpose of diagnostic assessment in classrooms should not be to simply determine deficiencies in students' language ability, but to gather information about both the strengths and areas needing improvement in specific components of language ability, in order to tailor instruction to their learning needs while capitalizing on their strengths. Diagnostic information from assessment is not only informative to teachers, but can also be used to help students modify their learning strategies. Some teachers avoid the term 'diagnosis' as it is charged with a medical connotation. Nevertheless, teachers need **diagnostic assessment competence** (the ability to diagnose individual students' strengths and areas needing improvement) (Edelenbos & Kubanek-German, 2004), and then plan for remedial actions for students. This competence is key to promoting the professionalization of teaching. Teachers' diagnostic assessment competence requires that teachers possess a deep understanding of pathways to language development, and this is the focus of Chapter 2.

Any language test has the potential for providing diagnostic information either at the macro or micro level (Bachman, 1990), and many existing proficiency and achievement tests have been used for this purpose. However there has not been much attention given to diagnostic assessment in the fields of language testing and assessment (Alderson, Clapham, & Wall, 1995). Diagnostic language assessment requires a profound understanding of pathways to language development. As an example of diagnostic assessment, **dynamic assessment** (Lantolf & Poehner, 2004) aims to address the gap between students' current ability and their future development. Teacher mediation is an integral component of dynamic assessment; through oral interactions, teachers can help students to develop proximal abilities (see Vygotsky, 1986).

Did you identify a language-dominance test as one of your examples while doing Activity 1.2? A language-dominance test is used to assess and compare bilingual children's language proficiency in both of their languages to determine whether they are equally proficient or whether proficiency in one of the languages is greater than in the other. The profile of language dominance and proficiency designed by Ortiz & García (1989) can be a useful way to gather information about children's language background.

Before delving into various uses of assessment and their effects, I would like to introduce some key concepts underlying language assessment practices which will guide us throughout the book. Note that these concepts will reappear throughout the book and we will have the opportunity to learn more about them in specific assessment contexts.

Preparing the Way for Our Journey to Language Assessment

We often say and hear, 'this is a valid test,' 'that test is not reliable,' or 'the test was so unfair!' These statements reflect the common misconception that test **validity**, **reliability**, and **fairness** are test properties. In fact, a test used to be viewed as valid for anything as long as the test **correlates** with it (Guilford, 1946). Later on, a test was viewed as valid if it measured what it is supposed to measure (as determined by the test maker). While the former definition reflects the view of validity as a test property, the latter highlights the test's congruence with theories used in its development.

- Does the test measure what it is intended to measure? (construct validity)
- How well does the test content represent the target knowledge that students learn in classrooms? (**content validity**)
- Does the test appear to measure what it is supposed to measure? (**face validity**)
- How well do the test scores correlate with well-established criterion tests that measure the same or similar **constructs**? (**criterion validity**)
- How well do the test scores predict students' future success? (**predictive validity**)

- What are the positive and negative consequences of the test use? (**consequential validity**)
- Are students' responses internally consistent? (**reliability**)
- How much variation in student responses is due to measurement error? (**reliability**)
- Do test items include any potential bias against certain subgroups? (**test bias**)
- How fairly is the test used for all students regardless of their background? (**fairness**)

These questions exemplify how the concept of validity has been expanded to embrace the social, political, and ethical functions of testing (Cronbach, 1988). Although understanding each aspect of validity (face, criterion, content, construct validity) is useful, it is best to understand validity holistically because its core idea is rather simple: it addresses the extent to which how we *interpret* and *use* test information is justifiable. Likewise, fairness addresses how the test results are used. Reliability is concerned with how consistently students perform on the test and how consistently their performance is judged.

Another common feature of these key concepts is that they are relative terms. They should be judged in terms of their degrees, and all or nothing evaluations are inappropriate because a test functions differently across different contexts in which it is used. Thus, it is misleading to state: 'This test is not valid' without qualifying why the test was used, for what purpose, and in what particular context it was used. The same test, well suited for a certain group of learners, may produce inconsistent test results when used with a different group of learners. When the test is misused for an unexpected or unintended purpose, its validity and fairness become questionable.

As I stated at the beginning of this chapter, we need to evaluate assessment practices based on the extent to which they are used appropriately, meaningfully, and ethically in a specific context (Bachman & Palmer, 2010). Researchers are increasingly acknowledging the need for a greater emphasis on a use-focused approach to assessment. For example, Fulcher & Davidson (2010) argue that 'tests have outcomes and impact on the world and it should be these test effects that drive the final decisions about crafting particular items and tasks' (p. 50). This use-focused assessment perspective helps us understand that the quality of an assessment instrument is insufficient for understanding the effect of its use, that is, how useful it is for achieving its intended goals and having a positive influence on both students and teachers. Bachman (2005) reminds us that:

> assessment qualities such as validity, usefulness, and fairness do not exist in the abstract; they pertain to specific assessments, indeed, to the way we interpret and use the test performance of each individual or group of test takers. Similarly, in any assessment, the intended uses and potential consequences of this use are essentially specific, local concerns that need to be addressed regarding the stakeholders in that specific assessment—the various individuals who will be affected in one way or another by the assessment and by the way we use it. We need to be able to justify the interpretations and uses we make of any assessment so that we can be accountable to the stakeholders. (p. 31)

No doubt you have come across the terms 'validity' 'reliability', 'fairness' in the past and have some understanding of what they mean. We are going to build upon this knowledge and by the end of this chapter, you will know more about basic principles of assessment for language learners and how they can be used to evaluate the students you are teaching. As you read the chapter and learn about these issues think about how these topics are relevant to you in your teaching context.

Using Assessment in Classrooms

In classrooms, teachers lead or participate in various assessment activities (both teacher-made and externally mandated). Through such activities, they constantly make interpretations about their students' level of achievement and language proficiency and use information from assessment to guide teaching and learning. Knowing how to use assessment results is as important as knowing how to interpret those results in evaluating the quality of assessment (Bachman & Palmer, 2010; Bennett, 2011). There is an increasing need for careful examination of how assessment results are used to improve teaching and learning (Nichols, Meyer, & Burling, 2009). This classroom use of assessment emphasizes its formative use, enabling teachers to improve their teaching and support students' language learning process.

Teachers increasingly recognize an on-going feedback loop as key to integrating assessment with teaching. Teachers can use this feedback loop to signal a gap in performance between students' current and desired levels of proficiency. Helping students identify this gap can motivate them to make more focused efforts to reaching their learning goals (Hattie & Timperley,

2007). As a result, students understand where they are in relation to their learning goals and are motivated to stay focused on tasks.

Teachers can employ different strategies for providing feedback to students. For example, when low-ability learners are engaged with cognitively complex language tasks, they may become overwhelmed. In such cases, teachers should use **scaffolding** strategies to provide mediated feedback to these learners. For example, teachers' scaffolding strategies can include breaking down a complex task into multiple steps, questioning learners to reorient their attention when they face difficulty, or demonstrating how to accomplish a task by modeling problem-solving procedures. Feedback from assessment encourages teachers and students to think of questions such as:

- What are my goals?
- How have I made progress toward my goals?
- What action should I take to make better progress? (Hattie & Timperley, 2007)

These questions can guide the instructional and learning processes by linking where learners are, where they are going, and how they can get there. Teachers can incorporate these questions into various types of feedback in order to facilitate students' critical reflections on own learning. Read Classroom Snapshot 1.2, in which a teacher gives students oral feedback during instruction or through student–teacher conferences.

Classroom Snapshot 1.2

The following transcript comes from a Grade 4 ESL classroom in the USA. Students in the class work in groups. Ms Deborah, an ESL teacher, sits with a group of students, showing the covers of three different versions of the book, *Frankenstein*. As you read the transcript, keep the following questions in mind:

- Do you think that the teacher assesses her students' comprehension in this interaction?
- What do you think of her questions?
- How does she respond to her students' answers?

Ms Deborah: Why doesn't he want his family to know what he is doing?

[The teacher waits.]

Ms Deborah: Why does he want to keep it secret?
Student: Because they will say, don't do it.
Student: Because he is going to be grounded.
Ms Deborah: He is a grown man. He's not going to get grounded. He's not a student. Why? Think of two reasons why he doesn't want his family to know it.

Student: Because this is nasty.

Ms Deborah: Is he proud of it?

Students: No. He doesn't want them to worry about this. Everyone will want to know it.

Ms Deborah: And what else?

[The teacher waits.]

Student: He wants to surprise the world.

Ms Deborah: Right, surprise the world. He does it in seclusion. What does that mean?

[pause]

Ms Deborah: Why do you think that he lives by himself? Have you ever heard of secluded?

[pause]

Student: Excluded.

Ms Deborah: All right, 'secluded' means live by myself away from others. He did it in a place where nobody would know what's going on.

(Jang, 2004) ▪

In this snapshot, the teacher uses questioning as a main instructional and assessment method. Teacher questioning is an essential part of instructional and assessment practice (Black, Harrison, Lee, Marshall, & Wiliam, 2003). Teacher questioning facilitates effective classroom discussions and is used to gather evidence of learning; it can also serve as an instructional cue to get students engaged in learning. When it is used in language learning classrooms, questioning helps students understand reading purposes, develop thinking skills, and monitor their own comprehension processes (Meltzer & Hamann, 2005).

The transcript in Classroom Snapshot 1.2 shows two key issues that are critical in evaluating the quality of teacher questioning: question type and wait time. Ms Deborah avoids simple, closed questions that assess students' recall because they fail to elicit students' deep thinking. Such questions raise the level of anxiety among students because they tend to assess factual knowledge where there are correct or incorrect answers. As a result, the teachers' feedback tends to be evaluative rather than descriptive. It is not an easy task for teachers to correct errors when a child puts his or her hand up enthusiastically and gives incorrect answers repeatedly. But Ms Deborah asks questions that assess students' critical reasoning, creativity, and application; she does not comment on students' responses using evaluative feedback such as 'good,' or 'excellent.' Instead, she engages her students through questioning that can potentially facilitate their deep, critical reasoning skills. She makes sure to assess their basic comprehension of the text through homework.

The second important aspect to note about Ms Deborah's instruction is her use of wait time (Black et al., 2003; Rowe, 1974). Wait time is the pause between questioning and student response. Rowe reported that teachers' average wait time was only 0.9 seconds, and that a wait time of less than one second hindered students' participation because it tended to elicit short, recall responses. Research shows that increasing wait time from less than one second up to seven seconds after asking higher-order questions results in longer student responses, student-initiated questioning, increased responses from at-risk students, and increased achievement (Rowe, 1974). As shown in the transcript, Ms Deborah uses wait time between her questioning and student responses. Along with questions that require higher-order thinking skills, her wait time is an excellent instructional and assessment strategy for students with language learning needs.

In addition to oral feedback, teachers spend a considerable amount of time providing written feedback on students' essays, presentations, or role-plays. Consider the endless hours of work teachers put into preparing report cards at the end of each instructional term! Teachers often wonder why their students repeat the same errors that they have previously corrected orally and in written form. They question if their students ever pay attention to their detailed comments. Some teachers are uncertain why a particular type of feedback works for one student but not for another.

This variability in the effects of feedback has given rise to research on various conditions that help or hinder the utilization of assessment information by teachers and learners. Research suggests that feedback is not fixed, but is subject to learners' interpretations and attitudes. It further suggests that the effects of feedback depend on differences in the types of tasks used and individual characteristics (Shute, 2008). The consensus from research is that when teachers provide summative scores relative to peers without giving descriptive feedback, it impedes learning.

Barringer & Gholson's review of feedback research (1979) examined the effects of the types of feedback and the combinations of different types of feedback on concept formation and concept identification. The most common combinations of feedback studied include feedback that follows:

1   both correct and incorrect responses (right/wrong)
2   only correct responses (right–blank) and
3   only incorrect responses (wrong–blank).

These combinations were presented in four different types of feedback: verbal feedback; symbolic feedback involving tones or light flashes; tangible objects involving tokens, candy, or money; and combined types of feedback.

The researchers conclude that verbal and symbolic feedback is more effective than tangible feedback because it is possible to redirect children's attention to relevant cues in learning materials. Giving only positive feedback is less facilitative than providing only negative feedback. This finding is due to the fact that the former does not provide the child with an opportunity to confirm or disconfirm his or her own hypothesis for solving a problem. Students tend to show greater interest in knowing what needs to be improved. Further, tangible feedback presented only to correct responses resulted in the poorest performance because it tended to distract the child's attention from the learning materials. The results were fairly consistent with both adults and young learners. Although the results are inconclusive because of other factors (such as individual learner differences), the review supports the claim that feedback can have facilitative or detrimental effects on students' learning.

Research on teacher responses to students' writing shows that teacher feedback can be distinguished in terms of whether an error is explicitly identified alongside its corrected form (direct or corrective feedback) or if errors are identified, but without the provision of the correct form (indirect or facilitative feedback). Indirect forms of feedback may be further categorized depending on whether the teacher uses a set of linguistic error codes. Classroom Snapshot 1.3 illustrates the use of indirect feedback type.

Classroom Snapshot 1.3

The following excerpts show a student writer's first draft and revision made based on the teacher's written comments on the first draft in a second language writing classroom. Read the excerpts, keeping in mind how the teacher's feedback affects revision in student writing. Ask yourself the following questions:

- What kind of feedback does the teacher give to the student writer?
- Do you think the student understood the teacher's feedback?
- Is the teacher's feedback effective?

Student's first draft: But is was unbelievable that when I visited New York City...

Teacher comment: INC SEN (But is was unbelievable that when I visited New York City...)

Student revision: It was unbelievable that when I visited New York City...

(Ferris, 2003, p. 27) ■

In this snapshot, the teacher uses a code, 'INC SEN,' which means 'incomplete sentence' to give feedback to the student writer. Ferris (2003) notes that if a teacher's feedback is too cryptic or too indirect in question form without a clear suggestion for revision (for example, 'Tense?' 'Agreement?'), it fails to lead to the desired result. In this example, the student writer removed the 'but' and changed 'is' to 'It.' It is possible that the student did not understand what 'INC SEN' meant, or understood the teacher's feedback, but could not correct the sentence fragment error.

Errors are not the only source of teachers' feedback. Evaluative feedback tends to rely on qualifiers, such as 'good,' 'nice job,' or 'excellent,' while tangible feedback (such as gold star stickers or smiley faces), commonly found in kindergarten and elementary school classrooms, is also evaluative. Descriptive feedback differs from evaluative feedback in that it provides detailed comments about the learner's strengths and areas needing improvement. Descriptive feedback may focus on either procedures or cognitive processes. Procedural feedback focuses on procedural mistakes specifically related to performance on assessment tasks whereas cognitive feedback focuses on misconceptions and cognitive strategies, which are important for understanding the extent to which students mastered target skills.

We have discussed different types of feedback that teachers use to give information to learners and guide their learning. Remember that you are not limited to using a single type of feedback to your learners, but that various feedback types may be used in combination. However, it is vital that you use the type of feedback that will most benefit individual students in meeting their language learning goals. Table 1.1 provides a summary of the different types of feedback that we have discussed.

Type of Feedback	Description	Examples
Descriptive Feedback	Detailed information that addresses qualities and informs future learning goals; involves the teacher and learner.	Your introduction is clearly stated and engages the reader. Provide another supporting detail from the text.
Evaluative Feedback	Non-descriptive; overall judgments on the quality of work.	Well-done; nice job; great effort.
Tangible Feedback	Objects used as rewards to recognize quality of work.	Gold stars; stickers; happy faces; candy; money
Verbal Feedback	Feedback that is provided orally to the student.	'You are correct.' 'Your answer is incorrect.'
Symbolic Feedback	A symbol is used to indicate if a response is correct/incorrect.	Sounds/tones; light flashes; music

Type of Feedback	Description	Examples
Procedural Feedback	Addresses procedural mistakes specifically related to performance on assessment tasks to address how to do something.	You need to enunciate your words more clearly. Try to include key words on your slides to help the audience during your presentation.
Cognitive Feedback	Targets students' knowledge and cognitive strategy use by identifying their strengths and identifying gaps in their knowledge.	You have great ideas in this paragraph, but you need to provide examples to clarify them.

Photocopiable © Oxford University Press

Table 1.1 Different types of feedback

Teachers often ask what makes feedback more or less specific and how specific is specific enough. Research shows that specific, elaborated feedback is more effective than general, evaluative feedback. When assessment takes place in the K–12 curriculum context, teachers' feedback needs to be aligned with the level of specificity in the learning objectives. Also, it is important to keep in mind the learner's level of cognitive maturity. Although more detailed feedback is desirable, if it is too fine-grained, it can be too complex for young or low-achieving learners. For example, young children may have difficulty understanding overly detailed feedback on abstract processing skills whereas older learners may appreciate detailed diagnostic feedback on specific skills that they need to improve.

As discussed earlier, feedback becomes more effective when it provides information about discrepancies between the learner's current level of performance and a desired goal that is specific, challenging, yet attainable. For feedback to be helpful, performance tasks should not demand overly complex cognitive processing. When such complex tasks are necessary, teacher scaffolding is a useful way of providing immediate feedback to support the learner.

But teachers also need feedback. Reflective teachers seek feedback from students during or after instruction in order to improve their teaching. For example, primary school teachers use techniques such as 'Traffic lights' or 'Thumbs up, thumbs down.' Before the lesson starts, each individual child is given three colored cups or cards. Each color indicates his or her level of understanding: red is for 'I don't understand and I really need some help'; yellow is for 'I'm not sure and I could use some help'; and green is for 'I understand and please proceed.' At key lesson points, the teacher asks students to show her a traffic light indication of the level of their understanding. Similarly, the teacher can ask children to give a thumbs up, thumbs down, or a sideways thumb to get feedback during the lesson. This instructional technique is often introduced through teacher professional development workshops.

For older students, the teacher may use technological devices like clickers, instant classroom response systems increasingly used in classrooms and campuses, to gauge their level of understanding during the class period and provide prompt feedback to students' questions. Anonymity helps the teacher to encourage students to provide input without fear of taking the public risk of being incorrect. Considering peer pressure among adolescents, using clickers in complete anonymity during instructional time may help them to actively give and receive feedback about their level of understanding.

In the following section, I survey various uses of language assessment across different contexts. As you learn about these uses, think of your own teaching context. Which approach has had a widespread impact in your school, community, or country? Are there any aspects of these assessments that you can draw from and use in your own practice?

Standards-Based Language Assessment

The most notable trend in language assessment for school-aged students is a standards-based approach to assessing students' progress in language and content areas related to curricular expectations. Standards are a set of benchmarks of curricular goals specified for students to achieve. In general, there are two components in standards: **content standards** which articulate what students should know in a particular subject domain and **performance standards** which describe how well students should be doing. These standards, working in tandem, are used to specify the knowledge and skills that students are expected to achieve and a range of proficiency levels each of which is elaborated by exemplars.

In standards-based assessment, teachers evaluate students' performance on tasks against a set of standards that include distinguishable descriptors of student performance, indicating a range of proficiency levels. These **proficiency-level descriptors** (PLDs) are widely used in writing rubrics or teacher observation checklists. In the classroom, teachers frequently use the PLDs to evaluate students' essays, role-plays, or oral presentations.

Teachers' use of standards-based language assessment has become a policy-supported practice in many parts of the world, including Australia, Canada, New Zealand, the United Kingdom, and the United States (Llosa, 2011). Furthermore, there has been a demonstrated need for these standards to be more specific to the characteristics of language learning (McKay, 2000). It is important that classroom teachers use language standards based on materials that recognize language learners' unique and positive learning paths. If the standards are developed based on learning trajectories of native language speakers only, assessment based on such standards will contribute to a deficit view of language learners (Neugebauer, 2008). Teachers may use standards developed specifically for language learners, such as the ESL Standards for Pre-K–12 students (TESOL, 1997) in order to assess students' language proficiency in content classrooms, as shown in Classroom Snapshot 1.4.

Classroom Snapshot 1.4

The following excerpt exemplifies the first step that a teacher takes to determine a student's English language learning proficiency and needs in a social studies classroom in the USA. As you read the vignette, reflect on the following questions:

- Do you agree with the teacher's assessment of Ling's English language proficiency? Why or why not?
- What do you think about the use of external standards to assess students' English language proficiency in content-area classrooms?
- How might English language learning demands vary depending on the subject area?

Ms Sampson, a social studies teacher in a Grade 10 classroom, uses social studies content and the *ESL Standards for Pre-K–12* students to determine the English language needs of a newcomer, Ling Fong, aged 15. She has received information about Ling's English reading, writing, listening, and speaking from her school's administration of the Woodcock-Munoz Language Survey. She now wants to determine Ling's language proficiency in her classroom using the rubrics drawn from the *ESL Standards for Pre-K–12 Students*. For three weeks Ms Sampson has been observing Ling interacting with his peers and participating in classroom routines and activities. Today, Ling is having a discussion with his peer, Max, about an upcoming presidential election.

Max: So, how do you say your name?
Ling Fong: You say, *Lee-am* Fong.
Max: Oh, cool name. Are you from China?
Ling Fong: No, I am Taiwanese.

Max: How did you get here? Boat?

Ling Fong: No, too far. I took a plane with my dad. He's a doctor here.

Max: Can you think of some words related to politics? How about congress, um ... election, senator? What is the guy called who is in charge of the state? He is like Schwarzenegger?

Ling Fong: Yeah, um ... Because of the terminator...See, how to say...

Max: Oh yeah, governor! What about a question?

Ling Fong: How to say about the politics?

Ling Fong also produced the following written paragraph based on the activity.

> At four years, the president becomes anew. America has one presidential this year. Not again for four years. Taiwan is same. Our presidential is the same.

(Case & Obenchain, 2006, p. 43)

In this Classroom Snapshot and many other activities, Ms Sampson assesses Ling's English language needs, using the social studies content and *ESL Standards for Pre-K–12* students (see Table 1.2 below). She determines that Ling is at the intermediate proficiency level because he fits the intermediate category, in which students depend heavily on their background knowledge of the theme or concepts in the text; they may present multiple errors though they can produce complex texts orally or in writing; and while they may be proficient with conversational language in daily situations they struggle with longer utterances.

Level of proficiency	Language skill	
	Reading and writing	**Listening and speaking**
Beginning	Reliance on pictures for meaning, can generate simple texts, may use invented spellings, syntax may borrow heavily from the native language.	May respond with single-word utterances or not at all. Simple phrases emerge as proficiency increases.
Intermediate	Proficiency varies but depends heavily on the student's background knowledge of or experience with the theme or concepts in the text. Although students can possibly write complex texts, their work contains many errors.	Students' speaking still contains several grammatical errors. They may have to hear something several times before understanding. They can use language in daily situations, but struggle with longer utterances.

Level of proficiency	Language skill	
	Reading and writing	**Listening and speaking**
Advanced	Students can read and produce texts written for academic or social purposes, but will struggle with texts that are abstract. Comprehension problems occur occasionally.	Students can easily converse on personal topics, but they will struggle to use and understand idioms and various figures of speech. It is difficult for them to express their understanding of abstract concepts.

Table 1.2 Summary of language proficiency levels (Case & Obenchain, 2006, p. 43)

Most standards-based assessment approaches are packaged with a set of **standardized tests** for teachers, and some are offered as a reference for teachers to use along with their own assessment in classrooms. Some are used to support teachers' classroom assessment, while others are used for high-stakes purposes. Because standards-based assessments tend to put more emphasis on teachers' judgments for assessing students' performance on tasks, the transparency of standards and consistency in using them are crucial for ensuring that information from standards-based assessment represents what students know and can do. **Teacher moderation** activities can be used to help teachers build a consensus on how to interpret and use standards.

NLLIA ESL Bandscales from Australia

In Australia, several standards-based frameworks, including the ESL Framework of Stages (McKay & Scarino, 1991), have been used by teachers. The primary purpose of the ESL Framework of Stages is to provide teachers with a planning tool for tracking ELLs' language development within the mainstream curriculum (McKay, 2000). The framework provides goals, objectives, and activities for students across three broad age groups. The goals include: communication, learning-how-to-learn, knowledge, and sociocultural goals. Teachers can use the framework as a reference document to identify students within stages of language learning (from beginner to advanced), but not for formal assessment or accountability purposes.

Experience with different frameworks eventually led to the development and use of the National Languages and Literacy Institute of Australia (NLLIA) ESL Bandscales (McKay, Hudson, & Sapuppo, 1994). The NLLIA ESL Bandscales provide information to teachers with the aim of developing their professional understanding of ELLs' language-learning development. Language-learning pathways are offered for students in junior primary, middle/upper primary, and secondary levels. Students' language development is further specified within seven or eight levels (for the secondary school-aged students) and across reading, speaking, listening, and writing skills. Like its predecessor (ESL Framework of Stages), the Bandscales are not intended to serve accountability purposes—instead they are used to help teachers understand the needs of ELL students within mainstream contexts.

Steps to English Proficiency in Canada

In Ontario, Canada, a new ELL assessment framework, **Steps to English Proficiency** (STEP), was developed for all classroom teachers in K–12 to assess, track, and support ELLs' language-proficiency development. Developed in collaboration with ESL content experts and teachers, the Ontario Ministry of Education initiated a policy to improve educational outcomes for ELL students. It was prompted by the concern that there was no consistent mode of assessing and tracking ELLs' developmental trajectories in schools. The STEP development team reviewed existing language-assessment continua (often referred to as benchmarks, standards, profiles, or stages of development) and concluded that they were inadequate for assessing ELLs' English-language proficiency in K–12 Ontario schools. The conclusion was based on the team's consideration of the school contexts in which Ontario ELL students represent diverse language groups speaking more than 100 different languages, including several Aboriginal languages and varieties of English (for example, Jamaican Creole). Together, Ontario ELL students represent more than 20 percent of the student populations in school settings. While the STEP development team appreciated other consortia's English language proficiency standards aligned with the curriculum in other subjects, they decided not to develop a large-scale standardized test because of its lack of congruence with assessment practices in Ontario schools, especially for younger students.

STEP includes three sets of descriptor-based developmental continua—oral communication, reading, and writing—for each of four different grade clusters. Each continuum includes six proficiency STEPs, characterized and differentiated from each other using a set of descriptors of **observable language behaviors** (OLB) specific to Ontario curriculum expectations and different age groups across grades. The OLB describes unique language behaviors that teachers can observe and evaluate in real classroom learning contexts.

A number of research activities took place between 2008 and 2011 to examine the validity of STEP. The first field research (Cummins, Jang, Stille,

Wagner, Clark, & Trahey, 2009) sought input from teachers who had the opportunity to use STEP in assessing their students. The study reported that teachers' knowledge of students' English-language development was augmented through the use of STEP, and the framework served both pedagogical and professional learning purposes. Although teachers appreciated that STEP provided them with a common language to use with other teachers, administrators, and parents, they were also concerned about increases to their workload (Cummins et al., 2009). In addition, teachers revealed that while the descriptors were interpretable and relevant to their tasks there were also inconsistencies in the continua. Teachers identified difficulties distinguishing between some STEPs, as well as some fairness issues (for example, inclusion of pronunciation in the descriptors). The need to revise descriptors served as the impetus for the subsequent phase of the STEP field research. Spotlight Study 1.1 illustrates how STEP can be used to describe an individual ELL student's language development and learning.

Spotlight Study 1.1

Jang, Cummins, Wagner, Stille, Dunlop, & Starkey (2011) worked with a group of 42 teachers and 159 students in STEP field research. The teachers selected between two and six students for whom they were providing ESL support and assessed their language proficiency using the STEP continua over a month. Based on classroom observations and interviews with teachers and students, the researchers provided rich descriptions of individual ELLs' language proficiency development to demonstrate how the STEP assessment framework can be used by teachers in assessing, tracking, and documenting ELLs' language development. Jana's language profile illustrates this process.

Jana's background

Jana is 10 years old. She came to Canada three months ago from China. She speaks Cantonese at home with her family. She is currently in Grade 5, and has been receiving ESL support in a half-day, self-contained ESL class for the past three months.

Jana's STEP assessment

Jana's teacher describes how Jana puts a great deal of time and effort into writing activities, evident in the progress she has made since arriving in Canada a few months ago. For example, samples from Jana's journal writing (shown below in Figures 1.1 and 1.2) illustrate some of the progress she made between March and May.

March 7

On the weekend I did my homework in my home. The homework was ~~pained~~ paint. Then I went to the supermarket with my mother. my mother bouse many food. We took the food go to the ~~KFe~~ KFC. Then I we were go home, My mother was cook dinner, I was do some housework. In the evening, We watched TV on the sofa, and we played cards. The day was happy day.

Figure 1.1 Jana's journal writing from March

Tuesday, May, 17th, 2011

To day is Tuesday. It's eight o' clock, it's time to get up, then I brush my teeth, get dress, make a bed clean. Also, I have a good breakfast time. Oh, no, it's eight twenty, late, I must go to school. In the school, when block one is over, I have a big red apple to eat. After go outside, is block two, I have two classes, first is French, second is math. It's time to eat lunch, I have a bread and a fruit. After lunch, I'm go to do a math practice. Then is block 3, in the block 3, I have Social Studies in my classroom, Social Studies is a fun class. When the class is almost over, I open my Agenda, write some thing I will do what today, then I go home.

Figure 1.2 Jana's journal writing from May

Jana's teacher describes her as 'very quiet' because she is still developing her confidence and her oral language abilities. However, when Jana can express herself in writing her teacher finds that she has 'tons of ideas' and that she can use resources such as the dictionary and Google Translate to find and use vocabulary at a higher level. Jana also incorporates pre-taught vocabulary and phrases into her writing. Evidence, such as these writing samples, assisted Jana's teacher in determining that she had demonstrated the ability to 'use sentence starters provided by the teacher to organize ideas' (Writing STEP 1 OLB), and 'write simple sentences following patterns provided by the teacher' (Writing STEP 1 OLB). Because Jana is new to her class, she is just beginning to contribute orally to class activities. Her teacher's STEP assessment shows that she can 'respond to personally relevant questions with a single word or phrase in English or L1' (Oral STEP 1 OLB) and 'use familiar words to express meaning' (Oral STEP 1 OLB). However, she is not yet able to 'use a small repertoire of conversational strategies to participate effectively in group work' (Oral STEP 2 OLB). She is beginning to develop peer relationships in class and at recess, and these will continue to support her development of conversational strategies.

Jana's English learning

Jana enjoys reading in English and thinks that reading helps to improve her language learning. Her teacher selects texts that she might like and Jana reads them in her free time. Jana says that reading new words is hard for her. She uses the dictionary and guesses the meaning of new words by looking at contextual cues such as the topic and pictures. Jana maintains a personal dictionary where she records new words that she wants to remember. She enjoys using the computer for writing at school not only because it helps her to practice typing in English, but also because 'it does not waste paper.' (Jang et al., 2011, pp. 100–3) ▪

There are several common features in the Australian and Canadian examples. Both assessment frameworks emphasize communication in language learning through an integrated task-based approach. Both are used by ESL and mainstream classroom teachers across all subject areas and grades. There is no formal standardized test associated with these examples, so no grades or percentages are used as markers of achievement. Instead, both utilize proficiency scales of progress toward age-appropriate target expectations. Teachers' concerns about increased workload and lack of professional development were documented in the evaluation of both the NLLIA ESL Bandscales (Brindley, 1998, 2001) and the STEP Assessment Framework (Cummins et al., 2009; Jang et al., 2011).

Council of Europe: CEFR

Another well-known example of standards-based assessment is the **Common European Framework of Reference for Languages** (CEFR) (Council of Europe, 2001). The CEFR was originally developed for assessing the language competence of adult migrants but it is increasingly applied to school systems (Hasselgreen, 2005). It includes six proficiency levels such as Basic (Breakthrough, Waystage), Independent (Threshold, Vantage), and Proficient (Effective Operational Proficiency, Mastery). Proficiency descriptors are used to illustrate language learners' progress through knowledge and skills.

Examples of the CEFR's application to young learner assessments are found with the **European Language Portfolio** (ELP) (Little 2002, 2005) and the Cambridge Young Learner (YLE) tests (Taylor & Saville, 2002). The ELP is used by teachers and students to document language-learning progress, and the CEFR's 'Can Do' descriptors are used as students' self-assessment tool. Hasselgreen (2003) examined the extent to which existing CEFR 'Can Do' descriptors could be adapted for young learners (ages 11–12) in primary and lower-secondary schools. The ELP is used as a self-assessment tool in several countries in the Nordic-Baltic region (Hasselgreen, 2005). For example, *My Language Portfolio* (Centre for Information on Language Teaching and Research, 2001) provides children with the opportunity to demonstrate what they can do with their foreign and second languages. Children at the beginning level can show what they can do for a wide range of simple functions, such as 'I can name the colors' and 'I can talk about what happened or is going to happen' (Hasselgreen, 2005, p. 343).

While the ELP is used by teachers and students in K–12 school settings (Little, 2005), the Cambridge YLE tests are designed to test the general EFL proficiency of children aged 7–12 at three proficiency levels, equivalent to CEFR's A1 and A2 levels: starters (age 7), movers (aged 8–11), and flyers (aged 9–12). Bailey (2005) reports that the YLE tests were taken by approximately 295,000 children from 55 countries. Children who complete all components of the test, including listening, reading, writing, and speaking, receive certificates. Instead of numerical scores, these certificates show children's proficiency mastery level in shield bands ranging from 1–5. Their teachers receive more detailed diagnostic information about students' achievement levels across different task types and components. We will review the use of the Cambridge YLE tests in Hong Kong in Spotlight Study 3.3 in Chapter 3.

All of the examples of assessment frameworks that have been reviewed so far utilize scaled proficiency descriptors. Despite their popularity, teachers are often uncertain about how to interpret the descriptors and use them to distinguish different proficiency levels. You too might wonder: Would my interpretation of a B2 level be the same as another teacher's? How well do the proficiency descriptors lend themselves to consistent interpretation? These are crucial questions in understanding the standards-based assessment approaches, considering their multiple roles, such as supporting teaching and learning, facilitating decisions about program placement and resource allocation, and monitoring students' language-proficiency development throughout their schooling. In Chapter 3, we will discuss issues that offer insights into teachers' interpretations of the standards in Spotlight Study 3.4

Language Testing in the Context of NCLB

Around the world, assessment is increasingly used to serve educational accountability policies, and information from student assessment is used to hold educators and schools accountable for student achievement. The No Child Left Behind Act (2001) in the United States is a case in point. The NCLB policy stipulates that a state shall approve assessment measures that are designed to assess the progress of ELLs in achieving English proficiency in speaking, listening, reading, and writing skills as well as annually measurable academic achievement objectives (Abedi, 2004;

Bunch, 2011). Various language tests were developed by a consortium of states in collaboration with test development agencies and academic institutes. Some examples of such assessments include: the Comprehensive English Language Learner Assessment (CELLA); the English Language Development Assessment (ELDA); the Mountain West Assessment (MWA); and Assessing Comprehension and Communication in English State-to-State for English Language Learners (ACCESS for ELLs®). According to Bunch (2011), these assessments share some common features in that they are based on curriculum content standards; they employ formal standard-setting procedures to determine a range of proficiency levels; and they commonly test reading, writing, speaking, and listening skills.

For example, the ELDA (English Language Development Assessment) was developed to measure both academic and social English language proficiency of ELLs in California schools. The ELDA determines students' language proficiency levels (1–5) based on composite scores derived from reading, listening, writing, and speaking. All K–12 students must repeat the ELDA until they reach Level 5 and are fully proficient in English.

ACCESS for ELLs® is a large-scale English language proficiency test based on WIDA's (World-Class Instructional Design and Assessment) English language development (ELD) standards which outline the development of academic language in five different content areas for each grade level. The tests are designed to measure academic English language proficiency across content areas and to identify students' language development along a six-level continuum. As of 2012, the tests are administered in 24 of the American states (WIDA, 2012) to over 840,000 students each year.

One interesting aspect of the ACCESS for ELLs® test, which also contributes to the complexity of its design, is that it accounts for the variability in students' English language proficiency development within each grade by introducing both a horizontal and a vertical dimension to explain English-language development. The horizontal dimension refers to the six-level continuum that identifies the learner as Entering (Level 1), Beginning (Level 2), Developing (Level 3), Expanding (Level 4), and Bridging (Level 5). The sixth level, Reaching, is reserved for ELLs who are fully proficient in English. The vertical scale provides teachers with information about students' progress in English language proficiency development over multiple grades on the same scale (Kenyon, MacGregor, Li, & Cook, 2011).

The use of these tests under the NCLB policy has resulted in high stakes for students, teachers, and schools. In some contexts, schools are subject to rewards or sanctions based on students' test performance, and teachers' incentives are based on their students' improvement in test scores. Test scores are also used to make decisions about grade-to-grade promotion or high-school graduation. One of the key controversies arising from the use of tests for these purposes is fairness and equity for all students, especially ELLs. Use of standardized tests as a requirement for grade promotion and high-school graduation has been a common practice since the 1970s and 1980s when minimum competence tests were widely used in the United States as a graduation requirement. Over 20 states in the USA require students to pass graduation tests (American Federation of Teachers, 1999). In Canada, students in Grade 10 in Ontario public schools must take the Ontario Secondary School Literacy Test (OSSLT) to meet one of 32 graduation requirements. Those who fail the test must either repeat it to achieve an acceptable score or take a remediation course. The OSSLT appears to have a low effect on English L1 students whose success rates are above 80 percent. However, ELLs' pass rates are slightly over 50 percent, as Figure 1.3 shows (Jang, 2010a).

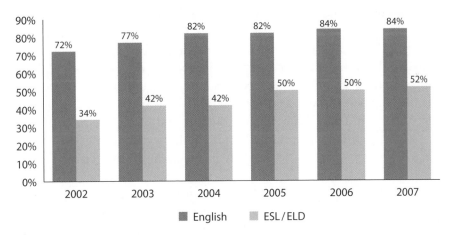

Figure 1.3 Success rates on the OSSLT

Indeed, significant gaps between the groups make us wonder whether they took the same test (Fox & Cheng, 2007). Although those who failed the test are provided with two options—to retake the test or take a remedial course—it is not difficult to imagine how such a testing experience can have a negative impact on adolescents' self-esteem and motivation.

Advocates for holding high standards for all students argue that they benefit disadvantaged students, including language learners, because they can be used to identify and improve resources for the students. However, there are potential negative consequences of such high-stakes testing on language minority students. Research shows that tests that measure students' academic achievement in content areas often include construct-irrelevant language factors (such as linguistically complex mathematics tests or culturally biased topics), deepening gaps in achievement between ELLs and non-ELLs (Abedi, 2004; Butler & Stevens, 2001; Solano-Flores, 2008). These issues concerning fairness and equity in assessing language learners will be further discussed in Chapters 3 and 4.

High-Stakes Testing in EFL Contexts

The impact of high-stakes testing on students is also found in many EFL teaching and learning contexts in which national English tests are used to select students for promotion to a higher grade or admission to university. For example, every year in China, millions of secondary-school students write the National Matriculation English Test (NMET) as part of a battery of tests required to gain entrance to university or college (Cheng & Qi, 2006). The NMET tests students' language proficiency in listening, reading, writing, grammar, and vocabulary knowledge. The test has also been used as part of educational reforms to influence English language teaching in Chinese high schools by introducing test items that measure students' productive skills (for example, writing). The NMET does not test speaking mainly due to cost and practical constraints. Students' unequal access to authentic language input is a great concern with the NMET in that students in larger cities in China (for example, Beijing and Shanghai) have greater access to English language through radio and television programs, while the rural students' access to English is much more limited or simply nonexistent.

The NMET has had significant impact on teaching and learning, as well as on society. Cheng & Qi (2006) describe an incident during the 1999 administration of the test during which parents blocked the roads outside of the testing center in Guangzhou city in order to eliminate the noise of traffic for test-takers. Within the school system, students' test performance is used as an indicator of the effectiveness or quality of teaching, schools, and various education departments. Teachers also report that their personal sense of efficacy and achievement is strongly linked to their students' performance on the NMET (Qi, 2003). Cheng & Qi (2006) describe the impact that the test has had on teaching in secondary schools by pointing to the fact that the curriculum has become limited to the test content, and even the delivery of the curriculum is modeled after the test format.

The use of high-stakes English language tests in Asian countries and elsewhere creates a tension between teachers' adherence to curricular policy on educational reforms and teachers' need to prepare students to write a test that is incongruent with the communicative focus stipulated by the new policy. For example, since the 1970s, Japan has recognized the English language as a means not only of bringing foreign culture and knowledge to the country, but also as a way to exchange information with those outside of Japan (Sasaki, 2008). Since 2001, Japanese elementary and secondary schools have shifted from teaching traditional knowledge and skills to a focus on academic abilities and the 'motivation/attitude for learning and the ability to solve problems as an autonomous individual responding to societal changes' (Kariya, 2002, translated and cited in Sasaki, 2008, p. 74). The purpose of English language teaching and learning is not only the acquisition of language knowledge and skills, but also involves 'fostering a positive attitude toward communication through foreign languages' (p. 74). However, these reforms to educational policies in Japan have met resistance, as teachers prepare students to succeed not only in the acquisition of the English language, but also on the high-stakes exam that they need to write.

In Taiwan, since the introduction of the General English Proficiency Test (GEPT) in 2000, more than four million Taiwanese have completed the test, including approximately 20,000 elementary school-aged children each year, until 2006 (Wu, 2012). The GEPT is intended to assess students' English language proficiency in an EFL context at various levels of schooling up to university graduates and beyond. Although it is not mandated, many parents choose to register their children for the test so that they can gain entrance to prestigious high schools. The test comprises five proficiency levels, each of which corresponds to a desired level at each key grade level. Similar to Chinese and Japanese contexts, the GEPT was developed with the purpose of bringing 'positive **washback** effects' to teaching and learning in EFL classrooms (Wu, 2012).

The term 'washback' or 'backwash' refers to both positive and negative impacts of testing on teaching and learning (Bailey, 1999; Wall & Alderson, 1993. Test impact is distinguished from test washback as it refers to various effects of testing on stakeholders and policies (Wall, 1997).

Because teachers use assessments in such a range of ways, research is inconclusive on the effect of testing on curriculum innovation (Andrews, 1994, 2004; Wall & Alderson, 1993). Wall and Alderson studied a new national EFL examination in Sri Lanka that emphasized the four language skills and expected teachers to adopt communicative approaches to teaching.

The new exam system entailed centralized reading and writing tests as well as teachers' classroom assessment of their students in all four language skills, especially oral and listening skills. Their key findings showed that the new exam system had its impact on the content of English lessons and teachers' classroom assessment methods. Wall and Alderson concluded: '... if an exam is to have the impact intended, educationalists and education managers need to consider a range of factors that affect how innovations succeed or fail and that influence teacher (and pupil) behaviors. The exam is only one of these factors' (p. 68).

What is common among the three EFL contexts discussed here is that national English tests strongly influence what is taught and how it is taught. While they are used for selection and promotion, they are also used as a lever for educational reform strategies, by introducing new kinds of assessment to the curriculum (Cheng, Watanabe, & Curtis, 2004; Linn, 2000). Policy-makers hope that such test-driven top-down approaches to curriculum change will have a positive washback effect on teaching and learning. Evaluating assessment practices requires a deep understanding of what happens as a result of using assessment in a specific local context (Frederiksen & Collins, 1989).

Summary

In this chapter, I have encouraged you to consider assessment from a use-oriented perspective. I have identified and discussed the primary uses of language assessment that will probably be familiar to most of you. Before surveying various language-assessment approaches being taken with language learners around the world, you had an opportunity to reflect on your own previous and current assessment practices, by specifically focusing on the use of assessment feedback in classrooms. Many of the emerging issues concern complex relationships among assessment, curriculum standards, teaching, and learning.

As you read about different assessment practices in this book, reflect on the issues discussed in this chapter and use the following general questions as a guide to your reflection:

• What view of assessment is conveyed?
• Is there an appropriate balance between summative and formative assessment in relation to the context of use?
• How evident is the formative assessment's pedagogical motive?

- What kinds of guidance are teachers given to enhance their knowledge about assessment generally and classroom language assessment in particular?
- How are teachers assessed?
- What specific tools are provided within the assessment framework (if any) to assist teachers' implementation of assessment?
- Are the standards both challenging and attainable?
- Are students provided with multiple ways to demonstrate what they can do?
- Are students tested in the same way they learn in the classroom?
- Is assessment information used in a pedagogically useful way?
- Does the assessment consider children's developmental characteristics?
- Do testing-driven curriculum innovations have positive effects?

(Adapted from Kiely & Rea-Dickens, 2005, p.179)

In Chapter 2, we will look at theories of language development that inform assessment practices. We will also focus on the development and assessment of the academic language proficiency of language learners, by reviewing salient features of language development.

2

What Teachers Need to Know about Theories of Language Development

Preview

High-quality language assessment for school-aged learners partly depends on an underlying theory of how students develop language proficiency. Unfortunately, not all existing language assessments are grounded in research on how second or additional language develops in young and adolescent learners. Furthermore, because the theoretical assumptions underlying the assessments are often implicit, they are inaccessible to users, including teachers. Typically, L2 proficiency is assessed in terms of the four **modalities**: listening, speaking, reading, and writing. However, such a modality-based definition of L2 proficiency is limited in providing information specific enough to help teachers or students understand the stages of language proficiency and improve it further. Additionally, most activities in language classrooms engage students in more than one language modality. For example, students may read a text out loud during a choral reading activity, and pause to discuss vocabulary, or key ideas. From the vantage point of assessment, in this chapter we explore key elements that make up L2 proficiency across the modalities necessary for school-aged students to succeed at school.

Let us begin the discussion of some of these issues by reflecting on Classroom Snapshots 2.1 and 2.2. As you read the two snapshots think about the following questions:

- What are the different types of language demands that students encounter in classrooms? For example, what kinds of vocabulary knowledge are students expected to have in order to participate in class discussions?
- What topics do teachers discuss with their students?
- How familiar are students with these topics?

Classroom Snapshot 2.1

The following dialogue takes place in a Grade 7 language arts classroom in a middle school in the United States. Elisa is a teacher with more than five years' teaching experience. Kim speaks Vietnamese and English at home, has been in the USA for more than four years, and shows oral fluency but struggles with academic tasks. The lesson is about the cause of the Black Plague.

Elisa: Look, in 1898, what did they realize the cause was?

[pointing to a page in a textbook]

Elisa: Read that to me.
Kim: In 1898, a French scientist solved mystery.
Elisa: Do you know what 'solved' means?

[pause]

Elisa: To answer the puzzle. What's a flea?
Kim: This bug on rats.
Elisa: OK. Where did the rats came [sic] from?
Kim: The boats?
Elisa: Yes. But why did people get disease?
Kim: I don't know.
Elisa: Because fleas would come off the rats and bite people because things weren't very clean. They found out that … what?
Kim: Where the disease come from.

Classroom Snapshot 2.2

Helen is a social studies teacher with over five years of teaching experience. Juan and Sara both speak Spanish. Juan has been in the USA for three years; Sara has lived in the USA for more than four years.

Helen: How did trade affect people after the plague? How did it affect their minds?
Sara: They wanted more!
Helen: OK, they wanted more. What else?
Juan: Trade flourished. Individualism.
Helen: What does that mean? Setting their own goals and did what they want?
Juan: Money, wealth!
Helen: This led into the …
Sara: Dark ages, middle ages?
Helen: No, the Renaissance. This means what? Renaissance, like *renacer* [Spanish: be reborn].
Juan: Rebirth!
Helen: Rebirth of … ? [pause] Of art and culture. A lot came as a result of more wealth that they got.

(Zwiers, 2007, p. 104) ▩

Even though these snapshots are drawn from two different classes—a language arts class and a social studies class—taught by two different teachers, there are similarities in the oral interactions among the students and their respective teacher. The teachers use academic words (realize, cause, affect, trade, flourish, wealth, rebirth), as well as content-specialized words (individualism, dark ages, middle ages, Renaissance), and they discuss historical events. In both snapshots, teachers use questions to engage students in lessons, but they differ in the type of questions they ask. In Classroom Snapshot 2.1, Elisa's questions focus on recalling information that students recently learned. She tells Kim to read a textbook to find specific information (the cause of the Black Plague) to find an answer to her question. She checks to see if Kim knows the meaning of the word 'solve' (though she does not wait long enough for the student to answer it. Recall the discussion of wait time in Chapter 1).

In the social studies class in Classroom Snapshot 2.2, Helen uses less structured questions to help students think about the cause and effect of trade. Her focus is not for learners to recall factual information from previous lessons, but to assist students in identifying causal relationships (such as connections between trade, people, wealth) and interpreting the consequences (for example, effect on the arts and culture).

These two Classroom Snapshots illustrate the language demands that students encounter in content classes as well as the characteristics of academic language used in classroom discussions. Clearly, adolescent learners' successful participation in these content classes requires knowledge of academic vocabulary, grammar, and a high level of cognitive functions (recalling and describing facts, identifying cause and effect, developing a perspective). In these Snapshots, teachers assess students' content knowledge and language proficiency through oral questioning during the discussions.

While historical content such as the Black Plague or the Renaissance might be familiar to ELLs with a Western background, students who have no such cultural knowledge often face significant challenges in content classes. For example, Duff (2001) argues that newcomer ELLs find it challenging to learn culturally unfamiliar content through oral interactions in class discussions. She describes the difficulties that the newcomer ELL faces during current events discussions, a major component of the secondary curriculum, as follows:

> …the interaction and topics in both courses favored local students' oral participation almost exclusively during open discussions; ESL students

were never observed to propose a topic and, when asked specifically for input, they often hedged and provided brief, partially audible responses. Participation in such spontaneous discussions requires familiarity with headlines in the news, including the English names of people, places, and events (usually from the city's main daily newspaper), plus sufficient content and confidence to introduce a topic, process information, and take turns quickly. (p. 116)

Not all subject teachers understand that some language learners' lack of active participation in class discussions is partly due to a lack of cultural knowledge, and this lack of understanding contributes to confusion when their assessment results show a significant discrepancy with other teachers, including ESL teachers (Duff, 2001). Teachers need to share their knowledge bases to understand ELLs' language learning needs and use a range of assessment methods to provide students with multiple opportunities to demonstrate their content learning, using linguistic knowledge and resources.

Language Proficiency Development

How do students develop language proficiency? What key linguistic knowledge and skills do students need for successful participation in academic learning? What should teachers consider in assessing students' language proficiency and its development while teaching content materials? The students themselves can help us answer these questions. Activity 2.1 introduces you to four ELL students. As you read about them, think about the similarities and differences in their language background profiles.

Activity 2.1

Do you recall the assessment framework Steps to English Proficiency (STEP) discussed in Chapter 1? In Spotlight Study 1.1, you read about the study in which STEP was validated in public schools in the Canadian province of Ontario (Jang et al., 2011). The 42 participating teachers each chose two to six students in their classrooms (totaling 159 students) and assessed their English proficiency based on a month-long instructional period. The teachers used STEP descriptors that illustrate observable language behaviors (OLB) in three language skills for each of four grade clusters.

Four of the ELL students who participated in the study are Jalissa, Omar, Ahmad, and Farooq. They are all English language learners, ranging in age from 9–14 and are in Grades 3, 6, 7, and 11 respectively. The three male students were born outside Canada; the female student, Jalissa, was born in Canada. Table 2.1 summarizes the students' background including information about their ages, the grade in which they are enrolled, gender, the country of birth, home language, and the number of years that they have been in Canada. Review this information carefully.

Student	Grade	Age (in yrs)	Gender	Country of Birth	First Language	Years in Canada
Jalissa	3	9	Female	Canada	Farsi	9
Omar	6	12	Male	Pakistan	Urdu	1.5
Ahmad	7	14	Male	Sudan	Arabic	1.1
Farooq	11	14	Male	Pakistan	Urdu	3

Table 2.1 Background information

Photocopiable © Oxford University Press

Figure 2.1 presents the students' language proficiency levels within the oral, reading, and writing skills based on their teachers' assessments. The vertical axis shows the number of OLB for which students have demonstrated mastery toward grade-level expectations. Note that each grade cluster has its own set of OLB on the six-step continuum. Before you look at Figure 2.1, what would you predict about the students' abilities in these three modalities based on the limited information you have about them? Write down your predictions; then look at Figure 2.1 and see whether the teachers' assessments of their proficiency levels match your predictions. Which student's skill profile was the most predictable and which one surprised you the most?

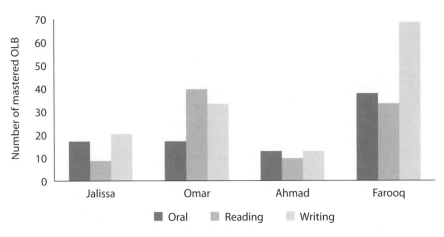

Figure 2.1 Jalissa, Omar, Ahmad, and Farooq's STEP skill profiles

These examples highlight both the diversity of ELLs' backgrounds and their non-uniform language skill development. For example, Ahmad has been in Canada over a year and shows the lowest mastery level, consistent across all the assessed skills. Omar, who has been in Canada four months more than Ahmad, shows a similar oral proficiency level to Ahmad. However, Omar shows higher proficiency levels in reading and writing skills. Farooq's profile is also interesting. He has spent three years in Canada and shows the highest proficiency level in writing. Jalissa, a Canadian-born girl in Grade 3, shows low English proficiency levels across all three skills, with a profile similar to Ahmad's. These domestic ELLs' struggles with literacy achievement have become a concern for educators and policy makers in North America. We will discuss these issues in greater detail in Spotlight Study 2.2.

Let us return to Activity 2.1 where you made predictions about these students' language proficiency levels according to three modalities. To see how the information from the STEP assessment is more finely tuned and specific to linguistic knowledge and skills, see Jana's STEP profile reported in Spotlight Study 1.1.

Keep these learners in mind as you continue to read this chapter. As we explore the characteristics of school-aged language learners' language proficiency development, pay attention to how theories of language development can inform assessment practices and instruction.

Is Language Proficiency Unitary or Multi-componential?

Language ability was once viewed as unitary, consisting of a single global construct that we cannot directly observe or measure (Oller, 1976), just like the traditional view of intelligence. A **unitary view of language ability** or intelligence endorses the either/or belief that one has either a good or poor command in language or that a person is intelligent or not. Such a unitary view applied to language assessments can be seen when a student's total test score is used to make decisions about the learner's overall language proficiency. Clearly, a unitary view does not reflect how language develops nor can it account for the diversity of language development of the four students presented in Activity 2.1. For example, there would be no way to discuss the differences among Omar, Jalissa, Ahmad, and Farooq's oral, reading, and writing development using one overall score for language proficiency.

Because it is difficult (if not impossible) to measure abstract human **traits** like proficiency and intelligence, we need to develop ways to describe them by identifying the parts that constitute the whole. For example, human intelligence is currently measured in multiple categories including spatial, musical, kinesthetic, and interpersonal in addition to two intelligences recognized traditionally—linguistic and mathematical (Gardner, 1983; Gardner & Hatch, 1989). These components together are used to make the abstract construct of human intelligence observable.

There has been much debate about how to measure L2 proficiency. The unitary view of language proficiency has been strongly contested and empirically refuted by researchers and educators (Bachman, 1990; Canale & Swain, 1980). For example, educators' use of the STEP assessment framework supported a **multi-componential** view. Over 90 percent of 192 teachers who participated in the STEP field research in 2008 reported that they observed significant differences in students' proficiency levels across the three language skills (Cummins et al., 2009). One elementary school teacher stated, 'I found one student where there were two STEP level differences—she was very high in Oral, STEP 4, and STEP 2 in Reading and Writing. All of the other students I worked with had about one STEP apart' (p. 9).

At the secondary level, students' non-uniform language development across the modalities becomes a critical concern for teachers when they place students into multi-level ESL courses. A secondary ESL teacher shares her experience as follows:

I think it is impossible [to make uniform progress across reading, writing, and oral], and I think, we know their oral skills. They are often sounding just like their peers orally, and then they are saying, 'Why am I in ESL? Because, look, I understand everything.' But, I think it will be useful to show them, all right, your oral skills are doing very well, [but gaps exist in other areas].

(Cummins et al., 2009, p. 9)

These teachers' observations coincide with current theories of language proficiency that characterize L2 development in terms of multiple components of linguistic knowledge and functional skills (Bachman, 1990; Canale & Swain, 1980; Cummins, 1979, 1983). The multi-componential view of language proficiency explains why two students whose overall test scores are similar to each other can, in fact, have starkly different language proficiency profiles.

This multi-componential view of L2 proficiency makes sense particularly when we consider the fact that school-aged language learners go through rapid emotional, physical, and cognitive development. As Activity 2.1 shows, language growth at an uneven rate across different modalities may result from the influence of a myriad of factors. Another important implication of the multi-componential view of language proficiency is its pedagogical potential—it enables teachers to diagnose students' strengths and areas for improvement in specific components and tailor their instruction to different students' needs.

What components of language development do you think are most relevant to your students' L2 proficiency? What specific knowledge and skills would you assess in order to understand the current stage of their language development? The following section explores these questions by examining each of the key components of **academic language proficiency** (ALP) and distinct characteristics of its development among language learners of different ages.

What is Academic Language Proficiency?

In school, students need both conversational and academic language proficiency to engage in meaningful learning through informal and formal interactions (Bailey, 2007; Gibbons, 2006). Cummins' (1981) **basic interpersonal communication skills** (BICS) are related to students' ability to use language for social interaction in familiar contexts. For example, students may demonstrate their use of BICS when they talk to their friends at school or when they converse with their teachers in school hallways or during recess. This everyday language enables students to participate in social conversations with peers about personal and familiar topics related to daily routine, personal experience, and interests. Students learn to use this social language skill to communicate with peers, teachers, and school staff about classroom activities, homework, and course materials.

In addition to these social aspects of language, young and adolescent learners need to develop academic language proficiency, the formal register of language used in the curriculum-learning context (Bailey & Butler, 2003; Cummins & Man Yee-Fun, 2007). Saunders & Goldenberg (2008) define academic language as 'the specialized vocabulary, grammar, discourse/ textual, and functional skills associated with academic instruction and mastery of academic material and tasks' (p. 47). Specifically, ALP allows learners to apply their grammar, vocabulary, and **discourse knowledge** and skills to meet language demands required to perform on academic tasks in content areas (Amstrom, 2010; Bailey & Butler, 2003; McKay, 2006).

Bailey (2007) notes that social and academic language can be differentiated based on the context of its use. In other words, it is not the differences in the quality or cognitive complexity between academic and social language that distinguish the two language proficiencies, but rather, the difference in the situation as well as the demands of learning materials that students encounter in that specific situation (Saunders & Goldenberg, 2010). The following section discusses various components of ALP in more depth, specifically the vocabulary, grammar, discourse knowledge, and the functional skills that students need in order to achieve mastery of language and curriculum content.

Vocabulary Knowledge

School-aged children regardless of their language background develop vocabulary capacity by increasing the size of their vocabulary (breadth) and later deepening their knowledge of vocabulary (depth) (Schoonen & Verhallen, 2008). Children begin to expand the size of their vocabulary by recognizing the most frequent 2000 words found in spoken and written text (Coxhead, 2006). They continue to expand their knowledge by learning academic vocabulary common across content areas and, later on, specialized vocabulary specific to content areas in secondary school (Stevens, Butler, & Castellon-Wellington, 2000).

Research shows that knowing the primary meanings of words is insufficient for content-specific learning and that students often fail to learn the secondary meanings, idioms, connotations, and words derived from other words (van Wyk & Greyling, 2008). Students need to learn specialized meanings and relationships of familiar words in different content areas and use them to understand technical processes and abstract relationships. For example, students learn that the word 'column' has different meanings in English and Mathematics classes. As students move to higher grades, they uncover new meanings and relationships of familiar words through the process of categorization, generalization, and abstraction (Miller, 1999; Schoonen & Verhallen, 2008). We will discuss research on young learners' vocabulary development and assessment in more detail in Chapter 3.

Activity 2.2

The following descriptors illustrate how language learners demonstrate their vocabulary knowledge. Think of students you know who are enrolled in a subject-specific course or program and assess their vocabulary ability, using the vocabulary skill descriptors. Note that they may be able to demonstrate some of these skills in some contexts but not others. Pay attention to whether they can demonstrate these skills consistently successfully across multiple tasks and contexts. Ask yourself whether they can:

- recognize familiar words and spell them correctly?
- use high-frequency general words?
- use general academic words?
- use specialized content-specific words?
- deduce the meaning of an unfamiliar word by using **semantic and syntactic cues** from text?
- understand lexically dense text?
- figure out the meaning of abstract, technical, and specialized vocabulary used in curriculum content?
- select words and phrases appropriate for conveying intended meaning?

Grammar Knowledge

In general, children's vocabulary development is closely associated with the development of grammar knowledge, in particular, knowledge of morphology and syntax. Morphology refers to an understanding of words' structure, such as the roots of words and the use of prefixes and suffixes. Learning about syntax refers to understanding the rules about how words are put together to make sentences.

Goodwin, Huggins, & Carlo (2012) note that 60–80 percent of words that children between Grades 1 and 3 encounter in texts are morphologically complex and involve affixes and stems (parts of words). Children can know or decode the meanings of the new words up to 60 percent if they pay attention to component morphemes and context (Nagy & Anderson, 1984). Anglin (1993) suggests that children in Grade 1 have limited knowledge of morphologically complex words, but they continue to increase their knowledge of morphology.

Gradually, students identify and use the grammatical features associated with specific text **genres**. They learn to identify the differences in sentence structures while dealing with increasingly dense text and abstract vocabulary (such as nominalization of verbs and adjectives into noun phrases, as in 'decide' to 'decision', 'applicable' to 'applicability') and conventions used in different text genres, such as **narrative** and **expository texts**.

Students need explicit instruction in order to learn different grammatical features of language used in different text genres. For example, if students have insufficient knowledge of the pronoun reference system and **collocations** frequently found in academic texts, it interferes with their textual comprehension (Scarcella, 2003). By acquiring grammatical knowledge, students learn to use appropriate linguistic features to accomplish a range of academic goals across content areas.

Activity 2.3

Think of students in your program (it may be the same students considered in Activity 2.2). Assess their grammatical competence by reviewing the following descriptors that illustrate skills associated with grammatical knowledge in **multimodal language learning** and assessment contexts. Is there any other grammatical skill you think should be included in this list? As noted in Activity 2.2, pay attention to whether the students can demonstrate these skills consistently successfully across multiple tasks. Ask yourself whether they can:

- discriminate sounds, stress, intonation, and pitch?
- apply knowledge of letter–sound relationships to pronounce words accurately?
- decode letters and single words?
- recognize characters and words by sight?
- understand that words are made up of sounds, including syllables, phonemes, or other units of sound?
- use parts of speech correctly?
- use a range of grammatical structures?
- understand text with nominalization strategies?
- form a sentence correctly?
- combine sentences using various connecting words?
- organize paragraphs logically?
- use conventions correctly?
- use transition words to link ideas?

Discourse Knowledge

As students progress to higher grades, they develop an understanding of the features of academic texts and discourse patterns. This discourse knowledge enables them to understand the structure of spoken and written text and participate in academic discourse in a socio-linguistically appropriate and effective manner. In other words, having discourse knowledge allows students to convey meanings that are appropriate to audiences and communicative purposes in a specific situation.

As children encounter a range of academic genres, they learn to identify text elements, conventions, intended audience, and the purpose of written text used in various genres. Through social interactions both in and outside of classrooms, students demonstrate their growing understanding of culturally appropriate language use. They pay attention to nonverbal cues and tones to interpret different meanings across different contexts. In high school, adolescent learners learn to use **cohesive devices** (phrases and words such as 'in the same way', 'nevertheless', 'furthermore') as transitions in academic discourse to produce academic writing in specific genres. They are expected to develop and express their perspective based on what they read and hear.

Activity 2.4

What linguistic behaviors best characterize discourse-level competence? Review the following descriptors that illustrate the core skills associated with discourse knowledge. Think about students you know and decide whether they can do what the descriptors entail.

Note that assessing students' discourse knowledge can be harder than assessing lexical and grammatical knowledge. Pay attention to whether the students can demonstrate these skills consistently in various language-use contexts. Some descriptors are more prominent than others in classrooms. Ask yourself whether the students can:

- speak cohesively in conversational interactions?
- understand explicit meanings from others' talk?
- understand implicit meanings from others' talk?
- understand an author's purpose?
- use culturally appropriate oral language skills to communicate with different audiences for various purposes?
- relate personal experience to textual information?
- appreciate the cultural relevance of a text topic?
- demonstrate an understanding of various text genres and features?

- organize ideas into paragraphs?
- identify the purpose of writing and its target audience?
- use a tone appropriate for the purpose?
- use a variety of organization patterns to structure writing?
- choose language appropriate for the context?

Language Functions and Skills

While school-aged language learners develop and expand their language skills in grammar, vocabulary, and discourse knowledge, they must also learn to use language to fulfill various communicative purposes. **Language functions** refer to the purposes of language use in the context of specific academic tasks across different content areas. Identifying the language functions specific to particular subjects (such as science or mathematics) is crucial for assessing and supporting language learners' ALP development across the curriculum (Christie, 2012; Schleppegrell & O'Hallaron, 2011). For example, students learn to ask questions, form and test hypotheses, make predictions, and draw conclusions based on empirical evidence in order to participate in discussions in a science class. Each subject area is shown to represent a distinct discourse community (Anstrom, 1997). Teachers need practical knowledge about language functions specific to the subjects that they teach; they should therefore provide explicit instruction on linguistic features and vocabulary used in particular subjects.

Research on classroom discourse features across content areas provides useful information about the language demands and necessary skills that students need to develop in content learning. Bailey, Butler, LaFramenta, & Ong (2001) reported, 'the language encountered in upper elementary science classrooms required students to comprehend language that was organized for specific purposes, namely explanations, descriptions, comparisons, and evaluations' (p. 186). Zwiers (2007) observed Grade 7 science, social studies, and language arts classes in a middle school and reported five core functional skills used during class discussions. They included: 'identifying cause and effect, comparing, persuading, interpreting, and taking other perspectives into account' (p. 99). This perspective is similar to what we saw in Classroom Snapshots 2.1 and 2.2.

Activity 2.5

Are there core language functions you expect students to master in order to achieve communicative goals? Work on this question yourself or with your classmates or colleagues and identify common language functions used in classrooms. Here are some language functions for you to consider in probing the question:

- Retell a personal experience.
- Recount information presented orally or in text.
- Categorize ideas.
- Identify relationships between events.
- Predict future events.
- Generate hypotheses to solve a problem.
- Explain a position with evidence.
- Identify evaluation criteria.
- Appraise various viewpoints.
- Determine the usefulness of resources.

Which language functions did you and your colleagues identify? Are there some language functions that are more prominent than others? Are there some language functions that are more difficult to teach than others?

Assessing ALP in Classrooms

So far, we have discussed the key components of ALP in terms of grammatical features, the depth and breadth of vocabulary, content-specific discourse knowledge, and language functions. When it comes to assessment, we need to break each component down into more specific skills to assess students' ALP mastery level.

What specific knowledge and skills do students need for each of the ALP knowledge components? What language functions are they be expected to master to achieve communicative goals? Based on a survey of existing theoretical models, curriculum materials, and assessment standards, Table 2.2 (on pages 54–5) presents an ALP Assessment Framework. The framework includes key descriptors that highlight core linguistic knowledge and skills. Teachers can assess students' academic language development at the grammatical, vocabulary, and discourse knowledge levels while students perform specific academic language functions.

In Table 2.2, 'interactive mode' refers to the channel of communication in learning curriculum content. As Gibbons (1998) noted, K–12 learning activities are multimodal, for example, students are asked to read a text, recount textual information orally, and then write a summary. This intertextual and interdependent relationship among the language modalities prompts us to be wary of the prevalent practice of organizing instruction and assessment in terms of listening, speaking, reading, and writing. Table 2.2 (on pages 54–5) uses mode as an organizing principle rather than the focus of assessment, and outlines how we can focus our assessment on grammar, vocabulary, textual knowledge, and functional skills that are foundational for academic life in multimodal learning.

The ALP framework can also be used to review an existing K–12 language assessment to uncover its underlying theoretical assumptions about ALP. It can assist teachers and educators in developing a new language assessment to be used in schools. To illustrate this use, Spotlight Study 2.1 introduces research by Heilman, Miller, & Nockerts (2010) and invites readers to apply the ALP framework to their Narrative Scoring Scheme (on page 56) to understand what elements of ALP are assessed.

Spotlight Study 2.1

Oral narration involves telling stories. Heilman, Miller, & Nockerts (2010) highlight how narration is a necessary skill for expressing intent, sharing information, and being an effective participant in classroom activities. The authors remind us that although telling stories is common across cultures, ELLs may need some extra support in order to successfully master the skill. To tell a story successfully, ELLs sometimes need to plan what they are going to say, and then use the appropriate vocabulary, grammar, and syntax to accomplish it. The researchers argue that there is a strong connection between language learners' reading achievement and their oral narrative skills. They also point out that although the development of oral language skills is included as part of most curricula, it is not a skill that is often assessed. Rather, teachers' time is devoted to assessing and tracking students' reading development.

Heilmann et al. (2010) examined various methods for assessing narrative organizational skills that were developmentally sensitive and that also informed characteristics of students' oral narrative skills. They concluded that the Narrative Scoring Scheme was the most developmentally sensitive measure of narrative organization skill. They used it to assess 129 young language learners in their oral narrative descriptions of a picture book by Mercer Mayer entitled, *Frog, Where Are You?*

Component	Interactive Mode		
	Oral	Reading	Writing
Grammar (morphology and syntax)	• discriminate sounds • discriminate stress, intonation, and pitch (i.e. prosodies) • apply knowledge of letter–sound relationship in pronouncing words accurately • use various grammatical structures with increasing accuracy.	• decode letters and single words • recognize characters and words by sight • understand that words are made up of sounds, including syllables, phonemes, or other units of sound • use knowledge of a range of grammatical structures for textual comprehension • understand text with nominalization strategies.	• form a sentence correctly • combine sentences using various connecting words • use parts of speech correctly • organize paragraphs logically • use a range of grammatical structures • use conventions correctly • use transition words to link ideas.
Vocabulary	• use a range of vocabulary relevant to context • expand vocabulary capacity from high-frequency general words to general academic words to specialized content specific words.	• use lexical knowledge for textual comprehension • use prior knowledge (e.g. first language) to deduce word meaning • recognize familiar words • use a range of cues (semantic, syntactic, and phonetic cues) to figure out new words • comprehend lexically dense text • figure out abstract, technical, and specialized vocabulary used in curriculum content.	• spell familiar words correctly • select words and phrases appropriate for conveying intended meaning • use a range of academic vocabulary to enrich intended meaning.
Discourse (textual)	• speak cohesively in conversational interactions • deliver well-organized speech in extended talk	• understand author's purpose • relate personal experience to textual information • appreciate cultural relevance of a text topic	• organize ideas into paragraphs • identify purpose of writing and target audience • choose an appropriate genre for the purpose

	• listen to, understand, and respond appropriately in a variety of situations for a variety of purposes • understand explicit and implicit meanings from others' talk • negotiate explicit and implicit meanings • use culturally appropriate oral language skills appropriately to communicate with different audiences for various purposes.	• demonstrate an understanding of various text genres (e.g. expository, narrative, causal, comparative) and features (e.g. literary, graphic, informational).	• use a tone appropriate for the purpose • use a variety of organization patterns to structure writing • use vivid language and innovative expressions to increase interest • use personal thoughts relevant to the topic of writing • choose language appropriate for sociocultural context.
Language function across modes	**Describe/summarize/synthesize** • retell personal experience • recount information presented orally by teacher or in text • recognize the author's main ideas with supporting details. **Analyze/classify/distinguish** • describe parts by separating them from whole • categorize ideas • identify relationships between events • identify causes and consequences • describe similarities and differences in ideas.	**Infer/hypothesize** • make inferences about implied meaning presented orally or in text • predict the ideas' implications • generate hypotheses to solve a problem. **Justify/persuade** • explain reasons for an action or ideas • support a position with evidence.	**Evaluate** • identify criteria for refining student work effectively • appraise the author's viewpoints • determine the appropriateness of text features and stylistic elements for the audience and purpose • determine the usefulness of other resources to enhance communication.

Table 2.2 Academic Language Proficiency (ALP) assessment framework

The Narrative Scoring in Table 2.3 Scheme provides teachers the means to assess seven aspects of narrative organization:

1 introduction
2 character development
3 mental states (the mental states of the characters in the story)
4 pronoun referencing
5 conflict resolution
6 cohesion
7 conclusion.

Each of these features is evaluated on a five-point scale that identifies the student as a minimal, emerging, or proficient user of these components of narrative organization.

Table 2.3 illustrates how the Narrative Scoring Scheme can be used to assess what a proficient child can do with narration organization skill (Heilmann et al., 2010, p. 623).

Characteristic	A proficient child can:
Introduction	• state place and time of the setting at appropriate place in story
Character development	• introduce main character with detail • distinguish main character from all supporting characters
Mental states	• describe mental states of main and supporting characters • use a variety of mental state words
Referencing	• use necessary antecedents to pronouns • use clear references throughout story
Conflict resolution	• identify all conflicts and resolutions critical to the story's plot
Cohesion	• keep the story in a logical order • distinguish critical events from minor ones • select smooth transitions between events
Conclusion	• conclude the story with clear concluding statements

Table 2.3 The Narrative Scoring Scheme

Using the Narrative Scoring Scheme, teachers can refer to the descriptions of the oral language behavior associated with each of the characteristics of the narrative organization. Here is a sample oral narrative produced by a child who had read *Frog, Where Are You?*

> The boy was looking for his frog. All day he looked for the frog and couldn't find him. Finally a beehive, the dog barked at a beehive in the tree. And the dog got in trouble. And so did the boy because the gopher and the owl. And ran away. And then he chased the dog. And he looked out from it. And then

he climbed on the branch. But it wasn't branches. It was a deer. And the deer shoved him off of the cliff. And then he went to the frog. And he had a family. And then a frog jumped out to get him. And then he took that frog home and left his old frog where his old frog was.

(Heilmann et al., 2010, p. 626)

This sample oral narrative received 14 points, based on the seven characteristics used to characterize the child's understanding of the story: introduction (1 pt); character development (3 pts.); mental states (1 pt.); referencing (3 pts.); conflict resolution (1 pt.); cohesion (2 pts.); and conclusion (3 pts.). ■

The study demonstrates how to assess children's oral language proficiency by focusing on the oral narration organization skill. Do you think that the Narrative Scoring Scheme is a potentially useful measure for assessing the discourse component in the ALP assessment framework in Table 2.2? When one takes a close look at the characteristics of the Narrative Scoring Scheme from the vantage point of the ALP assessment framework, it is not surprising to see that discourse knowledge is a key ALP component here. In addition to discourse-level skills, the scheme assesses vocabulary by focusing on whether a proficient child can 'state place and time of the setting' and 'use a variety of mental state words.' As such, grammar is assessed in terms of whether the child can 'use necessary antecedents to pronouns,' 'use clear references throughout story,' and 'select smooth transitions between events.'

Have you used oral narration to assess students' oral language proficiency in the classroom? Do you think that adolescent learners would benefit from oral narration activities? The secondary school curriculum tends to put more emphasis on written discourse than oral skills, and speaking practice is often limited to oral reading fluency. Furthermore, as indicated above, newcomer learners are often marginalized in whole-class oral interactions due to the lack of cultural familiarity and anxiety from peer pressure (Duff, 2001). At the same time, research shows that literacy development is influenced by students' oral and **metacognitive abilities** (Genesee, Lindholm-Leary, Saunders, & Christian, 2005). This positive relationship between oral and literacy skills becomes even stronger for older learners involved in more academic content learning (Genesee et al., 2005; Snow, Cancino, Gonzalez, & Shriberg, 1987). Nurss & Hough (1992) concur with many others that oral language is a key aspect of literacy development for language learners: 'Oral language competence is needed to actively participate in literacy instruction because most of the directions, explanations, and interactions that make up instruction in elementary and secondary classrooms are oral' (p. 281).

Language learners need frequent verbal interactions with teachers and with peers. Teachers should provide the academic and content-related language that students need, as well as the language related to classroom and learning management; whereas peers can provide socially appropriate ways of using language for communication. Both are necessary in order for newcomers to develop oral language competence in L2. Oral narration activities guided by teachers may provide newcomers with the opportunity to develop both oral and discourse organizational skills critical for academic language proficiency.

Key Features of ALP Development in Young and Adolescent Learners

As language learners move from grade to grade, they continue to develop academic language proficiency and confront language demands in increasingly specialized content areas. For example, Bailey & Butler (2003) reported five dominant language functions observed in Grades 4 and 5 science classrooms—explanation, description, comparison, questioning, and commenting. These language functions can be challenging for all school-aged students but ELLs in particular are expected to meet these demanding language functions in a language that they are currently developing. How do ELLs of different ages develop ALP? How about young children who have not yet mastered any language fully? Research supports some salient features of language development across the age span of ELLs in schools.

Young children aged 6 to 9:

- learn to recognize the most frequent 2,000 words of English that occur regularly in academic text. For example, Coxhead (2006) reports that these most frequent 2,000 words account for up to 75 percent of the words used in spoken and written text selected for the study.
- spend a significant amount of time in school developing oral language. They develop oral language skills at a rapid speed by participating in daily routines and social interactions with peers and teachers, and following instructions. The National Reading Panel (2000) reports that oral language skills are foundational for later reading proficiency development. Young language learners must develop literacy skills while simultaneously acquiring oral proficiency.

- begin to develop emergent literacy skills by acquiring print knowledge (understanding the relationship between the print form and purpose) and phonological awareness (August & Shanahan, 2006; Geva, 2006). Similarity in sounds and symbols between children's L1 and L2 can facilitate their development of knowledge of letter–sound associations (Bialystok, Luk, & Kwan, 2005).
- may have difficulty maintaining interest when language demands are too high or topics are not engaging. Young children tend to have a short attention span. Failing to consider the shorter attention span in assessment can result in the invalid interpretations of children's abilities and mistaking language development for cognitive delays.
- may show limited developmental vocabulary capacity in both English and home language possibly because of limited exposure to rich vocabulary use in both languages. Children may not yet fully benefit from the cognitive advantages of being bilingual because they have limited cognitive memory storage and limited ability to automatize information processing.

Early adolescent learners aged 10 to 13:

- experience a transition period in all aspects of their development, including cognitive and metacognitive maturation and physical growth. They are able to engage in abstract reasoning and strategic thinking. Research shows that bilingual learners demonstrate advantages in performing certain metalinguistic tasks (Bialystok, 2001). This increase in metalinguistic awareness facilitates the transfer of skills between languages (August, Calderon, & Carlo, 2002; Cummins & Swain, 1986).
- experience a shift from learning to read to reading to learn through being introduced to a full range of textual comprehension skills beyond word decoding skills (Smith & Wilhelm, 2002). Reading and writing abilities become important skills to demonstrate what children can do in content learning (Meltzer & Hamann, 2005).
- may show decrease in interest in literacy (Eccles, 1993) possibly due to increasingly challenging and lexically dense academic texts. Students may experience the 'fourth grade slump' (Chall, Jacobs, & Baldwin, 1990, p. 45) in which achievement gaps among subgroups of students from different socio-economic and linguistic backgrounds become wider. In particular, students from economically disadvantaged backgrounds show the greatest difficulty with academic vocabulary.

- expand vocabulary knowledge by acquiring general academic vocabulary beyond the most frequent vocabulary (Stevens et al., 2000). Early adolescent learners also deepen their vocabulary knowledge by learning specialized meanings of familiar words used in content areas by dealing with conceptually abstract or experience-distant ideas beyond first-hand experience.
- learn a wide variety of genres including narrative and expository. Students begin to identify and use the grammatical features associated with specific text genres across the curriculum. ELLs tend to show more difficulty with narrative texts than with expository compared to L1 students, partly because narrative texts require an understanding of social and cultural contexts in which narration takes place in the text (Cheng, Klinger, & Zheng, 2009).

Adolescent learners aged 14 to 18

- develop and refine their identities with new roles and responsibilities in peer groups and communities (Guthrie, 2001). Even though adolescents crave independence and autonomy, they also try to conform to expectations they perceive from their peers and adults (Hume, 2008).
- engage fully in abstract thinking on values, beliefs, and propositions. Adolescent language learners acquire advanced language proficiency that allows them to use language to convey non-literal meanings and participate fully in academic content learning through interactions (Byrnes, 2002; Shohamy, Inbar-Lourie, & Poehner, 2008).
- acquire control over a full range of language functions with extensive use of 'appraisal' with critical perspective (Christie, 2012). Students develop advanced metalinguistic ability to verbalize their abstract thinking and use language in more sophisticated ways. They further develop and benefit from metalinguistic awareness to apply to a variety of language functions across content areas (Bialystok, 2001; Cummins, 2001). They are capable of setting communicative goals, monitoring and using various linguistic resources, and assessing the achievement of the goals they set.
- use a range of registers and genres associated with specific content areas. Students' written language becomes more grammatically complex and conceptually abstract. They write expository essays for reporting, summarizing, analyzing information, and expressing different perspectives as they transition to high schools.
- develop specialized vocabulary, including technical and subject-specific terms. Students express abstract ideas with grammatical nominalization and abstract and technical vocabulary in academic texts (Schleppegrell & O'Hallaron, 2011).

These key developmental features of academic language proficiency among learners of different ages illustrate a learning continuum in which learners make progress at different rates as a result of a range of factors associated with their life experiences, cognitive maturation, and the social and cultural settings in which they are situated. These features are neither exhaustive nor exclusive. Rather they should be considered on the developmental continuum as a guide for teachers to understand individual learners' unique language development profiles.

How Long Does it Take to Acquire ALP?

Learning a new language is a complex and challenging task that takes a considerable amount of time for people of any age. It is a particularly demanding process for children who experience substantial cultural change—especially for immigrant children. Research suggests that ELLs can achieve conversational fluency within two years of learning English, but they will need between five and seven years to catch up with their mainstream L1 counterparts to succeed in academic school life (Collier, 1987; Cummins, 1981). While both young and adolescent learners experience rapid growth in cognitive, socio-emotional, and physical development, young learners' growth rates may vary significantly depending on a range of factors. What becomes the most critical factor for these learners is the amount of available support at home and school for acquiring language proficiency in both English and their home language (RAND Reading Study Group, 2002). For example, parents' motivation and ability to support children's language development accelerates children's literacy development. A home environment rich with literacy activities in both the first language and English advances students' language development at a higher rate (August & Shanahan, 2006; Genesee et al., 2005). Let us read more about these issues in Spotlight Study 2.2.

Spotlight Study 2.2

Jang, Dunlop, Wagner, Kim, & Gu (2013) investigated differences in reading achievement and reading skill development among over 100,000 Grade 6 students with different language backgrounds in Ontario public schools. The researchers applied a statistical skill-profiling method to large-scale reading achievement test data. Their investigation started by examining overall reading achievement levels among subgroups of students, using the percentage of students who met or exceeded the provincial standard (levels 3 and 4) on a standardized reading test. The subgroups were formed on the basis of multiple background variables, including immigration status, the number of years the students had been living in Canada, and **home language environment**. The home language environment variable (based on students' responses to the home language survey) identified three groups: '(1) those who hear and speak only English (*n* = 92,619) at home; (2) those who hear (*n* = 13,897) and speak (*n* =13,815) another language(s) as often as English; and (3) those who hear and speak only (*n* = 14,251) or mostly another language(s) (*n* = 7,957) (Jang et al., p. 408). Figure 2.2 illustrates overall reading achievement levels between monolingual and multilingual groups in terms of the length of residence and immigration status.

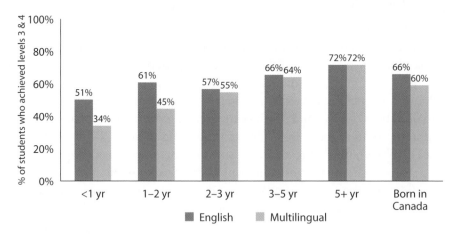

Figure 2.2 Reading achievement levels among language subgroups ▪

As the figure illustrates, the results show that earlier gaps in reading achievement among immigrant ELLs disappear as the length of residence increases. This finding holds true for all immigrant students regardless of their home language environment. However, students who have spent more than five years in Canada and whose home language environment is monolingual or bilingual—English and home languages are equally available—demonstrate the highest achievement level among all of the language groups, including domestic students who were born in Canada, but speak and hear mostly another language at home (see the domestic multilingual group in Figure 2.2).

Jang et al. (2013) further examined the mastery patterns of six reading skills (against the grade-level expectations) among the subgroups of students from different language background profiles. Let us review two specific skills, vocabulary and grammar skill mastery patterns, among four home language groups:

- EnEn (those who hear and speak English only at home)
- EqEq (those who hear and speak both English and another language equally)
- OtOt (those who hear and speak another language only at home), and
- EqEn (those who hear both languages but speak English only at home).

Figures 2.3 and 2.4 show the vocabulary skill and grammar skill mastery patterns among the subgroups. The vertical axis shows the skill mastery probability, and its value of 0.6 and above is considered to represent skill mastery. The horizontal axis shows five immigrant groups and one domestic group.

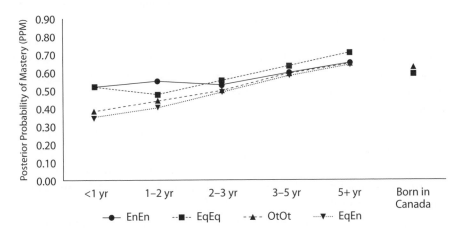

Figure 2.3 Mastery patterns of vocabulary knowledge

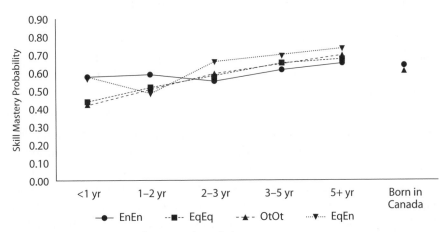

Figure 2.4 Mastery patterns of grammar knowledge

These two skill mastery patterns are similar to the overall reading achievement illustrated in Figure 2.2. The immigrant students who hear and speak other languages only at home (OtOt) with less than a year of residence in Canada showed the lowest skill mastery levels. It took approximately three to five years for immigrant students to reach the mastery level (0.6 and above) of the vocabulary skill while it took two to three years for them to achieve the mastery level of the grammar skill. The findings suggest that students' home language environment affects immigrant students' reading skill development in the early years. However, as the length of residence increased, the early years' gaps among students with different home language backgrounds disappeared, 'canceling out any initial advantage that the monolingual immigrant students had' (p. 419). Of all the home language subgroups, those who hear both English and other languages and speak English (EqEn) show the highest level of reading skill mastery (both vocabulary and grammar). The same pattern was observed with four different home language subgroups within Canadian-born students. The researchers conclude:

> A minimum of 3 years of language immersion appears to be a tipping point for immigrant students to achieve grade-appropriate reading comprehension ability across skills. Once students reach the grade-appropriate reading proficiency level, their reading skill development becomes speedy, possibly because of bilingual advantages such as greater mental flexibility and creativity, efficient concept formation, and metalinguistic skills that allow students to reflect on their language and its use… It is possible that, as explained by Cummins' (1996) interdependence hypothesis, multilinguals' cognitive advantages become available when students reach a certain threshold level of language proficiency. Further research is necessary for examining whether students with different language background profiles follow different skill mastery paths and whether there are specific skills that are readily transferable. (Gunderson, 2007).

(Jang et al., 2013, p. 427)

One notable finding, as shown in Figure 2.2, was that the achievement level of domestic ELLs is behind both domestic English-speaking and immigrant students with more than five years of residence in Canada. This finding is confirmed by their skill mastery patterns in Figure 2.3 and 2.4. These patterns imply that time alone is not a sufficient condition for reading development, nor is the home language environment. Do you recall Jalissa, the Canadian-born student in Grade 3, in Activity 2.1 of this chapter?

Although she is younger (Grade 3) than the studied population (Grade 6), her profile fits the domestic multilingual students' reading achievement pattern. This underachievement in reading may be partly because domestic ELLs are often not identified as language learners in schools (possibly because of their relatively fluent oral language skill). As a result, they are less likely to receive formal ESL support. This assertion is corroborated by a case study by McGloin (2011) in which none of eight domestic ELLs she studied received ESL support; instead, three were placed in the special education program. Despite the policy that domestic students are also entitled to support in developing English proficiency, such support does not seem to be available for all domestic ELLs.

The findings from Spotlight Study 2.2 encourage us to reconsider some commonly held views that ELLs lag behind in their academic and literacy attainment, and that ELLs are a homogeneous group with identical challenges and similar language-learning trajectories. For example, the No Child Left Behind Act of 2001 in the USA demands equivalent academic progress for all ELLs regardless of their backgrounds, reflecting an overly simplistic view of ELLs. The study also highlights that immigration status and a first language used for identifying students' ELL status may not provide sufficient information for teachers to understand the diversity and complexity of ELLs' language profiles. Identification and assessment can be a daunting task for teachers in schools with a high proportion of ELLs. Teachers' professional knowledge about language development is crucial for making assessment appropriate and meaningful for school-aged students.

The researchers in Spotlight Study 2.3 examine similar issues by focusing on adolescent learners' writing skills development. Developing writing skills is a long-term process. Although writing develops along with reading, many adolescent learners may find writing difficult despite their relative competence in reading. They continue to 'learn to write' by expanding and deepening the knowledge of vocabulary and mastering the conventions of grammar. They learn to approach writing tasks strategically by brainstorming, organizing ideas, revising, and evaluating their essays. At the same time, writing becomes a key means to learn and demonstrate their content knowledge (Graham & Perin, 2007; Shanahan, 2004). This second role, writing to learn and to show what they have learned, places significant pressures on adolescent language learners who are still learning to write.

How do adolescent language learners develop writing skills? How do their first languages assist in developing L2 writing skills? Are there different rates in development during the adolescent years? These questions are addressed in Spotlight Study 2.3.

Spotlight Study 2.3

Schoonen, van Gelderen, Stoel, Hulstijn, & de Glopper (2011) investigated the development of the English writing proficiency of close to 400 Dutch students over a three-year period. They were interested not only in tracking the development of students' writing proficiency, but also examining the extent to which the development is related to students' metacognitive knowledge about reading and writing, vocabulary knowledge, grammatical knowledge, spelling knowledge, speed of lexical retrieval (or typing fluency), and speed of sentence construction.

The researchers assessed students' first language (Dutch) and foreign language (English) writing proficiency through a series of three writing tasks completed in each language and in each of three years of the study when students were in Grades 8, 9, and 10. By the time the students were in Grade 8, they had been learning English for approximately 3.5 years. Researchers selected writing topics relevant to adolescents' lives and experiences and scored the students' writings holistically, which means that students were given a single mark based on how well they were able to express themselves.

The researchers' informative findings raised some key discussion points about students' writing proficiency development:

- Students' English language writing proficiency was related to their metacognitive knowledge, grammatical knowledge, spelling knowledge, and typing fluency. In other words, each of these aspects of students' knowledge or ability could be used to predict students' L2 writing proficiency. During the second year of testing, when students were in Grade 9, there was an even greater relationship between their grammatical knowledge and L2 writing proficiency than when they were in Grade 8.
- Overall, students' Dutch writing proficiency increased only a little and by the same amount between Grade 8 and Grade 9, and Grade 9 and Grade 10. Students' English writing proficiency improved more between Grade 8 and Grade 9 than between Grades 9 and 10.
- In Grade 8, there was a strong relationship between students' first language writing ability and English writing proficiency, and this relationship remained the same in Grade 9 and Grade 10.

The researchers concluded that by the time students were in Grade 8, their first language writing proficiency had developed enough that they were able to successfully complete the writing tasks presented to them in this study, but that their L2 writing proficiency was still in the early stages of development. Recall that on average, the students had been learning English for approximately 3.5

years. With this in mind, what might be the implications for how you organize your writing instruction and assessment? In Chapters 3 and 4, we will discuss issues associated with various approaches to assessing young and adolescent learners' language proficiency. ▧

Differentiating Language Development from Exceptionalities

Considering the growing number of language learners in classrooms, it is not surprising that teachers experience difficulty in differentiating between students' difficulty with language development and exceptionalities arising from cognitive delays—either in general learning or specific to reading (Paradis, Genesee, & Crago, 2011). In general, early indicators of poor reading development are related to poor phonological processing skills, such as phonological awareness and decoding (Stanovich, 1986). This is observed in children's lack of knowledge about alphabet sounds and letters and difficulty linking sounds to letters. They may make errors when reading common words and experience difficulty connecting textual understanding to their own experiences. The National Reading Panel (2000) reports that phonological awareness and letter–sound knowledge account for up to 40 percent of variation in word-level reading test scores among L1 students.

Research suggests that both L1 and L2 students with **reading disability** tend to perform poorly on measures of phonological awareness, syntactic awareness, and working memory (Lipka, Siegel, & Vukovic, 2005). Children with learning difficulties in their first languages may experience similar difficulties in English (Cummins, 1979). At the same time, distinct features in the characteristics of language scripts between L1 and L2 may lead to difficulties unique to different subgroups of L2 students. It is also possible that L2 students experience temporary language imbalance where one language may be more dominant at a certain point in time as children become bilingual (Genesee, Paradis, & Crago, 2004). In addition, considering that early reading development in young language learners is facilitated by their oral proficiency in L1 and L2 (Bialystok, 2002; Gottardo, 2002), L2 students' lack of oral skills presents a significant challenge for teachers in determining whether the challenges the students experience are due to their potential exceptionalities. Teachers need to consider students' oral and literacy skills in their first languages as a first step to understanding whether their difficulty is based on cognitive impairment or rather is a reflection of their current L2 development.

The question of when is a good time to identify learning and reading difficulties among language learners is highly contested. Without considering their language development stages and onset of L2 exposure, early identification of reading difficulties can result in over-identification resulting from a failure to differentiate language development from learning disability (Cummins, 1984). On the other hand, the longer teachers wait to identify reading difficulties, the harder they are to overcome (Geva, 2000). This is due to the increasingly higher language demands in content areas as students progress to higher grades.

Some students may have multiple learning difficulties, and the ability to accurately identify these cannot be a sole teacher's responsibility. Clearly, this problem requires teachers to collaborate with others (ESL teachers, students, parents) particularly those who have knowledge of the students' first languages in schools. Genesee et al. (2005) insist that collaboration among ESL teachers and special education professionals is crucial to ensure that students' language needs are accurately identified. They recommend that teachers use multiple evidence-gathering methods to develop a comprehensive language profile that includes strengths and weaknesses in both first language and English.

An example of such collaborative approaches can be seen in a project at the York Region District School Board (YRDSB, 2012) in the province of Ontario, Canada. The board initiated an ELL policy and program implementation project to guide the identification of ELLs with special needs. The project was intended to meet the policy requirement that 'school boards will develop a protocol for identifying English language learners who may also have special education needs' (Ontario Ministry of Education, 2007, p. 18). In collaboration with teachers, psychologists, speech pathologists, and other key education agents, the board developed a framework that includes an examination of the following factors:

1 Personal and family issues/context (Pre- and post-migration experience)
2 Previous schooling (continuous/disrupted)
3 Physical, developmental, emotional, and cognitive development
4 **Acculturation** process
5 Language and literacy development (L1, oral skills)

Understanding personal and family factors can contribute to understanding how to differentiate between L2 development and exceptionalities. When new ELLs arrive in school, teachers can orally interview or survey their parents in writing to gather information about their family backgrounds. If parents do not speak or read English sufficiently well, social service workers can assist with the interview by arranging a translator for the parents. In gathering personal and family background information, teachers need to ask about students' previous schooling experience in terms of the amount and quality of instruction in both first and English languages. Teachers also need to continue to track students' physical, emotional, and cognitive development in relation to their language development and academic growth, through ongoing observations of students' interactions within and outside the classroom.

Activity 2.5

Review the framework developed by the YRDSB. For each factor, identify what kind of specific information would be useful. From whom would you seek this information? What method would be appropriate for gathering such information? Are there other factors that you think should be considered? Discuss these factors with your colleagues, special education professionals, and parents in your school.

ELLs go through various stages in the process of acculturation. It is not surprising for teachers to find that some new ELLs remain silent for an extended time while others adapt themselves quickly to the new learning environment. Tabors & Snow (1994) describe the silent period as the second stage of a development sequence in second-language acquisition following a first stage when young children persist in using their home languages for a brief period even when others do not understand. When children realize their home languages do not work in the new environment, they become nonverbal. This time is a critical period for young children to learn the new language. Assessment during this period may underestimate or misrepresent young children's potential language ability (Tabors & Snow).

It is possible that adolescent language learners with two years of immigration experience cope with the challenge arising from the new school environment in ways similar to young learners. Unlike young children, these adolescent ELLs may have prior educational experiences in the L2 although the degree varies to a great extent. If they remain silent in the classroom, it may be because they are experiencing identity conflicts, a negative attitude to L2 language learning, and anxiety from peer pressure. This situation is well portrayed in Danzak's (2011) case study that illustrates two distinct patterns associated with adolescent Mexican students' perceptions of L2 learning:

The first pattern, *bilingual identity with positive views of bilingualism*, was exhibited by Carolina and Juan (from Puerto Rico) and Diego (from Mexico). From the participants' perspective, *bilingual* was understood as having a certain level of (oral) language proficiency in both Spanish and English. These three students reported that they regularly spoke and felt confident using both languages, enjoyed/valued both languages, and felt happy living in the United States. Despite their self-identification as bilinguals, these participants elected to write or speak in Spanish when given the option, as discussed above ... The second pattern, monolingual (Spanish-speaking) identity with negative views of bilingualism, was demonstrated by Edgar, Sara, and Manuel (all from Mexico) ... These students felt that they did not speak enough English, English was difficult, they did not want to learn English, and they were not happy or comfortable living in the United States. Additionally, all of these students expressed a desire to return to live in Mexico.

(Danzak, 2011, p. 512)

Danzak's detailed analysis helps us understand individual students' identities and perceptions of L2 learning. For example, Edgar demonstrated academic language proficiency in L1 at the lexical, syntactic, and discourse-level skills; however, his limited experience and negative attitude to English prevented him from transferring such academic language skills to writing in the L2. On the other hand, while Manuel had negative feelings about L2 learning, he struggled with writing in both L1 and L2. Danzak notes that Manuel could have an undiagnosed language learning disability.

There are numerous formal measures used for identifying learning and reading difficulties. For example, the Wechsler Individual Achievement Test (WIAT-III, Wechsler, 2009) is often used to assess students' reading ability and to further identify a discrepancy between the student's current proficiency level and a grade/age norm. Another example is the Woodcock-Johnson III test battery (Woodcock, McGrew, & Mather, 2001), which is used to assess cognitive and oral language levels, and achievement levels. Given the complexity of the linguistic and cultural learning that ELLs experience, teachers need to be cautious about using existing standardized measures typically normed for L1 students. There is a great need for linguistically and culturally sensitive assessments for ELLs.

In particular, the assessment of bilingual children should not be used to confirm the double-deficit view, that is, they are not as proficient as monolinguals in either of their languages. Instead, it should take into account additive effects of learning multiple languages. Assessing the bilingual/multilingual students' linguistic repertoire as a whole can provide more comprehensive information about their linguistic and cognitive potential on the continuum of multilingual competence (Grosjean, 2001; Jessner, 2008).

Although it is imperative to identify language learners who may have exceptionalities as soon as possible in order to arrange appropriate programming for them, teachers should take careful steps before referring them to psycho-educational tests. Through initial language assessments, teachers should arrange language support programs for students, and monitor them if they are not making adequate progress in the programs. If they are not, even after receiving sufficient support to develop language skills, teachers may initiate a pre-referral process in which they conduct a systematic assessment of the students' strengths and needs by documenting their responses to differentiated instructional strategies and tasks. This pre-referral process can help minimize the chance that language learners are inaccurately referred to psycho-educational tests for exceptionalities (Ortiz & Yates, 2001).

Although a lack of attention to identifying students' learning needs and necessary interventions is detrimental, negative consequences from mis- and over-identification can also have a profound impact on the lives of language learners. The purpose of assessment in this regard is not to label students with deficits but to provide them with support tailored to their actual needs. Teachers can gather information from multiple assessments to develop comprehensive language profiles that detail not only students' areas of needs but also their strengths. These actions will send a positive message to students about assessment and about themselves as learners.

Summary

In this chapter, we have examined different ways of conceptualizing language proficiency. We have also looked at research, using different approaches to describe school-aged language learners' proficiency development. Throughout, it has been emphasized that in planning, interpreting, and using assessment results, teachers need to take account of individual students' unique developmental paths from a long-term perspective. We have also discussed the difficulties of assessing language proficiency separately from content knowledge and skills in the curriculum-learning context. Because most existing language assessments may not be sensitive enough to assess students' academic language proficiency in content-specific areas beyond social uses of language, we paid close attention to the key components of

ALP. This chapter illustrated ways in which the ALP assessment framework can be used to identify knowledge and skills assessed by existing tests and guide the development of a new assessment tool.

Teachers need to take care in distinguishing children's language learning needs from special needs arising from developmental disabilities or delays, emotional impairments, and/or physical disabilities. Because young language learners develop their first language literacy skills while simultaneously developing an L2, teachers need to consider a range of factors including students' home language use when assessing them for exceptionalities. Considering the complexity of L2 students' language development and a myriad of factors associated with it, we should be careful when using existing standardized measures. In Chapter 3, we will examine key principles for assessing young language learners and discuss various assessment approaches based on research evidence and practical applications in classrooms.

3

Principles for Assessing Young Language Learners

Preview

Thus far, we have explored how language assessment is used in many different parts of the world. We have also discussed theories of language development that teachers need to know in planning, implementing, and using assessment results for language learners. In this chapter, we will focus on key principles for assessing young language learners in schools (we will discuss some principles for assessing adolescent learners in Chapter 4). Let us begin the discussion by exploring some assessment issues in Classroom Snapshot 3.1.

Classroom Snapshot 3.1

Anna is a full-time elementary school teacher and is pursuing a Master's degree in Education. She chose to take a graduate course entitled, Assessing School-aged Language Learners, as her second last course for her degree. Here is a conversation between Anna and her course instructor (myself) during the first class. Think about what assessment issues she raises and compare her questions and concerns with yours.

Eunice: Why are you interested in this course, I mean, assessments?

Anna: I work with ELLs and students with special needs. There is no formal identification of exceptionalities in my school because it's a private school. But we use many different tests throughout the year. Some are standardized, and some aren't. But we have so little information about the tests.

Eunice: What kind of information do you wish to have?

Anna: For example, we don't know which test is better for our students. Shouldn't there be a set of criteria that can guide us with test selection and use?

Eunice: OK. Can you please elaborate on the criteria? What comes to your mind when you think of such criteria?

Anna: I would like to know if the test I am using (or am asked to use) really measures my students' language ability. Especially when I use a

	standardized test, I want to know if it is relevant to what my students learn in my classroom. Also I feel teachers' marks are too subjective.
Eunice:	Why so?
Anna:	Because we know individual students well, it may be hard for us to be objective.
Eunice:	OK. Let me write down some of your questions on the board so that we can revisit them later.
Anna:	Another question I ask myself a lot has to do with assessment methods. What assessment method should I use? Depending on assessment methods, such as essay, multiple-choice test, presentation, students' marks fluctuate. I'm pretty sure it has to do with assessment methods. Obviously some need some additional help or accommodations. But I'm not sure if it's even fair to give accommodations, such as extra time or a dictionary, to some students but not to all. ■

Anna asked some important questions; unfortunately, answering them is not simple. Do any of your own questions overlap with hers? In Chapter 1 we touched on some of the key concepts that Anna is struggling with here. Building on these key concepts of assessment, we will discuss specific assessment principles that can be used to evaluate young learners. As you read the chapter and learn about these issues, think about how these topics are relevant to you in your teaching context. How will you use the information in your assessment and instruction of the young language learners in your classrooms?

Mapping out Assessments

What kinds of assessment are appropriate for assessing young learners? When should teachers use external language tests to inform them of their students' language proficiency? How is the use of external language tests and the information that they generate different from teacher-designed classroom assessment? In Snapshot 3.1, Anna mentions various assessments such as standardized external tests, student term papers, and informal assessments. These assessments differ in many ways, including their purposes, task types, scoring, and interpretations.

Take a look at Figure 3.1. Each of the four dimensions illustrates how an assessment can be characterized according to its purpose and degree of standardization. For example, an assessment in Dimension 1 serves more of a formative (than summative) purpose, and is unstandardized. An example of an assessment in this dimension would be a teacher checklist used to evaluate students' language use during group work. As discussed in Chapter 1, the purpose of each assessment falls somewhere along the continuum of formative (i.e. providing on-going feedback on teaching and learning) to summative (i.e. evaluating and reporting students' overall achievement) functions. Standardization is a procedure taken to make test administration and scoring uniform. A standardized test means that students take the same test under the same test condition, and their performance is evaluated based on predetermined scoring schemes or rubrics (Popham, 1999). This process allows test score users to compare individual students against pre-established references.

Activity 3.1

Let us revisit the assessments you used to complete Activity 1.1 in Chapter 1. Use those assessments as exemplars to answer the following questions: What is the purpose of each assessment? To what extent is it standardized? Now situate each of your assessments in one of the four dimensions illustrated in Figure 3.1. Is there any assessment that appears in more than one dimension?

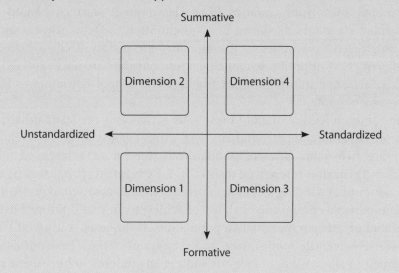

Figure 3.1 A framework for mapping assessments on the continua

Many classroom language assessments are informal in that they are not standardized. For example, spelling tests that you create before starting a new unit could appear in Dimension 1. If you administered a vocabulary test from PPVT-IV (Peabody Picture Vocabulary Test, 4th ed.), it would appear either in Dimension 3 or Dimension 4 depending on your use of the test results. If students submit portfolios that they worked on throughout the term, they may be found in Dimension 2. If teachers assess students' portfolios using state, provincial, or national standards-based rubrics, they may be found close to the vertical axis within Dimension 2. It is entirely possible that the same assessment (for example, a portfolio) is found in two different dimensions, because it is the *use* of the assessment (not the assessment itself) that will help to determine its placement along the vertical axis.

Let us discuss the term 'standardization' in more detail. Take a look at the language tests you placed in Dimensions 3 and 4. There are many standardized language tests used for both summative and formative purposes. International language tests, such as the Cambridge Young Learners English Tests and TOEFL Junior Tests are examples of standardized language tests. They are increasingly used in schools in EFL contexts in which the tests serve a need from local EFL educators to provide evidence of student progress in the development of English proficiency by offering certification or providing information used for admission and placement decisions (see Spotlight Study 3.3). Standards-based language tests mandated by educational authorities (such as ELD Classroom Assessment, based on Californian standards, as shown in Spotlight Study 3.4) are also examples of standardized approaches to testing. They are mainly used to evaluate the effectiveness of public school education, but they are also expected to provide formative information for teachers and school educators to plan improvement strategies.

One common feature of all of these tests is that they are standardized in order for users to compare students' test scores against certain references. There are two main types of standardized tests: **norm-referenced tests** (NRT) and **criterion-referenced tests** (CRT). Recognizing this distinction is crucial for understanding assessment practices. NRTs are used to rank order students across a continuum of ability or achievement that is normed using a national or other representative population. If the tests you use at your school use percentile scores, they are examples of NRTs. These norms are developed to allow users to measure individual students' achievement and ability with reference to a larger sample, often a nationally representative sample of students. Therefore, those NRT scores are meaningful only with reference to the norms. Some external tests use scaled scores by translating raw scores to a scale of a **mean** and a **standard deviation**. For example, in a well-known test used with older learners, the Test of English as Foreign Language Internet-Based (TOEFL iBT) total scores are reported on a 0 to 300 scale. Overall, the norm-referenced tests are based upon the principle of normal score distributions in which the distribution of students' scores looks like a symmetrical bell curve. This normal distribution should remain the same across occasion and time, which is problematic when the NRT is used to measure students' achievement after instruction. Teachers would surely not want to see a highly skewed distribution of their students' scores as an indication of effective instruction and growth in students' learning!

While NRT scores can tell you where one of your students stands in reference to a national norm, they cannot tell you how well he or she has achieved curricular goals, which is the goal of CRTs (Hudson & Lynch, 1984). CRTs differ from NRTs in that they are used to determine what students have achieved and can do in relation to a set of pre-specified criteria, including the educational standards that we reviewed in Chapter 1.

NRTs and CRTs differ not only in terms of the purposes of testing but also in the principles used to guide test item development. Most NRTs use selected-response test item types (multiple-choice, true false, matching) because of efficiency in administration and scoring, which are crucial conditions for large-scale testing serving educational accountability. In addition, because discriminating among students is the prime goal of the NRTs, test items are developed and validated based on rigorous technical scrutiny to ensure high quality discriminating power for differentiating high- from low-proficient learners.

Items for the CRTs are also carefully designed and validated based on their capacity to measure core curricular skills and knowledge that students have learned. The CRTs prefer performance assessment because they directly elicit students' target language output. They are more difficult to standardize mainly because of the variability in human scoring procedures and fewer tasks used (Bailey, 1998).

How often do you use standardized NRTs in your school? The most frequent uses of standardized tests used for young language learners in schools are to identify students for referral for special education and to track academic achievements in content areas in order to meet the accountability policy demands. Because both uses are considered to have significant consequences for students, standardized tests used for those purposes should be developmentally, culturally, and linguistically appropriate for young language learners. I caution here that most standardized NRTs used for referral to special education, or tracking students' academic achievement are normed against a population which may not adequately represent language learners. In addition, normative scales for these tests are inappropriate for judging language learners' eligibility for special education and further identifying their learning needs. As we learned from the York

Region District School Board project in Chapter 2, educators need to take a holistic perspective when considering special education services for language learners instead of basing referral on the results from standardized NRTs. They should consider multiple aspects of language learning potential, collecting data using multiple assessment methods, and by seeking input from parents and teachers in addition to formal standardized test results.

When tests are standardized against a large norming group, they are not best suited to provide information about individuals' strengths and areas of needs. Rather, they are efficient for rank-ordering students against the normed population and make comparison easier. When norm-referenced standardized tests are used for assessing young and adolescent language learners, the test results are more prone to errors because the tests tend to be long, and time-constrained, and to favor multiple-choice test questions. As we discussed in Chapter 2, young learners have a much shorter attention span than older learners and they may also have limited experience with multiple-choice tests in some contexts. It is common to hear elementary school teachers talking about the many hours they have spent before a mandatory external test helping to familiarize their younger learners with multiple-choice tests! Let us now discuss specific principles for assessing school-aged language learners.

Assessment Should be Cognitively Rich Enough to Elicit Knowledge and Skills

One indication of the quality of language assessment is whether it involves children in rich cognitive activities. Learners need to understand what the activity is asking them to do and then cognitively process information presented in them. Cognitively rich activities require students to draw on their linguistic resources and background knowledge including both content and world knowledge. Learners also need to recognize the context of the task (for example, is this a conversation between two students in the school hallway?) and text genres (is it from a science textbook or a magazine?). In some tests, a cognitively rich task asks students to predict what a text will be about from the title or pictures included in the task. Presented either orally or in written format, such tasks can help students to create mental images to synthesize information from the text and use metacognitive ability to monitor their problem-solving strategies. As you can see from these examples and descriptions, cognitively rich tasks engage learners by asking them to draw upon various linguistic, cognitive, and metacogntive skills.

The creation of a cognitively rich language assessment begins with the development of assessment specifications that identify core linguistic knowledge and skills that proficient students are expected to demonstrate in the target language (Davidson & Lynch, 2002). The assessment developers then identify language behaviors and functions associated with each element of the core linguistic knowledge and skills. For example, vocabulary knowledge plays a key role in young learners' language proficiency development. One of the vocabulary processing skills may be the ability to figure out the meaning of a low-frequency word from the context of its use in an academic text. The mastery of this skill may be observed when students use such low-frequency vocabulary in their essays. Subsequently, assessment tasks are created to simulate learning contexts in which this language function can be observed.

How effectively do assessments elicit target language skills? Do elicited skills represent the target language construct? How authentic are testing contexts? What kind of evidence should we seek in order to answer these questions? Answering them is critical for understanding principles associated with test validity. Test validation is a process of seeking and accumulating evidence to support claims we make about a test (Bachman, 2005; Messick, 1989). For example, a main claim may be that a test offers meaningful information about students' language ability and useful information upon which we can make instructional and programming decisions. We then need to seek **validity evidence** to support this claim.

One method of collecting such evidence is to examine whether assessment tasks elicit rich cognitive processes and activate linguistic knowledge. In other words, do students actually use knowledge and skills that assessment tasks are purported to elicit? Are they congruent with how they use the language in real life? This understanding of the relationship between the actual skills that are tested and those which the assessment aims to test is called cognitive validity (Field, 2011; Glaser, 1991; Weir, 2005). It concerns the breadth and depth of linguistic and metalinguistic knowledge students draw on during mental processes, as well as the effectiveness of the cognitive processes on successful task performance (O'Sullivan, 2011). Cognitive validity offers crucial information for teachers in assessing young language learners who experience rapid growth in developing linguistic abilities and cognitive skills. Empirical evidence from students' verbal descriptions of their thinking processes helps build the connection between how students think (cognition), how tasks elicit cognition (observation), and what inferences are made about students' ability (interpretation) (The National Research Council, 2001).

Think-aloud can be a useful method of gathering evidence of cognitive validity and for understanding the complex nature of cognitive processes and strategies that students use during task performance (Ericsson & Simon, 1993; Gass & Mackey, 2000; Jang, 2005). Teachers can indirectly observe students' thinking processes and strategy use by prompting them to say aloud as they work through problems. Students may think aloud concurrently while performing the given task or recall their thoughts after completing it, prompted by some retrieval cues (for example, video clips, pictures, or students' own work).

Considering that reading aloud is a common learning activity in young learners' classrooms (Beck & McKeown, 2001) and that teachers increasingly use think-aloud as an instructional tool to model problem-solving processes to students, students' verbalized accounts of their own problem-solving processes offer useful information for teachers and researchers. In Activity 3.2, I introduce two Grade 6 students, Ellen and Sam and share parts of their think-aloud reports. Let us take a close look at their cognitive processes in Activity 3.2.

Activity 3.2

Ellen and Sam took a provincial Grade 6 literacy test a month before the think-aloud session and were invited back to select two passages and verbalize their thought processes. The transcripts in Tables 3.1 and 3.2 show excerpts from their think-aloud reports produced while reading the passage, *Popcorn under pressure*, and answering reading comprehension questions. I divided the reports into two parts. Table 3.1 illustrates the students' verbalizations of their thoughts while reading the text and Table 3.2 shows their answers to the corresponding reading comprehension questions. Italicized transcripts refer to the original text, and 'I' refers to the interviewer. Use the space provided next to the verbal reports to make notes of your ideas and thoughts as you read the transcripts. When you read their reports, consider the following questions:

- How do the students process textual information?
- How do they differ in solving reading comprehension tasks?
- How effectively do you think the reading comprehension tasks elicit reading skills?

What did you notice while you were reading the transcripts of the students' verbal reports? How do they process the textual information and use that information in answering the comprehension questions on pages 81–2? Do their thought processes reveal their reading abilities? Who do you think had a better understanding of the text?

Ellen's verbal report	Sam's verbal report	Note
Ellen: I think I want to do 'Popcorn under Pressure,' because the other stories I still kind of remember and I didn't really, I'm not really into those kinds of stories, like poems.	**Sam:** This one. "Popcorn under Pressure." I was thinking like, what do they mean by Popcorn under Pressure, like, when the popcorn pops, it flies.	How do the students choose the text?
It looks like kitchen magic. **Ellen:** It's kind of like, there's magic in the kitchen. *You take a handful of dried corn kernels, small and hard as ladybugs.* **Ellen:** Um, there's like, dried corn kernels, and they're really hard and small, like ladybugs. …	*It looks like kitchen magic. You take a handful of dried corn kernels, small and hard as ladybugs. Throw them into a hot pan with a little oil, and soon they're jumping, spinning and exploding into shapes like freeze-dried clouds. That's popcorn. Don't forget to put on the lid. But why does popcorn pop?*	How do the students chunk the text while thinking aloud?
That's popcorn. Don't forget to put on the lid. **Ellen:** I would think that because if you don't put on the lid, it will go all over the place and the popcorn will fly out and make a big mess. …	**Sam:** Maybe popcorn pops because of the name, the pressure of like, what they put inside with the popcorn. Or maybe because of the fire, it makes heat and then they pop, 'cause in the beginning they're just kernels and then they pop into popcorn.	How much attention do they pay to details in the text?
Each kernel of popcorn has a hard outer shell around a pocket of starch. **Ellen:** Um, a popcorn has an outer shell and inside there's a pocket of starch. …	*Each kernel of popcorn has a hard outer shell around a pocket of starch. This pocket is called an endosperm, which means "inside the seed." If you could take off the shell, the starch in the endosperm would feel and taste a little like a raw potato. There's a lot of water in that starch: in fact, the perfect piece of popcorn is about 14% water.*	How do the students infer about the author's intent to mention potatoes?
If you could take off the shell, the starch in the endosperm would feel and taste a little like a raw potato. **Ellen:** If you open it and take off the shell, inside it would feel and taste like a raw potato …	**Sam:** So, I'm wondering how that small kernel has so much water in it. It looks like more amount of water than the kernel. …	Do the students show interest in reading the text?

Ellen's verbal report	Sam's verbal report	Note
Interviewer: What are you thinking? **Ellen:** Well, it's really interesting 'cause um, in the starch, I didn't know that there would be 14% of water in it. I thought it would be less. …	*But the expansion of steam is only half the story. When most things are heated, the water in them just boils away. That's why foods with a lot of water in them, such as mushrooms or tomatoes, usually get smaller when you cook them. Popcorn is different because of the hard shell. The shell keeps the hot steam inside the popcorn like air inside a balloon. The pressure builds up. You can picture the fast-moving molecules of steam pushing and hitting against the hard shell until the shell can't hold them in. Like a balloon, the shell flies apart all at once: it pops.*	How do the students understand why the author mentions mushrooms, tomatoes, and a balloon in the text?
But the expansion of steam is only half the story. **Ellen:** The expansion of steam is only half of the story, only half of the cycle. …	**Sam:** So, you can imagine the pop, the kernel hitting the pan from side to side, and when it can't take it anymore, it just pops into a popcorn, but not like a balloon, a balloon just pops and goes smaller, it doesn't grow bigger when it pops.	
That's why foods with a lot of water in them, such as mushrooms or tomatoes, usually get smaller when you cook them. **Ellen:** So, um, like, food, mushrooms or tomatoes, they get smaller when you cook them. Like, when my mom cooks them, it actually does get smaller. …	*Popcorn is a tasty example of the science of pressure. It may not be magic, but it is magical.*	
The shell keeps the hot steam inside the popcorn like air inside a balloon. **Ellen:** The shell around the popcorn, it keeps the steam from exploding out of it. …	**Sam:** How is popcorn magic? It's just, like, natural. It's like a box, when you put something in that box, something really big, and the box can't take it so… in the beginning it can take it, but after some time, it just opens and becomes big. So, that's not magic.	How do the students interpret the author's mention of 'magical'?
Popcorn is a tasty example of the science of pressure. **Ellen:** It's a really good example of science of pressure. …		
It may not be magic, but it is magical. **Ellen:** It's not magic but it could be really cool and magical, like that.		

Table 3.1 Thinking aloud while reading the text (Jang, Dunlop, Park, & Vander Boom, 2013)

A number of themes emerge from the analysis of the transcripts. For example, it is interesting to observe how the two students chose the same text for different reasons. As I explained above, both the students took the test a month prior to the think-aloud session and were asked to select two passages they would like to re-read for their think-aloud. Ellen explains she chose the text because she could not remember as much detail about it as she did with the other texts. It seems that she wanted to work on a text that was not repetitive and more challenging. She also considered the text genre by stating that poems (one of the texts provided) are not her favorite type of reading material. On the other hand, Sam seemed to be intrigued by the title *Popcorn under pressure* and wanted to know what it means (although he had read the same text before).

The most obvious difference between the two students is how they chunk the text during the think-aloud; that is, how they break down the text into smaller parts to help with comprehension. It is one of the reading strategies used to break down challenging text into more manageable pieces. You might think that more proficient readers, like Ellen, would work with longer chunks. It is quite the contrary. Ellen worked with much shorter chunks, constantly paraphrasing what she read, identifying key words, and paying attention to details. Sam, on the other hand, worked with much longer chunks throughout the text, with little information drawn from the text.

The excerpts presented in Table 3.1 shows how the students processed the textual information. From their verbal reports, how do you think the students will perform on reading comprehension tasks? Which student do you think will have performed better? Let us take a close look at the excerpts presented in Table 3.2 on page 84.

Ellen and Sam's verbal data show a distinct difference in their ability to comprehend textual information by searching and locating the key idea (starch) in the text. For example, while answering the first question, what is at the center of the corn kernel? Ellen verbalized, "it would be starch because it says so in the text. Here, 'each kernel of popcorn has a hard outer shell around a pocket of starch.'" On the other hand, Sam responded, "Potato! That's what brings most of the taste to the popcorn." Clearly, Sam needs to work on differentiating details from the main idea in the text because he failed to understand why the author mentioned the word 'potato' in the passage. He also needs to work on improving the inferencing skills he requires for understanding implied meaning. As such, differences in cognitive skills between these two students are evident throughout their reports. I am sure your notes include many more salient differences. I encourage you to share the notes with your colleagues and discuss your analyses in more detail.

Ellen's verbal report	Sam's verbal report	Note
(Q1) What is at the center of the corn kernel? **Ellen:** It would be starch, 'cause it says so in the text.	*(Q1) What is at the center of the corn kernel?* **Sam:** Potato. That's what brings most of the taste to the popcorn.	Do the students refer back to the text when answering the question?
(Q2) What is the purpose of the colon in line 11? **Ellen:** It'd be A, 'cause it has like, some really, it relates a little.	*(Q2) What is the purpose of the colon in line 11?* **Sam:** Usually when you start a paragraph you start with one subject, and then you start another paragraph and you start a different subject.	Do the students understand the use of the colon in the text?
(Q3) But the expansion of steam is only half the story. What is the other half of the story? **Ellen:** It's not the pot lid, 'cause the shell keeps it in.	*(Q3) But the expansion of steam is only half the story. What is the other half of the story?* **Sam:** The shell cracks open from the pressure. The pressure becomes stronger and it pops.	Do the students use any test-taking strategies?
(Q4) Describe a safety issue related to popping popcorn. Use information from the text and your own ideas to support your answer. **Ellen:** In the text, it did say you have to keep the lid on, otherwise it will explode all over the place and it's going to get messy, and it's happened to me before, so yeah.	*(Q4) Describe a safety issue related to popping popcorn. Use information from the text and your own ideas to support your answer.* **Sam:** So if you don't keep the lid on while the popcorn is popping, it can pop in your face and like, hit your hand, somehow. So you could get burnt on your hand it can hit your eye or your face, and you can get burnt.	How do the students use their background knowledge in solving problems?
(Q5) How does this text make a complicated process understandable? Use information from the text and your own ideas to support your answer. **Ellen:** Um, I know how to pop popcorn, and it's a pretty simple how-to-do list. If you know how to do it. Like, check it out on the computer and stuff.	*(Q5) How does this text make a complicated process understandable? Use information from the text and your own ideas to support your answer.*	Do the students understand the prompt?

(Q6) The text as a whole answers which of these questions? **Ellen:** It would be C, 'cause it does talk about how the pressure makes a corn kernel explode. *(Q7) Where would this text most likely be published?* **Ellen:** It'd be in a science textbook, because it is science related. **I:** All right, that's it, and thank you very much. How were the passages? **Ellen:** Um, they're good, I liked them, the stories were interesting, the texts. And the questions were really specific, so I can remember.	**Sam:** 'Cause people usually just put the ingredients in the correct place. People don't usually think about the stuff that they do, they just follow the ingredients on the back of the plastic where you get the popcorn, or they just cover it. *(Q6) The text as a whole answers which of these questions?* **Sam:** How does popcorn cook differently from tomatoes? **I:** What are you thinking? **Sam:** How do tomatoes fit in that thing? Is it like, small pieces of tomatoes or is it like, big? *(Q7) Where would this text most likely be published?* **Sam:** In a science textbook, 'cause all this is science, 'cause popcorn isn't magic, it's a tasty example of the science of pressure. It may not be magic, but it's magical. That's why it should be in a textbook. **I:** All right, great! So how were the passages and questions? **Sam:** Good. I understood them all.	Do the students understand details mentioned in the text (e.g. tomatoes, balloon, potatoes)? Do the students have the genre knowledge? How do the students evaluate their work?

Table 3.2 Thinking aloud while answering the reading comprehension questions (Jang, Dunlop, Park, & Vander Boom, 2013)

As shown above, students' think-alouds can be an important data source for teachers. They provide evidence that helps to understand individual students' cognitive strengths and areas for improvement, which is a critical function of assessment in school contexts. They also provide information about whether the difficulty level of assessment tasks is associated with cognitive complexity.

Furthermore, think-aloud can complement teachers' diagnostic assessment and instructional interventions. For example, Kletzien & Bednar (1990) used think-aloud approaches in dynamic assessment (see our discussion in Chapter 1) to understand struggling students' strategy use and attitude to reading. Based on Vygotsky's conceptualization of assessment, dynamic assessment is used to assess children's current ability, and identify and cultivate their learning potential through mediated instruction. Based on iterative dynamic assessments procedures, Kletzien and Bednar show how Suzana, a Grade 10 student, who initially performed lower than her grade level and showed low self-efficacy, could enhance her reading comprehension ability, using a visualization strategy (which was determined as Suzana's strength by her teacher during the mediated intervention).

These studies illustrate that detailed analysis of students' cognitive processes can provide rich descriptions of their performance, elicited from assessments and evidence to account for the relationship between their task performance and language proficiency levels. Messick (1994) argues that 'the level and sources of task complexity should match those of the construct being measured and be attuned to the level of developing expertise of the students assessed' (p. 21).

In fact, think-alouds are widely used by teachers as a useful teaching tool in classrooms. For example, during teacher–student conferences, teachers can observe how students like Ellen and Sam engage in tasks and offer scaffolding feedback to help students test, reinforce, and renew their problem-solving strategies (Jang, 2010b). Teachers may use information from the observations to refine assessment tasks, adjust their difficulty levels, or plan subsequent interventions to address differential performance among students.

Assessment Tasks Should Measure Essential Core Skills

In Chapter 2, we discussed the various components of academic language proficiency that learners need to apply in order to meet language demands and master tasks in curricular contexts. Specifically, we focused on grammar and vocabulary knowledge, and discourse skills. Different assessment methods are appropriate for measuring different aspects of ALP. For example, let us think about how we assess young learners' vocabulary ability. When young children enter school, emphasis tends to be on oral and aural skills development rather than literacy skills. This oral primacy of classroom interactions requires children to develop the receptive knowledge of new words and the ability to produce the words in order to participate in classroom learning activities.

Early writing measures used for young children are largely at the word level. Have you ever administered a dictation test? In an elementary classroom, teachers use a dictation test to measure young children's spelling ability (Bailey, 1998). Teachers read words aloud, and students write down the words they hear. Although it is often used to measure children's spelling ability, it also measures listening ability as well as phonological awareness. If the target language does not have a simple match between orthography (spelling) and phonology (sound), a dictation test can be challenging for young language learners. When teachers are expected to dictate more than words or phrases, they should adjust the difficulty level of the test by considering the lexical density of a text. They can also use their speed and pause to control the difficulty level (Bailey, 1998).

Children continue to expand their lexical and syntactic knowledge. For example, once they have learned the word, 'friend,' and gain increasing awareness of the morphemic structure of words (Goodwin et al., 2012), they start to manipulate the word structure to acquire new words, such as 'friendly' and 'unfriendly.' Teachers may test students' vocabulary, grammar, and listening skills using integrative tasks. For example, teachers may use a dictogloss task where they read aloud a text while students take notes (Wajnryb, 1990). Students work together to recreate the text. Research shows that dictogloss has the potential to facilitate multiple skills at the syntactic, semantic, and discourse levels (Swain & Lapkin, 1998; Vasiljevic, 2010).

In the earlier grades, young learners focus on increasing the size of their vocabulary knowledge by acquiring new words every day and, accordingly, teachers' assessment focuses on the breadth of vocabulary knowledge (Nation, 2001; Read, 2004). Schoonen & Verhallen (2008) point out that measuring vocabulary size, focusing on: How many words do you know?, is 'deceptively simple, because different definitions of "a word" and "knowing a word" can lead to quite different estimates of a person's vocabulary size'(p. 212). The question of 'How much do you know of a word?' concerns the depth of vocabulary knowledge. For example, consider the word 'field.' We can talk about a field of study, or a baseball field, or fielding questions, which are only a few of the ways that this word can be used. As students are exposed to increasingly complex academic text, teachers need to measure whether students know multiple meanings of a word, its grammatical feature, including morphological derivations, pragmatic usage, and collocations. Schoonen & Verhallen (2008) note that measuring the depth of vocabulary knowledge is more challenging than vocabulary size.

Think about how you assess vocabulary knowledge in your classrooms. Do you use vocabulary tests? If yes, what aspects of vocabulary knowledge do they measure? If you do not use such tests, then how do you measure vocabulary knowledge? Spotlight Studies 3.1 and 3.2 invite you to read about two different methods used to assess young learners' vocabulary knowledge. Think about which method provides pedagogically more useful information to teachers.

Spotlight Study 3.1

Jiménez Catalán & Terrazas Gallego (2008) investigated the receptive vocabulary knowledge of primary students using the Vocabulary Levels Test (VLT). The authors describe this test as designed with "a pedagogical aim in mind" (p. 175). This vocabulary measure uses words from lists of the most frequently used words in English, for example, the 2000 or 3000 most frequent families of words, as well as those from the Academic Word List that includes 570 word families (Coxhead, 2006). Each of the word lists is used to create a different level of the test, and there are five different test levels. As Jiménez Catalán and Terrazas Gallego explain:

> The main assumptions underlying the test are that the most frequent words in a language will be the first learned, and the vocabulary growth will take place in scalable order: that is, knowledge of words in a particular band implies knowledge of words in all lower bands, but not of those in any higher band. To put it another way, testees' knowledge of uncommon words implies knowledge of the most frequent words but not the other way around.
>
> (Jiménez Catalán & Terrazas Gallego, 2008, p. 175)

The test measures decontextualized knowledge of vocabulary words (Nation, 2012, p. 3). Here is an example:

'soldier':
He is a soldier.

a person in a business
b student
c person who uses metal
d person in the army

Jiménez Catalán and Terrazas Gallego focused on investigating the overall receptive vocabulary of 270 year four primary school Spanish learners (average age of 10.3 years) studying English. They used two tests to measure receptive vocabulary of young learners: a 1000-word receptive test (Nation, 1993), and the 2000-word frequency band from the receptive version of the VLT (Schmitt, Schmitt & Clapham 2001, version 2). They further investigated if there were correlations between this vocabulary measure and a **cloze** test. Each student participant completed the two vocabulary measures and the cloze test, which was a subtest of a standardized language test developed for young learners. Learners were given 15 minutes to complete each task during class time. As part of the instructions, students were told that they would be penalized for wrong answers to reduce chances of learners' guessing.

The results indicate that the young learners had mastered about 559 words out of 1000 on the 1000-word level test, and 178 words out of 2000 on the 2000-word level test. The researchers suggest that these findings indicate that students have a 'reasonably good vocabulary size' (p. 184) considering their age and the amount of instruction that they have received (total of 419 hours of instruction in English). They conclude that information about students' receptive vocabulary is integral to teachers' lesson planning and instruction of vocabulary, and point out some of the limitations of their study, one of which is that the test only measures learners' basic knowledge of word meanings, and not deep word understanding.

Spotlight Study 3.2

Schoonen & Verhallen (2008) investigated the reliability and validity of a vocabulary measure called the *Word Association Task (WAT)*, adapted for use with young English language learners. As the authors state, researching measures of deep word knowledge has been used with adolescent and adult language learners but not younger ELLs. The purpose of this vocabulary measure is to test deep word knowledge. The young ELLs in Grades 3 and 5 are presented with word webs. At the center of each word web is a stimulus word that is surrounded by six associated words. Students need to decide which words are related to the stimulus word. For example, the stimulus word, foot, is related to leg, toe, and body part, but it is not related to cup, as illustrated in Figure 3.2.

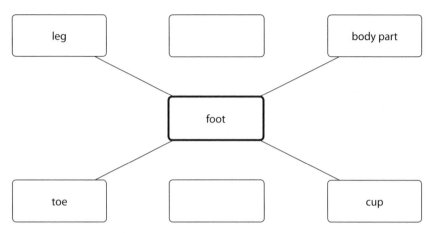

Figure 3.2. Word Association Task (WAT) example

The researchers administered two versions of this test (WAT-A and WAT-B) to over 400 students in each of Grades 3 and 5 (total of 822). They recorded which connecting lines were drawn to each stimulus word presented to the students, and if students were able to correctly identify all three connecting lines for each stimulus word, then they were awarded points for the test item.

Overall, the young language learners did not have difficulty with the test; they were able to understand and complete the word connection tasks and the probability of guessing correct answers was low. Additionally, as Schoonen and Verhallen (2008) point out, the test is suitable for administration in classrooms, as it can be completed in a short period of time (20–30 minutes). The authors concluded that, with respect to difficulty, the test is appropriate for young learners in Grade 3, and slightly less so for students in Grade 5. ■

Now that you have read a little bit about these two vocabulary tests and have become familiar with them, take some time to compare the two measures based on our discussion of ALP, and the vocabulary knowledge that students need in order to successfully meet school language demands and master curricular content. How do these two tests differ in assessing young English language learners' vocabulary knowledge? Do you agree that Schoonen & Verhallen's (2008) investigation focused primarily on measuring the depth of vocabulary knowledge, while Jiménez Catalán & Terrazas Gallego (2008) study focused on the breadth of vocabulary? Do you value one type of vocabulary knowledge more than the other? While teachers need to measure both the breadth and depth of young ELLs' vocabulary development, it is possible that teachers focus more on assessing children's vocabulary size during primary grades (1–3) when they show a rapid growth of vocabulary knowledge by acquiring new words every day. As students are exposed to more academic texts across subject areas and deepen their vocabulary knowledge, it is crucial that their teachers assess their growth in depth of vocabulary knowledge as well. Therefore, both measures reviewed in the Spotlight Studies are potentially useful for assessing young learners' developmental growth in vocabulary knowledge.

Assessment Should Promote Positive Learning and Assessment Experiences

One of the characteristics that distinguishes young learners from older ones is how they are affected by their educational and personal contexts. Unlike older students whose learning is often structured by tangible goals they strive to achieve (for example, going to college, applying for a scholarship, or maintaining high GPA), young learners are likely to be affected by whether or not learning materials and tasks are 'interesting.' The adjective, 'interesting,' is a common word that children use when asked about their thoughts on assessment tasks (Jang et al., 2013). What they may mean by that is that assessments are meaningful (i.e. relevant to their school and personal life), challenging enough (not repetitive of old information), and still achievable (not too difficult). If assessment tasks fail to engage students enough to fully demonstrate their competencies, results from the assessment will under-represent their abilities. If assessment tasks trigger severe anxiety in students because of either misfit difficulty levels of the tasks or restrictive administration procedures, their validity must also be called into question. Kathy, a Grade 4 bilingual student, expresses her enjoyment while reading the passage about popcorn by saying "So I might feel excited if this ... if I'm making popcorn and they keep popping and then they might pop everywhere so I might be excited to eat them after they're done" (Jang, 2009, p. 37). Even if this comment is made in a testing situation, it is evident that the child enjoys reading to learn about a new concept. We learn more about her excitement as she continues to verbalize her thoughts and says, "so it sounds interesting to me since I'm learning all this while I'm reading all this so I kind of want to read even more about this. It gets me interested in all this" (p. 37).

Unfortunately, not all students show as much interest as Kathy does in reading the popcorn passage. The student in Classroom Snapshot 3.2 is clearly distracted by the line numbers that appear on the margin of the passage, as we can see by his verbalization as he reads the popcorn passage.

Classroom Snapshot 3.2

Travis (T), a Grade 4 student, thinks aloud while reading a passage about how popcorn pops and answers C's reading comprehension questions.

T: What's with all these numbers beside it?

C: Um.

T: I was wondering what these numbers are for?

C: OK, well what do you think? What um…

T: I don't know. Maybe it's time. Like after five minutes or so or after ten, fifteen, twenty or so to see what's happening.

…

C: OK. Turn the page. OK as you're answering the questions tell us what you're thinking about. OK?

T: What is at the center of the corn kernel? Uh…

C: OK. Why is the question asking this question?

T: Like what's in the popcorn kernel.

…

T: Question number two. What is the purpose of the colon in line 11? (Unintelligible) I get it now. That what that is.

C: Mm-hmm.

T: That's the fifth line, line eleven.

(Chun & Jang, 2012, p. 72) ■

Travis is being distracted by line numbers that run alongside the text margin. He becomes fixated by those numbers though he eventually understands their purpose. Line numbers in the texts are not authentic, as we do not find them in non-testing situations. They are test features, and young learners who are writing a test for the first time may not be familiar with them, as Travis illustrates.

Compared to adolescent and adult learners, young children tend to have shorter attention spans and can get easily distracted from learning and assessment. Instruments used for young learners should be user-friendly and interesting to them. Green, Hamnett, & Green (2001) examined the user-friendliness of national reading comprehension tests by interviewing 24 children in Year 6 to understand their perceptions about the test stimuli and answer booklets of the tests. Their findings show that:

• Children enjoy learning (new) things from the stimulus.
• If children feel familiar with the topics of the stimulus, they feel more confident and at ease.

- Less proficient children (judged by their teachers) tend to make remarks about the text length and express their concerns about remembering the texts rather than referring to the content of the texts when answering test questions (lack of test-taking strategies).
- Children find factual texts boring and prefer stimulus materials with humor.
- Children find questions asking about facts stated in the text boring because they just need to remember the text instead of drawing on their own thoughts.
- Children prefer illustrations and pictures with captions.
- Some children find 'non-traditional' question types, such as matching, table completion, bullet points, speech bubbles, and ticking encouraging, while other children prefer multiple-choice questions as they are quick and involve less writing.

The researchers conclude that the level of engagement with the stimulus is crucial, as children's motivation influences their test performance. Topic familiarity is also an important factor to be considered, as children tend to feel more confident when answering questions on familiar subjects. Overall, less proficient children feel more threatened by text length and topic unfamiliarity. They highlight the importance of user-friendliness from children's perspectives, as it has impact on test validity.

While user-friendly assessment for young children is crucial, the negative impact of high-stakes testing on children is of concern to teachers across countries. So far, little attention has been paid to the impact of testing on young children's affect and attitude to assessment. Considering that anxiety negatively influences achievement in L2 (Gardner, Tremblay, & Masgoret, 1997) and that test-taking populations have become much younger in recent years, the affective consequences of testing on young learners should not be overlooked. Depending on the context, they hold different power and influence over individuals, practices, and policies. Spotlight Study 3.3 examined the use of commercial international language tests for young language learners in Hong Kong.

Spotlight Study 3.3

Chik & Besser (2011) investigated the use of the Cambridge Young Learners English (YLE) tests in Hong Kong. This test series is just one of many commercial international language tests that are available for the assessment of young learners' English language proficiency. Chik & Besser summarize the characteristics of these tests by identifying their four commonalities:

1 they measure the English language proficiency of learners between the ages of 5 and 12

2 they are standardized, so that students all over the world can take them, and the results can be compared across countries and cultures

3 they are marketed as products available for purchase

4 there is a cost associated with taking the test.

As Chik & Besser explain, the Hong Kong context provides an ideal setting in which to examine the use of commercial international language tests for young language learners partly because of the high social status attributed to English language proficiency. In fact, in Hong Kong, increasing numbers of young learners take the test. The researchers report that in 2006, 18,000 students took the test, reflecting an almost two-fold increase from 2002, when 10,000 students participated in the examination. Furthermore, in Hong Kong, the age of administration was lowered to five to accommodate the 'popular demand' for the test.

Before delving into the specifics of the study, it is also important to briefly summarize the English language-learning context for young learners in Hong Kong. Chik & Besser explain that all schools in Hong Kong (both public and subsidized) follow a standardized curriculum; however, at the secondary level, the language of instruction may be Cantonese Chinese or English depending on the school. Schools in which English is the primary language of instruction are highly sought after by parents, so gaining entrance to them is much more competitive. Parents are faced with intense pressure to help their children access placement in these schools. In order to decide who gains access to these privileged placements, schools adopt a 'Discretionary Placement system' (p. 77) in which they have the freedom to allocate a pre-determined percentage of placements to students who meet their advertised set of admission criteria. These criteria include evidence of participating in extracurricular activities, as well as demonstration of English language proficiency.

In studying the increasing popularity of English language testing among Hong Kong children, Chik & Besser investigated the perspectives of different stakeholders. The investigation entailed conducting in-depth case studies of two primary schools where students were preparing and competing for entrance to secondary schools. The case studies involved interviewing principals, teachers, parents and students at the schools. Additionally, they interviewed the principals of two different English-medium secondary schools. They refer to all of the people involved with test taking and test use (including students, parents, teachers, and principals) as stakeholders. The researchers examined three questions:

1 Why do young learners take international language tests?
   The primary reason learners take commercial tests such as the Cambridge YLE is to increase their chances of gaining entrance into English-medium secondary schools. These secondary schools are not permitted to administer

their own language tests; therefore, parents opt to have their children write the tests and subsequently, 'volunteer' the information as part of the evidence of their children's academic merit. In general, only those who are socioeconomically advantaged are able to afford the costs associated with preparing their children (through commercial test preparatory courses), and then subsequently taking the test. In Hong Kong, these tests are considered "'indisputable' proof of competence in English" (p. 87).

2   How are the results of international language tests used in this educational context?

Chik & Besser highlight the fact that users of test information––the stakeholders who make entrance decisions––are primarily concerned with the scores that students have achieved on the tests, and give little attention to how the results can be used for further learning and development. As the authors eloquently state:

International language tests are not being used for the assessment of language proficiency from a teaching/learning perspective. Instead, international tests in Hong Kong are being used for academic advancement purposes, which are not necessarily tied to learning. This focus on the artifacts of certificates, rather than on the learners, is contrary to the learning focus of literature on young learner assessment (Cameron, 2001; Chik & Besser, p. 87).

3   How important is test taking and what are its social consequences?

Chik & Besser point out that the use of these commercial language tests may be perceived as a positive endeavor, if it is viewed from a perspective in which the tests are a means of providing students with an opportunity to demonstrate their language skills. However, the authors claim that the power does not rest with the stakeholders who participated in the study (parents, students, teachers, and principals), but with the testing agencies. Chik & Besser contend that 'These agencies are profiting from the parental worry over their children's future education opportunities' (p. 88). As a consequence, the test-taking context in Hong Kong advantages groups who have the resources to participate in the process, and disempowers all others. ■

Are commercial language tests used where you teach? How are they used? Are high-stakes decisions based on students' test scores? The local context we reviewed in Spotlight Study 3.3 presents a complex dynamic involving multiple stakeholders (students, parents, teachers, elementary school and secondary school principals) across the elementary to English-medium high school systems.

The study also highlights the importance of considering social consequences of test use in test validation. Test use has impact on individuals including students and teachers, the curriculum, educational systems, and society (McNamara & Roever, 2006; Shohamy, 2001). As the power of tests increases, the concept of consequential validity has become central to building arguments for valid interpretations and fair use of test results (Moss, 1994). This has contributed to expanding the traditional view of test validity based on construct, content, and criterion validity. Evaluating assessment in terms of its use and effects helps us recognize various users who will be affected as legitimate role players in test validation.

Assessment Should Provide Consistent and Reliable Information on Proficiency

Most teachers, like Anna, express concerns about the subjectivity of assessment. Are you also concerned about subjective assessment? Test subjectivity is associated with issues of test reliability. Do you think that we will get the same scores if we administer the same test to the same students multiple times? If so, the reliability of the test in providing the same scores will be perfect. However, it is almost impossible to get exactly the same scores because of a range of sources of error in assessment (Alderson & Clapham, 1995).

Suppose that you just administered a vocabulary test and are now about to review your students' test scores. You wonder how reliable the test is. A reliable test is believed to provide consistent results within an acceptable margin of errors. Therefore, reliability describes the error associated with testing. There are two different sources of error that affect the degree of reliability. There may be **systematic errors of measurement**, for example, when a wrong answer key is used for scoring student responses, affecting all students. As another example, imagine a situation where students take a listening test in the classroom while loud music is played in the next classroom. The distraction generated from the music affects all the students' test performance.

On the other hand, some errors are random. Some students may be feeling sick or feel bored; others may have a better day on a testing day. These fluctuations are more random than systematic, as they do not affect all student performance in one direction (such as lowering or increasing everyone's scores). Traditionally, tests that limit students' responses (multiple-choice, true/false, or matching tests), were believed to provide more accurate information about students' ability because they are free from bias associated with personal investment. Assessments that are open to subjective marking were avoided because they are less reliable and more prone to bias.

Theoretically, an increase in reliability is expected to increase validity. In practice, however, decisions made to increase reliability often result in decreasing validity. For example, a multiple-choice test is often favored over a writing test in assessing students' vocabulary knowledge, because the former produces higher reliability; however, its validity is likely to be compromised because of its limitation in assessing students' ability to *use* vocabulary in a specific context. This is a classic example of a validity and reliability paradox (Brennan, 2001).

Validity concerns outweigh reliability concerns in current assessment culture, and this prioritization is reflected in teachers' increasing use of performance assessments. Performance assessments allow teachers to directly assess students' language ability from their performance on tasks. Some examples of performance assessment used in elementary classrooms include role-plays, presentations, and written texts (for example, letters to newspaper editors, lab reports, fiction). Performance assessment methods provide ample opportunities for students to demonstrate their language proficiency, which has the potential to enhance the validity of interpretations about students' actual ability (Linn, Baker, & Dunbar, 1991). They are relatively more difficult to administer, and they are time-consuming. As a result, compared to traditional selected-response tests, fewer tasks are used for assessing students' performance.

Moreover, subjectivity associated with teachers' assessment in classrooms is of great concern. It reflects the common belief that teachers' judgments are influenced by their opinions, feelings, or beliefs. If two teachers, one who knows a student very well and the other who has no prior knowledge about the student, judge the students' test performance, any discrepancy in their judgments may tell us whether or not teachers' knowledge matters in assessment. We call this type of consistency 'inter-rater reliability.' However, the discrepancy itself does not tell us which teacher's judgment is more or less valid; that is, we do not know if the teacher's knowledge about the student has resulted in a biased judgment in assessment. In addition, it is uncommon for more than one teacher to score students' performance.

Internal consistency in an individual teacher's scoring of students is a more common concern for teachers and students than consistency in scoring between teachers. If the same teacher assesses the same student repeatedly at different occasions, any discrepancy in the assessments indicates inconsistency in the teacher's judgments as long as the student remains the same. We call this type of consistency 'intra-rater reliability.'

Teachers' changing mood or different interpretation about evaluation criteria may contribute to their intra-rater reliability.

How can teachers maintain self-consistency when scoring students' work in classroom assessment? One effective approach is to offer students multiple opportunities to demonstrate what they can do, using different assessment methods. Looking for consistency in their performance across tasks and occasions is a great way of ensuring both validity and reliability in teachers' assessment. For teachers, using rubrics that describe evaluation criteria in assessing students' performance on a language assessment task will help them assess students' work consistently across different learners. There are two different ways to score students' writing: holistically and analytically. With holistic scoring, teachers may assess students' writing by assigning a single score based on the overall quality of the writing (Weigle, 2002). The rubric used for holistic scoring contains a set of benchmarks that distinguish among proficiency levels with descriptive criteria. Because of its efficiency over the other scoring methods, the holistic scoring method has been widely used in large-scale standardized assessment. However, as you know, assessing writing (and providing feedback) is an extremely time-consuming task for many teachers.

Analytic scoring is preferred when the purpose of performance assessment is to provide fine-grained information about students' proficiency in several related skills. For example, in analytic scoring, teachers may rate students' writing by focusing on some key writing features such as content development, organization, vocabulary, grammar, and discourse. Teachers may give different scores to these aspects of writing, but researchers warn against differential weighing (for example, placing more value on content development than accuracy of grammar usage) because the resulting scores may change what the construct was originally intended to assess (Hamp-Lyons, 1991). Even after using analytic scoring procedures, teachers often aggregate subscores and use the resulting total score for communication with students. In such instances, the diagnostic value of analytic scoring may be lost (Weigle, 2002).

Which scoring method have you used in assessing students' performance? Activity 3.3 introduces an elementary school student in Grade 5 and one of his three writing samples. I invite you to assess his writing using two different scoring rubrics.

Activity 3.3

Adam is a Canadian-born Grade 5 student. His parents emigrated from South Korea and the Philippines. His family speaks English and other languages at home. He can read and write in French. He enjoys comic books, computer games, YouTube videos, and learning new things. In Jang et al.'s 2013 research project, he wrote three texts in class. Here is a prompt, his notes, and his writing.

Prompt

Most people enjoy special events. Write a journal entry about your favorite special event. Explain why you enjoy this event.

Ideas for My Journal Entry

watching TV/eating hamburgers and Korean food/drinking bubble tea/going to Blue Mountain every year/reading comics

Adam's Writing

I like on Friday nights watching TV and when I watch TV I always need to eat popcorn. My favorite movies are: Salang Bi (Korean movie), Neverland, and Billy Madison. Another thing I like is eating hamburgers and Korean food. My favorite hamburger is The BACONATOR. And my favourite Korean food is Soon tofu and Ramen. Whenever I go to the Mall I like dinking bubble tea. My favorite is passion fruit with tapioca. Every year I go to Blue Mountain. I like doing high ropes, the roller coaster, and swimming. Another thing I like doing is reading comics. My favorite is Naruto. I also make comics with my Friends.

Score	Proficiency level
4	**Advanced** • Response is developed with sufficiently clear ideas and is clearly related to the assigned task • Control of conventions is evident in written work • Uses extensive vocabulary and sentence types
3	**Good** • Response is somewhat developed with some simple ideas and is partly related to the assigned task • Errors in conventions do not distract from communication • Uses a variety of vocabulary and sentence types
2	**Developing** • Response is minimally developed with few ideas and is partly related to the assigned task • Errors in conventions distract from communication • Uses limited vocabulary and sentence types
1	**Beginning** • Response is not developed, and ideas are unclear and • Errors in conventions interfere with communication • Uses simple repetitive vocabulary with no varying sentence types

Table 3.3 Holistic scoring rubric

Scale	Student can:	Mastery	Transition	Needs help
Organization	Organize ideas logically			
	Use some common transition words to link ideas			
	Clearly express main ideas with relevant supporting details			
	Generate ideas relevant to audience and appropriate for the purpose			
Conventions	Choose appropriate words for conveying the intended meaning			
	Use parts of speech correctly to communicate meaning			
	Combine sentences in a variety of ways using various connecting words			
	Use conventional spelling, punctuation and grammar			
Vocabulary	Spell familiar words correctly			
	Select words and phrases that make meanings clear			
	Can make word choices are appropriate for the purpose			
	Use a tone appropriate for the purpose			
Content	Write a topic relevant to the writing task			
	Use vivid (figurative) language and innovative expressions to enhance interest			
	Use relevant details, personal thoughts and effective word choices to make writing interesting and engaging			

Table 3.4 Analytic scoring rubric (Jang, Dunlop, Park, & Vander Boom, 2013)

What were the outcomes of your rating of Adam's short text using the holistic and analytic scoring rubrics? How did you use the holistic scoring rubric? How was your experience using the analytic scoring rubric with can-do descriptors in four writing skills, organization, conventions, vocabulary, and content? Which scoring method do you think provides the opportunity to deliver more consistent results? Detailed analysis of Adam's written texts shows that he needs to improve all four skills, especially organization and content, as shown in Figure 3.3.

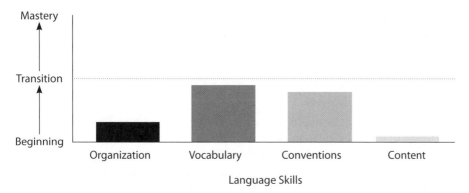

Figure 3.3 Adam's writing profile

As Activity 3.3 illustrates, the use of assessment results should be considered when teachers decide which scoring method they want to use. If the purpose of the writing assessment that Adam took is to make a summative judgment about his overall writing proficiency, teachers may consider using the holistic scoring rubric. Otherwise, teachers may prefer the analytic scoring rubric as it provides detailed information about the strengths and weaknesses of Adam's writing ability in specific writing skills. Regardless of which type of rubric is used, teachers should specify the criteria for evaluating students' performance before administering the assessment, and share this information with students.

It is common for teachers to engage in teacher moderation activities when an assessment is administered across classrooms involving multiple teachers. During these moderation activities teachers have the opportunity to develop common understandings of what students can do at each proficiency level and enhance the reliability of their judgments. In fact, this shared understanding among teachers is key to enhancing the inter-rater reliability of teacher assessment. Therefore, teacher moderation is a crucial validation process in large-scale standardized testing. In Spotlight Study

3.4, the researcher examines the validity and reliability of a standards-based classroom assessment based on teacher judgments.

Spotlight Study 3.4

Llosa (2008) brings together the findings from two previous research studies to investigate the quality of teacher judgments of students' English language development, on a Californian standards-based classroom assessment called the English Language Development (ELD) Classroom Assessment. The ELD assessments have multiple purposes: the results are used by teachers in classrooms to guide teaching and learning (formative purposes), and they are also used to make high-stakes decisions about ELLs' achievement toward the California state standards. The standards define students' development on any of four points on a scale ranging from 'Limited Progress' towards mastery of standards to 'Advanced Progress' which defines students as exceeding the standards for an ELD level.

Why is it important to investigate the quality of teacher judgments? The answer to this question is another validity issue. The use of test scores and assessment information depends on the extent to which teachers' judgments may be interpreted as *valid* and meaningful indicators of students' performance (Llosa, 2008). These scores, which are rooted in teacher judgments, are used to make important decisions about students' language ability that impact them in multiple ways (for example, type of instruction and support they do or don't receive). One major issue that emerges when studying the quality of teacher judgments of ELD is the fact that teachers interpret 'language ability' differently. Interestingly, Llosa cites research which reveals that teachers use a number of factors, not related to language, to make decisions about students' language ability.

In her research, Llosa asked, "To what extent do the ELD Classroom Assessment and the CELDT [California English Language Development Test], the statewide standardized test, measure the same construct of English proficiency as defined by the California ELD Standards?" (p. 35). Recall that teachers make the decisions about students' language ability using the ELD Classroom assessment, but that the CELDT provides a different reference of students' language ability since it is a state-designed standardized test. Therefore, comparisons of students' performance on these two indicators will reflect the extent to which teachers' scores are reliable. Llosa (2008) analyzed ELD Classroom Assessment and CELDT data for 1,224 fourth grade ELLs for three consecutive administration years. Her findings showed that, overall, the ELD Classroom Assessment data was consistent with the CELDT performance data.

Llosa also asked, "When scoring the ELD Classroom Assessment, how do teachers make decisions about students' English language proficiency as defined by the California ELD standards?" (p. 35). Based on a qualitative study with 10 Grade 4 teachers who thought aloud while scoring students' ELD Classroom Assessment, Llosa reported that teachers did not depend only on students' language ability while they scored; they were also influenced by students' personality and behavior. For example, students who participated less in class or were quieter tended to be scored lower than their more overtly engaged peers. Furthermore, teachers' scores also reflected their assessment beliefs. For example, one teacher refused to place any student on a level 1 or level 2 on the standard scale, as she believed that these scores represent a 'fail' and she does not believe in failing students. The accountability pressure also played a role in some teachers' scoring, and they felt the need to demonstrate that their students were showing improvement and advancing through the standard levels. ■

Now that you have read this study, think about your own practice. How do you evaluate your students' written work? Do you think that all of the teachers in your school mark consistently? How often do you feel that teachers' assessment results are influenced by their knowledge about students' personality and traits other than language ability? Have you participated in teacher moderation activities at your school? We will discuss the influence of teachers' beliefs and attitude to assessment practices in Spotlight Study 4.1 in Chapter 4.

All assessments are subject to error, regardless of methods used. Moreover, it is possible that a test can provide consistent yet invalid information about students' abilities (Moss, 2004). If multiple-choice tests that measure limited factual content knowledge are used to infer students' overall language proficiency, the inferences are potentially invalid despite consistency in students' scores. On the other hand, inconsistent judgments about students' performance on language tasks affect valid interpretations and fair use of test scores. Therefore, teachers should strive to make their assessment reliable in order to provide meaningful interpretations of students' language ability.

Assessment Should Promote Students' Ability to Self-Assess

As we discussed above, young learners should have positive experiences with assessment. One way to ensure this is by engaging them in the assessment process through self-assessment. Self-assessment has gained increasing attention for its potential to promote self-regulated learning (Butler & Lee, 2010; Cohen, 1994; Dann, 2002; Oscarson, 1989; Zimmerman, 1990). This practice reflects the shifts in assessment culture from mainly focusing on measuring learning outcomes (assessment *of* learning) to assessing the learning process to inform instruction and guide student learning (assessment *for* learning) and to using assessment as a means of facilitating students' self-regulation and autonomy (assessment *as* learning) (Assessment Reform Group, 2002; Earl & Katz, 2006). In this expanding view of assessment, students are viewed as critical agents of their own learning. Self-assessment is increasingly used as a tool to provide opportunities for young learners to become metacognitively aware of their own learning process, to be more confident about their learning process, and to have a better sense of control over own learning pace and the actions taken for learning. Such opportunities for self-assessment help children develop positive attitudes to language learning and assessment (Paris & Paris, 2001).

Despite the potential advantages of self-assessment, teachers wonder if students can actually assess themselves validly. Can students' self-assessment be more or less accurate depending on the domain of skills being assessed? How early and in which grade should students be encouraged to assess their own learning? What evidence should teachers seek in order to evaluate the validity of self-assessment? Ross (1998) reports that adult learners can self-assess their receptive skills more accurately than their productive skills, but is the same true for young learners? Butler & Lee (2010) reason that there is relatively less research on self-assessment for young learners because of the belief that children are not capable of accurately evaluating their performance or regulating their learning (p. 8). They further note:

> It has been reported that children younger than 7 years old appear to be excessively optimistic and naïve about their own ability, and that they lack the ability to reflect upon their performance. However, their ability to self-reflect and self-assess their performance appears to improve around years 8 to 12 (Paris & Newman, 1990). Butler and Lee (2006) also found that 6th grade students (11–12 years old) could more accurately self-asses their performance in English as a foreign language than their 4th grade (9–10 years old) counterparts. Butler and Lee (2006) also found that 4th grade students as well as 6th grade students could improve the accuracy of their self-assessment if their assessment items are directly tied to classroom tasks and are formulated and delivered in a contextualized manner.
>
> (Butler & Lee, 2010, p. 9)

Activity 3.5

How accurate are young learners' self-assessments? How do they correlate with other assessments administered by teachers? Here is a self-assessment tool developed and used for Grades 5 and 6 students in a Canadian elementary school by Jang, Dunlop, Park, & Vander Boom (2013).

Self-Assessment of Reading Comprehension

Read each statement carefully and fill in the circle (○). Here is a practice statement:

	Never	Rarely	Sometimes	Usually	Always	Not sure
I get up early on Saturdays.	○	○	○	○	○	○

Great! Let's get started!

		Never	Rarely	Sometimes	Usually	Always	Not sure
1	I can understand grammatically complicated sentences.	○	○	○	○	○	○
2	I can summarize the main points of a text with some supporting ideas.	○	○	○	○	○	○
3	I can figure out the author's lesson or purpose of a text.	○	○	○	○	○	○
4	After I read a text, I can understand the main point.	○	○	○	○	○	○
5	I can understand what the writer is trying to say even though it is not directly written in a text.	○	○	○	○	○	○
6	I can draw appropriate conclusions after I read a text.	○	○	○	○	○	○
7	I can guess the meaning of unfamiliar words using my knowledge and experiences.	○	○	○	○	○	○
8	I can understand the writing conventions (for example, period, comma, colons, etc.)	○	○	○	○	○	○
9	I know most of the vocabulary words in the textbooks we are using.	○	○	○	○	○	○
10	I can remember detailed information stated in a text after I read.	○	○	○	○	○	○
11	I can retell the main ideas from something I read.	○	○	○	○	○	○
12	I can predict what will happen next based on the evidence in a text as I read.	○	○	○	○	○	○

The results of the study by Jang et al. (2013) show that 44 students' self-assessment of their vocabulary skill was statistically significantly correlated with their reading comprehension test scores ($r = .31$). The self-assessment of the grammar skill was also highly correlated with their test scores, but the relationship was not statistically significant ($r = .25$).

Do the students' self-assessment results surprise you? Are you skeptical about the validity of self-assessment given its lack of correlations with other measures? However, remember that the value of self-assessment is not due to its accuracy as determined by its correlation with other measures, but because of its potential to advance students' learning.

To better understand the function and role of self-assessment, we need to take into account a few factors that influence the validity of students' self-assessment. First, research shows that students' self-assessment ability is highly correlated with their overall ability levels. In other words, higher-proficient learners show higher metacognitive ability, which enables students to accurately assess their performance and ability (Zimmerman, 1990). Jang et al. (2013) suggest that higher-proficient students tend to underestimate their skill proficiency whereas lower-proficient students tend to overestimate them. Butler & Lee (2010) offer some insights that may help us understand this interaction:

> It has been noted that children's perceptions towards academic
> competence changes as they go through school. While younger children
> have very positive views towards their academic performance, by the
> time they finish elementary schools, the perception of their academic
> performance becomes much lower (Nicholls, 1984). (p. 25)

As young learners acquire a higher level of language proficiency, they may develop the ability to differentiate their perceived ability in finer details, resulting in harsher self-assessment. Lower-proficient learners, like younger learners, appear to have a less differentiated perception of their own ability, resulting in an overestimation of their ability.

It is possible that students' less positive view of their ability at higher grades in elementary school reflects their realistic understanding of their own ability. However, teachers need to consider this changing perception in association with the *fourth grade slump* that we discussed in Chapter 2. The fourth grade is a critical transition period for all students, as the purpose of reading shifts from 'learn to read' to 'read to learn.' While this transition is a difficult period for all children, research shows that students from socio-economically disadvantaged backgrounds start to show greater difficulties with academic vocabulary during this period (Chall, Jacobs, &

Baldwin, 1990). These increasingly difficult academic language demands can be attributable to students' changing perceptions about their ability and decreased interest in reading and learning.

Furthermore, students do not naturally develop the ability to self-assess their performance. Self-assessment requires teachers' careful guidance. Students should understand why they are asked to assess their own work (not because their teachers are being lazy!). They should be taught how to assess their own work. Evaluation criteria should be communicated prior to students' self-assessment. It is a great idea to invite learners to brainstorm criteria for assessing their work. Instead of waiting until students develop the ability to self-assess with accuracy, teachers should view self-assessment as an important skill whose development should be facilitated. Research shows teachers' views about student self-assessment have an effect on students' positive learning outcomes (Butler & Lee, 2010).

Another important consideration is whether to let students assign marks to their self-assessment or incorporate them into summative assessment for reporting purposes. Both can present tricky problems. Teachers observe that if no mark is assigned, some students do not make the needed effort. Students tend to devalue self-assessment if it has no weight in teachers' summative assessment. It is especially true when students are exposed to competitive learning environments (Butler & Lee, 2010; Dann, 2002).

We see this conflict everywhere, don't we? It is common to hear and perceive tensions between formative and summative assessments. We are aware of tensions among various assessments, not only between student and teacher assessments, but also between teachers' classroom assessments and external standardized tests. The issue of whether to assign marks to students' self-assessment should be understood in the same vein. Marks are not likely to resolve the tension. They may keep students motivated to focus more on the outcome of performance than process and mastery of necessary skills. Teachers should focus on the principles of self-assessment, that is, to promote students' self-regulated learning and autonomy, and to help students themselves witness the empowering effects of self-assessment. Although it may take longer to see such positive effects of self-assessment on students, it is certainly worth investing instruction time on this!

Assessment Should Provide the Support Needed

Good assessment should provide fair opportunities for all students to demonstrate in a meaningful manner what they can do best. In addition, decisions and uses made on the basis of students' test performance should not be biased against a certain group of students based on their gender, ethnicity, language, economic status, or cultural background knowledge. Test fairness concerns both values underlying decisions made (i.e. which skill should be valued more for deciding admission, scholarship, and placement) and consequences of the decisions (i.e. what changes are made as a result of test use) (Kunnan, 2005; Jang, 2002; Madaus, 1994; Willingham, 1998).

A common misconception about testing in general is that objectivity is the solution to test fairness. As discussed earlier, traditional tests that are free of subjective human scoring are thought to be more objective and therefore fairer than alternative assessment approaches that require human judgments. However, the scope of test fairness has been expanded beyond the technical matter of assessment methods. For example, the APA/AERA/NCME Standards (1999) describe the characteristics of test fairness in four broad features that concern all aspects of the testing process:

1   absence of bias
2   equitable treatment of all test takers in the testing process to ensure comparability
3   the equality of testing outcomes for test taker subgroups (in terms of ethnicity, gender, disability, and other characteristics)
4   equity in opportunity to learn the material.

Much emphasis has been given to point 1, ensuring that the test is free of bias. Content experts' test sensitivity reviews are usually used to identify potentially biased test items, and statistical bias-detection methods, which we will discuss in detail in Chapter 4, are used to screen test items. Another important principle of fairness in testing is the extent to which students receive equitable treatment in the testing process. The last two characteristics, the equality of testing outcome and equity in opportunity to learn, concern issues associated with educational and social equity rather than test unfairness. In theory, students with equal abilities should be expected to have equal learning outcomes. As we have seen, construct-irrelevant factors may differentially affect students with the same abilities yet from different background memberships. Messick (1998) notes that 'given current educational and social realities, the idea that test fairness requires overall passing rates to be comparable across groups is not generally accepted in the professional literature' (p. 14). He further notes:

> It is also important to distinguish between equality (the state of being the same) and equity (treatment that is just under the circumstances)

and to recognize that not all inequalities are inequities. Indeed, in education as in medicine, the watchword should not be equal treatment but, rather, treatment that is appropriate to the characteristic and sufficient to the need (Gordon, 1998). From this perspective, it was important that the Standards phrased one of the alternative views of test fairness just considered as equitable, not equal, treatment of all examinees in the testing process, thereby allowing room for accommodation to the different needs of examinees with handicaps or allowing use of tests translated into an examinees' best language. (Willingham et al., 1988) (p. 15)

Point 4 (equity in opportunity to learn the material), is another important issue for language teachers and students. For example, ELLs learn English as a foreign or second language in various learning contexts where access to authentic language input varies, language learning materials are limited, and various varieties of English are heard and spoken. Students' performance is greatly affected by their varying opportunities to learn the test material when the test is standardized, based on a particular variety of English (British vs. American accents, for example). This situation becomes a serious fairness issue when the test results are used for making high-stakes decisions.

In contexts where teachers should assess language learners' academic achievement in subjects such as mathematics, science, and social studies, teachers are concerned about the extent to which the results of the subject-matter tests accurately reflect students' content knowledge, and further what type of accommodations they should provide for students to demonstrate their content knowledge despite difficulties in L2. Test accommodations refer to adjustments made to a test administration procedure in order to facilitate student access to test materials without changing the test construct (Butler & Stevens, 1997). Most accommodations provided in mass testing are primarily for students with special needs, and policies on test accommodations for ELLs are not well established (Pennock-Roman & Rivera, 2011). There are two types of accommodation for ELLs. *Direct support* involves adjustments to the language of the test by using students' L1 or simplifying test directions in English. Teachers may provide *indirect support* by allowing students to take additional time or a break. Accommodations should provide a fair opportunity for ELLs to demonstrate what they can do without giving them advantages over other students or altering the construct of the test (Abedi, Hofstetter, & Lord, 2004).

Test **modifications** differ from accommodations in that they may alter the content of the test and/or a testing procedure. They may lower learning expectations/standards for students with exceptionalities. The current accountability systems, such as NCLB in the USA or EQAO in Ontario, Canada, do not permit test modifications, to ensure that all students are expected to achieve the same standards; therefore, no modification is permitted to statewide or provincial tests.

There is a validity concern that test accommodations inflate L2 students' abilities when they are excessively provided. Careful research is necessary for examining whether L1 students benefit from accommodations that L2 students receive. In principle, they should not affect L1 students' test performance if they do not need them (Abedi et al., 2004; Sireci, Li, & Scarpati, 2003).

Research on the effects of accommodations on language learners' performance is inconclusive. Sireci et al. (2003) reviewed over 150 studies on test accommodations for ELLs and students with exceptionalities and concluded that extra time provided for students with disabilities was the only effective accommodation strategy. Abedi et al. (2004) reported that reduced linguistic complexity of a test (which is actually a test modification) effectively accommodated ELLs without affecting its validity, as determined by its lack of influence on non-ELLs. However, it is unclear how the effectiveness of these accommodation strategies may vary for different age groups, ELLs with different language needs, or school contexts. Black-Allen (2011) points out that the conflicting results from research on the validity of different types of test accommodations is attributable to "the contradiction between the 'quest for a one-size-fits all' accommodation, on one hand, and the diversity of ELLs, students with special needs and school contexts, on the other hand" (p. 22).

Each accommodation approach requires careful research as it can potentially alter the construct that the test is intended to measure or over-boost students' test scores, invalidating the test results. Let us take as an example a translation method. First of all, this method would probably not be feasible unless the majority of ELLs share the same L1 background. In urban schools where ELLs include students from many different places, the use of a test translated into students' L1 whose orthography is starkly different from L2 is neither practical nor theoretically justifiable (Geva, 2006). Furthermore, if students have not learned academic vocabulary in their L1, translation would actually impede their performance.

When teachers assess language learners' academic achievement in subject areas, they should provide appropriate accommodations for students to demonstrate what they know and can do. Research shows that not all accommodation types are equally effective for supporting language learners. It is also critical to ensure that accommodations provided for language learners do not alter the construct being tested. Teachers should consult with students and other teachers to determine their needs and provide on-going communication regarding how students' needs are being met through the accommodations provided. Teachers, especially of older students, express their concern that test accommodations are unfair to students who do not receive them, and they make it hard to compare among students. This perspective is important yet also problematic. As we discussed earlier, accommodations should not affect performance of students who do not need them, and more importantly, students who need them have the right to receive them.

Summary

In this chapter, we discussed six key principles for assessing young language learners:

1 Assessment should be cognitively rich enough to elicit linguistic knowledge and cognitive skills.
2 Assessment tasks should measure core language skills essential for young learners' successful participation in school learning.
3 Assessment should promote positive learning and assessment experiences.
4 Assessment should provide reliable information about young learners' language proficiency.
5 Assessment should promote students' ability to self-assess and monitor their own language proficiency development.
6 Assessment should provide the support needed for young learners to demonstrate what they know and can do.

Many of the principles we have discussed for younger learners are also applicable to the adolescent learners who will be in focus in Chapter 4. In discussing these principles, we reviewed various assessment methods specifically used for young language learners. Using the four-dimensional continua shown in Figure 3.1, I have reformulated Figure 3.4 for your review.

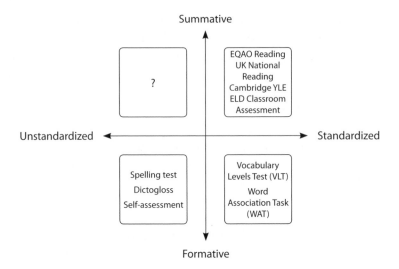

Figure 3.4 Map of assessment examples reviewed for young language learners

Interestingly, there is no assessment in Dimension 2. Unstandardized language tests used for the summative purpose are relatively less common in elementary classrooms compared to secondary. However this finding may vary across contexts.

At the beginning of this chapter you were introduced to Anna, who asked about the criteria necessary for choosing a good language test for young language learners. The principles discussed in this chapter can be used in making that choice. In summary, assessments useful for young language learners should mirror ways in which they learn and 'enjoy' learning. They should be congruent with your educational philosophy and useful for meeting your teaching goals. Children's experience with assessment in their early years can shape their life-long learning and affective attitude to assessment. Assessments should not be used only to highlight deficits in children's language development. Instead, they should identify both the strengths and areas needing improvement. Any assessment should also serve as a tool that children need to master to become self-regulated learners. In Chapter 4, we will discuss key issues and principles relevant to assessing adolescent language learners in schools.

4
Principles for Assessing Adolescent Language Learners

Preview

In Chapter 3, we discussed the key principles for assessing young language learners. Specifically, we focused on the purposes of assessment and its degree of standardization. In this chapter, we turn our attention to some of the essential principles of assessment that are relevant to adolescent language learners. These principles are grounded in the broader ecological system that influences adolescent learners' experience with and performance on language assessment.

As we briefly reviewed in Chapter 2, in general, adolescents face challenging physical, cognitive, social, and emotional transitions in their lives (Hume, 2008). Advanced cognitive skills allow students to organize abstract information in their minds and reflect on their own thoughts, feelings, and motivations. For example, adolescents acquire the ability to use language with abstract or non-literal meanings (for example, sarcasm and humor) and develop the metalinguistic ability to verbalize their abstract thinking. They are expected to use language in more sophisticated ways, as written language used in schooling becomes more complex and abstract.

Adolescents further develop their identity as they assume new roles and responsibilities in peer groups and communities. They crave independence and autonomy, shifting away from their families to their network of friends. They may struggle to fit in, try to conform to peer pressure, and show anxiety about their changing bodies and expectations of others. These developmental characteristics of adolescents are deeply intertwined and co-influence their experience with and performance on assessment.

Assessing adolescents in these transition years requires careful consideration of contextual factors from immediate and distant environments. In order to discuss assessment principles for adolescent language learners, we will consider assessment activities and contextual influences on their experience with and performance on assessment, drawing on Bronfenbrenner's ecological systems theory (1992). This theory will provide us with a lens through which we can evaluate and discuss the complex context of assessment. Bronfenbrenner's ecological systems theory identifies contextual factors that influence students in terms of four types of systems: a microsystem, a mesosystem, an exosystem, and a macrosystem, as shown in Figure 4.1.

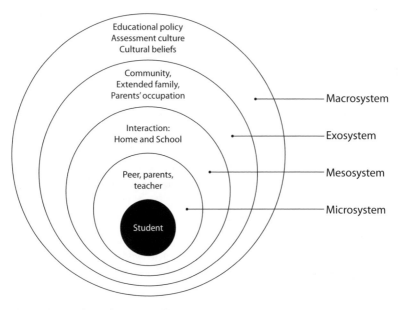

Figure 4.1 Ecological systems of language assessment

In the microsystem, we consider the most immediate environment that directly influences adolescents' experience with and performance on assessment in positive or negative ways. This environment includes the people with whom the student forms immediate relationships including peers, teachers, and family. There are of course numerous ways in which parents and teachers directly and indirectly influence adolescents' experience in and outside of school. One example of the influence of peers would be a task in which students are involved in a collaborative group presentation or a peer assessment activity.

In the mesosystem, we consider how different agents identified in the microsystem interact with each other. For example, adolescents are expected to make various decisions related to their education and future careers, including the selection of programs (for example, academic vs. vocational/humanities vs. science courses), and extracurricular activities. The mesosystem describes how parents interact with teachers to inform and guide students during such decision-making processes. This interaction would include, for example, teachers' reporting practices. Take a moment and reflect on your current reporting practices and evaluate the extent to which it provides parents with useful information about their children's learning progress and achievement.

Adolescent language learners, especially immigrant students, face linguistic and cultural transitions that demand considerable acculturation (Berry, Kim, Mine, & Mok, 1987). They also become aware of family relationships and ethnic and racial community memberships (Markstrom-Adams, 1992). Such challenges draw our attention to the exosystem that describes an environment in which an individual is indirectly involved, including parents' workplaces, extended family members, and the community in which they reside.

Lastly, the macrosystem describes the larger social and cultural context in which educational policies and the testing culture (the social history and beliefs about testing) affect adolescents' experience either positively and/ or negatively. This ecological system is also relevant to assessing young language learners.

In this chapter, we will discuss various assessment activities in this larger ecological system in which adolescent language learners participate. In the following section, we will focus on specific assessment activities to understand the principles and issues related to assessment of adolescent language learners in this large ecological system. For example, teachers use various forms of performance assessments in K–12 classrooms. Such assessments include oral presentations, group debates, videotaped performances, portfolios, and self- and peer- assessment (Darling-Hammond, 1994; Lynch & Shaw, 2005; Shohamy, 1996). The wide use of these **alternative assessments** in the classroom signals a shift from testing discrete linguistic knowledge to communicative competence that allows for meaningful interaction in a specific context relevant to students' lives (Brindley, 2001; Chalhoub-Deville 2003; Shepard, 2000). Lynch & Shaw characterize this changing assessment culture as follows:

> [Assessment] involves an investigation of developmental sequences in student learning, a sampling of genuine performances that reveal the underlying thinking processes, and the provision of directions and opportunities for further learning. Assessment culture also assumes that teaching, learning, and assessment practices are inseparable and integral; students should be active participants in the process of developing assessment procedures, including the criteria and standards by which performances are judged; both the process and product of

assessment tasks should be evaluated; and the assessment results should be reported as a qualitative profile rather than a single score or other quantification.

(Lynch & Shaw, 2005 p. 265)

One common assessment activity that teachers use with adolescent learners is portfolio assessment. Portfolio assessments provide us with an example of a relevant activity that reflects local assessment cultures. The use of portfolio assessments varies from classroom to classroom and gives us a rich opportunity to discuss key principles and issues specific to adolescent language learners.

Portfolio Assessment Should Promote Learner Autonomy

Among the various forms of alternative assessments, portfolio assessment best reflects the changing assessment culture described above. A portfolio is a purposeful collection of students' work samples that demonstrate learning progress, efforts, and achievement, and a systematic evaluation against a user-specified set of criteria or rating scales (Arter & Spandel, 1992; O'Malley & Valdez Pierce, 1996). Portfolios may include various materials, such as students' writing samples. These writing samples are not necessarily just the final polished copies, but may also include multiple earlier drafts of a piece to demonstrate improvement in writing or reports in different genres, such as lab reports in science or research papers in social studies. Teachers may select materials to be included in portfolios or students can, with their teachers' guidance, select exemplars of their 'best' work.

Portfolio assessment allows teachers, students and parents to appreciate the learning process as well as the outcomes. It documents concrete evidence of the learning process, which can be used for substantiating learning outcomes. Portfolio assessment also gives students an opportunity to collaborate with their peers through self- and peer-assessment. You will recall our discussion of the value of self-assessment with young language learners in Chapter 3. While portfolio assessment has become increasingly popular around the world, its applications to classroom settings vary from context to context. Have you used portfolios to assess language learners? What were the advantages and disadvantages of portfolio assessments? What do you think about students' attitude to portfolios? Before we discuss their use in adolescent language learners' classrooms, let us take a moment to reflect on our experience with portfolio assessment using Activity 4.1.

Activity 4.1

While portfolio assessment is widely used in classrooms, not all portfolios reflect an alternative assessment culture (Hamp-Lyons & Condon, 2000). Lynch & Shaw (2005) suggest that portfolios should demonstrate the features outlined in the chart below. Let us evaluate the use of portfolios you have used with your students in relation to these features. Indicate the level of experience you have had with each of the portfolio features listed below by checking off 'rarely' 'sometimes' or 'always'.

Portfolio Feature	Rarely	Sometimes	Always
1 The students actively participate in the selection of the portfolio components.			
2 The students reflect on this selection process, and their reflection is included in the portfolio.			
3 The process of creating and selecting the portfolio components is included in the evaluation.			
4 The evaluation contains elements of peer and self-assessment.			
5 The portfolios are evaluated by persons familiar with the individual students and their learning context.			
6 The students participate in deciding the criteria for evaluating the portfolios.			
7 The evaluation is reported qualitatively, as a profile or other detailed description of what the student has achieved.			

Teachers often face challenges when using portfolio assessment. They may wonder whether their students' work samples in the portfolios either under- or over-represent what they can do. Evaluation criteria may fail to assess the most relevant aspects of the learning task. As we discussed in Chapter 3, some teachers fear that students cannot evaluate their own work or that portfolios cannot be used for summative purposes when students evaluate their own portfolios. Have you ever experienced any of these issues?

One critical issue sometimes encountered in portfolio assessment is a conflict arising from its use for both summative reporting and formative learning purposes. Standardization, as we discussed in Chapter 3, is a necessary condition for making assessment results comparable among students across classrooms and schools. When portfolio assessment is used for tracking students' academic achievement in comparison with other groups, teachers are expected to follow a standardized guideline that specifies the contents of a portfolio. However, the standardizing of content and evaluation procedures becomes incompatible with the potential for promoting student autonomy through self-assessment.

Alternatively, teachers may moderate the selection procedure by identifying broad categories of contents while leaving room for students to choose the specific contents of their portfolios. For example, in a study describing the use of portfolios with EFL high-school students in Iran (Barootchi & Keshavarz, 2002), the portfolios included core and optional items as well as students' learning goals and comments on the aspects of learning demonstrated by each work sample they chose.

Another critical issue with portfolio assessment is the role of students. Ideally, in portfolio assessment, students should be actively participating in setting their own learning goals, selecting the contents of portfolios, and evaluating them through self-assessment. Needless to say, self-assessment is an integral component of portfolio assessment (Little, 2005). Self-assessment should involve analysis of the work and self-reflection in the form of a written or oral report. Research supports the validity of student self-assessment based on its correlations with other measures (criterion validity) (Blanche & Merino, 1989; Ross, 1998). Furthermore, the more direct learning experience students have with the content of self-assessment, the more accurate its results become (Ross, 1998). Therefore, it is crucial for assessment to be fully integrated into students' learning tasks.

Nevertheless, not all students appreciate opportunities to choose the contents of their portfolios and to self-evaluate their work. For this to happen, students need to be exposed to a learning environment in which they are encouraged to demonstrate learning in various ways, to cooperate with peers by sharing ideas, and to develop autonomy by making their own choices. When teachers communicate the evaluation criteria to students before they assemble their portfolios, this helps students develop the ability to distinguish good from weak performance and use the criteria for improvement.

One of the most significant developments in portfolio assessment is the European Language Portfolio (ELP) by the Council of Europe, which has garnered much attention across the European countries (Little, 2002). I initially introduced you to the ELP in Chapter 1, and will now review the ELP in detail, as it will help us understand both the potential and challenges of portfolio assessment in language learning contexts.

The ELP has three basic components:
1   a language passport
2   a language biography
3   a dossier.

The language passport is a summary of the portfolio owner's linguistic identity with the records of language education background, significant experience and qualifications, and the student's self-assessments of language proficiency levels with reference to the CEFR. The language biography is a record of language-learning goals and progress as well as key cross-cultural language learning experiences. The dossier is a collection of the work samples that best represent the student's own language proficiency. The self-assessment in the ELP is based on six language proficiency levels of the CEFR for languages, in five communicative activities: listening, reading, spoken interaction, spoken production, and writing (See Appendix for the Council of Europe's self-assessment grid).

While the Council of Europe's ELP project was initiated to fulfill the reporting function for adult migrants' second and foreign language certifications, the ELP pilot projects involved a range of language learners, including school-aged and university students as well as adult learners. Little (2002) reports overall positive experiences of both teachers and students with the ELP. Most teachers found the ELP useful for teaching and learning, while students found the self-assessment component of the ELP innovative and motivational. However, the ELP's implementation varied significantly across regions, depending on whether or not the educational authorities promoted large-scale implementation. Nevertheless, the reporting function of the ELP caused controversy arising from questions about the validity of the ELP's self-assessment in its use in the final evaluation of language-learning achievement and diplomas.

Perclová (2006) provides rich accounts of how teachers and students experienced the ELP in primary and lower secondary schools in the Czech Republic. The study involved 53 teachers of English, German, and French and their 902 students, from 1999 to 2002. Based on multiple data sources from teacher and student questionnaires and interviews, class observations, and documents, the study confirmed that overall, the ELP helped enhance students' self-confidence. Most teachers appreciated the descriptors of communicative activities which served as standards for assessment. However, some students viewed the ELP as additional work or a folder that they just had to check. While teachers found students' self-assessment innovative, it felt detached from their daily instructional practice when it was first introduced. Classroom Snapshot 4.1, drawn from Perclová's study, introduces various classrooms in which adolescent language learners used the ELP in learning a second or foreign language.

Classroom Snapshot 4.1

In Perclová (2006), there was much variation in the use of the ELP across classrooms. Examples from different teachers in four classrooms were chosen for this snapshot. These teachers used the ELP in teaching different foreign languages to adolescent learners ranging from 11–14 years of age. As you read the descriptions of how these teachers used the ELP in their classrooms:

- think about some positive aspects of their use
- make a note of any issue(s) relevant to your teaching context.

Teacher ID 8 with 8 students (11 yrs), L2=English

The teacher planned the whole class work on the descriptors of communicative activities in level A1. She wrote all descriptors on posters and led much discussion about how to achieve 'can-do' objectives. The students indicated their achievement by signing a particular descriptor. They planned additional practice activities for peers in need of help. Achieving all the A1 objectives was the goal of the whole class initiated by students and supported by the teacher. Parents appreciated their child's ELP for its transparency of learning process.

Teacher ID 24 with 16 students (13 yrs), L2=English

The students worked frequently on the Dossier and especially enjoyed making a newspaper collage by highlighting new expressions in different colors. The students recorded mostly on spoken interaction and writing tasks (not on listening and reading 'can-do' tasks). There was a mismatch between students' work included in the Dossier and descriptor activities.

Teachers' use of ELP in classroom

Teacher ID 39 with 12 students (14 yrs), L2=German

The students created their own lists of what they had learned and what they had not yet learned, and they found the lists useful. The lists included grammar elements. The students found it hard to communicate in the target language. There was much variation in the achievement level among students. The teachers' evaluation suggested that the observed variation among students did not reflect real difference in the students' proficiency levels; rather, it was attributable to the fact that students focused on different activities and different L2 languages (German and English).

Teacher ID 47 with 20 students (14 yrs), L2=German

All students could reflect on their learning process, and three made their own lists of achievements using free pages. The students included various materials in their Dossiers: surveys of German spelling and grammatical structures, tests, and pages from German magazines. The students' ELPs showed variations in terms of the quality and number of entries. It was observed that the teachers' evaluation of the students' attainment was different from the students' own assessment.

Figure 4.2 Use of the ELP in the classroom, summarized from Perclová (2006) ■

Classroom Snapshot 4.1 shows rich examples of the use of the ELP. In particular, the examples show how the ELP promotes students' autonomy. For example, students created their own lists of what they learned by signing or coloring relevant descriptors and planned additional activities for low-achieving peers. Teachers' support is also well demonstrated. They planned the entire class work on descriptor activities, and also created posters and questionnaires, or refined descriptors for students.

While these examples highlight positive and encouraging aspects of ELP use, they also raise some important concerns. One issue is related to discrepancies between teachers' evaluation of their students' language proficiency and students' self-assessment. In some of these classrooms, students' dossiers did not reflect descriptor activities led by teachers. Some students skipped a certain proficiency level (such as A1) and self-assessed using descriptors in a higher proficiency level (B1). Though variations in the use of the ELP in classrooms may be unavoidable, these observations suggest that teachers need to provide more explicit instruction on how to use the ELP and portfolios in general. You will recall that in Chapter 3 we discussed the importance of teacher guidance of young learners to support their self-assessment competencies. Adolescent learners need similar training and support.

Furthermore, the study result suggests that students in the same classroom tend to share similar attitudes toward the ELP. It is possible that the class atmosphere shapes students' perceptions about the usefulness of the ELP either positively or negatively. The teacher's role is pivotal for creating a classroom culture that is consistent with or favorable to the principles underlying portfolio assessment. As we discussed at the beginning of this chapter, the finding illustrates how various factors associated with microsystem–classroom environment have an immediate influence on students' experience with and performance on assessment.

However, the classroom culture and learning environment depend on many factors, some of which are out of the teacher's control. One of the most significant external influences on assessment practices is a top-down policy directive. When a nationwide curriculum innovation is introduced to the education system, it also introduces changes to the ways in which students' L2 proficiency is assessed (East & Scott, 2011). This shift was the case with portfolio assessment that was introduced to many classrooms as part of large-scale educational reforms. Research shows that this top-down, macrosystem-level change to assessment practice brings significant challenges to teachers (Cheng, Watanabe, & Curtis, 2004; Hamp-Lyons, 2007). The potential of the newly introduced assessment along with new curriculum policies may be compromised if it fails to engage teachers in making critical decisions about the development and implementation of the new assessment system (Hamp-Lyons & Condon, 2000). Collaboration among teachers, including those who are experts in assessment, is essential for the effective implementation of portfolio assessment (Bachman & Palmer, 2010; Hamp-Lyons & Condon, 2000).

Assessment of Oral Proficiency Should Consider Dynamic Peer Interactions

Group work is often a substantial component of secondary classrooms because teachers take advantage of students' increased cognitive maturity and ability to work collaboratively. We frequently ask students to work in pairs or small groups to discuss topics and complete both small and large tasks. How do you form these groups in your classroom? Is the grouping random or is it purposeful? If it is the latter, do you organize students according to their proficiency levels, their personalities, their skill levels, or another attribute? Read the interaction among four students in Classroom Snapshot 4.2 for an introduction to these issues.

Classroom Snapshot 4.2

Students in this classroom have recently watched the movie *Forrest Gump*. Their teacher has organized them into small groups and asked the learners to choose a gift for the main character, Forrest Gump. Listen to an excerpt from students Keith, Warren, Henry, and Jesi as they work together on this assignment.

As you read the students' interactions:

- think about how the students were grouped
- think about whether their organization provided maximum opportunity for students to express their ideas and for the teacher to evaluate facets of their oral language production.

Keith: Let's discuss the present to give to give to the main character of *Forrest Gump* which is Forrest Gump himself. Do you have any suggestion?

Warren: Okay. Maybe first we talk about what film we have watched.

Keith: Okay?

Henry: Of course *Forrest Gump* so it's a biography of Forrest Gump himself?

Warren: Yeah

Jesi: It's a very touching movie.

Henry: Yes?

Warren: and kind of comedy.

Henry: Yeah so first we if we have to decide to give a gift for a person, I think we better consider what's his background or what impression does he give you. Like Forrest Gump I think he is a very optimistic guy. Well and…

Keith:	He do.
Henry:	He never gives up
Keith:	Yeah he do things very straight forward. What he thinks what he'll do straight way.
Jesi:	I think if he's not optimistic, if he is… He was permistic he won't have this bright future.
Henry:	Yeah? And I'm especially impressed by one of his motto. He says, always said that life is like a box of chocolate. You will never know you what you get. So I decide, I think I have thought of giving him a box of chocolate hah! as a gift since it's so meaningful to him. And even it's like it's a symbol of his life?
Jesi:	Well chocolate is sweet. Sometimes you may get a bitter one.
Henry:	And that's life.
Jesi:	Yea, just like life.
Keith:	I could see that in the film that Forrest Gump really likes chocolate because once he wanted to give a box of chocolate to his girlfriend in the university under the heavy rain.
Jesi:	Jenny[1].
Keith:	He ate a few one and told Jenny, 'I'm I have I have a present to give to you and but I ate a: few candies inside.' And er I think chocolate is a quite good idea.
Warren:	But can't you see he always hold chocolate and when he showed up. So why don't we consider other presents to give him.
Henry:	So…
Warren:	How about photo album. So let him take some photos and put in the photo album, yea.

[1]Jenny is the name of the female protagonist in the movie.

(Gan, 2010, pp. 590–1) ▪

What did you notice about the students' interactions? Did this grouping allow all of the learners to contribute equally to the conversation? How did you assess each of the group members' oral proficiency? Do you think each student participated equally in the discussion?

Assessing oral proficiency is a challenging task because it involves various factors associated with task formats, such as a solo oral presentation, one-on-one direct interview (by interviewer's elicitation) or indirect interviews (by audio-taped elicitation), or a pair or group discussion (O'Loughlin, 2001). O'Loughlin reports that compared to the indirect interview format, direct interviews generate more bidirectional interactions and elicit a wider range of prosodic features, such as more varied intonations and richer vocabulary. One-on-one semi-direct or direct interviews are more likely to be used for a standardized testing situation, whereas teachers tend to favor a group oral discussion or a role-play format in classroom assessments.

Group oral assessment typically involves a group of three to four students in discussion about an assigned topic while the assessor observes the group discussion without interacting (Ockey, 2009). Group oral assessment is believed to elicit more authentic language output than the one-on-one interview format that differs from natural conversation (Fulcher, 1996; Lazaraton, 2002). Group oral assessment is also considered to promote positive washback for communicative classrooms through the simulation of group discussions. Nonetheless, there remains a critical concern about the effect of grouping on student performance, that is, how students' personality traits influence the other members' test performance (Bonk & Ockey, 2003; He & Dai, 2006). In a study involving Finnish students, Liski & Puntanen (1983) reported that the more talkative the students were, the fewer mistakes per utterance they made, indicating a positive correlation between students' dominance of group discussion and oral test scores.

Ockey (2009) investigated the extent to which the level of assertiveness of other group members affects non-assertive students' scores. He concluded that assertive test takers tended to receive higher scores than expected when they were grouped with non-assertive members. However, they received lower scores than expected when grouped with equally assertive members. He & Dai (2006) questioned the validity of the group oral assessment because test takers in their study failed to engage in the group discussion when the examiners were present; instead, the students chose to interact with the examiner, indicating the importance of students' familiarity with the format of the group oral assessment. Ockey describes the setting of the group oral assessment as follows:

> Groups of four test takers are seated in a small circle and given about one minute to read an assigned prompt and think about how they will respond before one of two raters says, 'Would someone like to begin.' Once test takers begin, they are expected to sustain a discussion on the assigned topic for eight minutes. The two raters, who are not involved in the group's discussion, sit outside of the group and provide ratings on a nine-point scale for each of five oral communication subscales: pronunciation, fluency, grammar, vocabulary, and communication strategies.
>
> (Ockey, 2009 pp. 169–170)

Fulcher reports that students in his study responded to the group discussion format favorably because they felt more confident and natural with oral speech. He concludes that the group discussion format appears to help students overcome affective disadvantages they may have during a one-on-one interview format.

Let us think about how to apply this research information to the assessment of adolescent language learners in classrooms. How do students with different language proficiency levels perform on these types of group oral assessment? What criteria do classroom teachers use to assess students' oral presentations or other forms of oral language production? Sometimes, mainstream teachers confine their classroom assessment of students' oral communication skills to formal presentations, and use criteria such as 'eye contact', and 'rate of speech' to evaluate the quality of the oral performance. However, such qualities are a poor indication of skill development underlying students' language competence; consider the fact that many fluent speakers may also have problems making eye contact and speaking slowly. Assessing students' interactions during group work can be an opportunity to observe core language skills and can serve to inform our instructional and pedagogical choices (for example, how to group students so that they have the maximum opportunity to interact).

Oral assessment tasks can be evaluated on the degree of interactiveness, the extent to which tasks allow students to draw from their knowledge of both the language and the topic, and use their strategic competence and emotional response (Bachman & Palmer, 1996). Successful interactions further involve knowledge co-constructed through the interaction with other participants beyond interaction with the task. Let us delve deeper into the characteristics of interactional patterns from the oral assessment of higher- and lower-scoring groups as described in Spotlight Study 4.1. As you read it, think about how this research can inform your decisions about grouping adolescent learners to ensure that they have optimal opportunities for interactions and that you are able to assess their oral communication language development.

Spotlight Study 4.1

Gan (2010) investigated the oral interactional patterns of two groups of Grade 9 learners in order to characterize the differences between higher- and lower-scoring groups, and to gain insights about the use of groups to assess students' oral language production. In this research investigation, Gan selected two videos to analyze the interactive communication among Cantonese students studying English in Hong Kong (aged from 14–17 years old). The students in the first group comprised learners whose oral English proficiency was scored at a Level 4 along a six-level continuum. Their assessment task was to discuss the film *Forrest Gump*.

The second video that Gan analyzed comprised four learners who had scored Level 3 or lower on the assessment scale. The assessment task for these students was to discuss prompts related to a different movie called *About a Boy*. The assessment of oral proficiency was focused on four main areas of language performance: Pronunciation and Delivery; Communication Strategies; Vocabulary and Language Patterns; and Ideas and Organization. Gan used a method called 'conversational analysis' to analyze the interaction patterns of each of the two groups. Table 4.1 summarizes the analyses of the two groups' interactions.

Group 1 (Higher-Scoring)
• Group work begins with students focusing on the task. • Clarification of the task is integrated throughout the discussion. • The task is well achieved as students move forward by continuously '(re)formulating task demands' (p. 591). • Students monitor the content of their discussion to ensure that it is appropriate and relevant to the task. • Students engage critically with each other in various ways including: expanding ideas, agreeing/disagreeing, clarifying or challenging each other.
Group 2 (Lower-Scoring)
• Group work does not begin with explicit discussion of the task requirements at the beginning of the interaction. • Students' speech sometimes includes long pauses indicating that they are struggling to either formulate ideas or use appropriate vocabulary and language structures. • Students react 'minimally' to each other (e.g. a typical minimal response may be 'oh yeah') indicating that the development of the discussion on the topic is minimal. • The discussion is more structured as students heavily depend on the sequence and content of the teachers' task questions to guide work. • Students monitor each other's language, and the 'linguistic problems' that students face provide them with an opportunity to collaborate on the construction of the language or dialogue.

Table 4.1 Summary of the analyses of the higher- and lower-scoring groups' interactions

Based on these findings, Gan suggests that group work allows students to engage in substantive discussions and authentic communicative tasks that give them the opportunity to demonstrate a wide range of language functions. One of the biggest differences between the higher- and lower-scoring groups was that the former group critically engaged with the task through fluent discussions while the latter group negotiated their conversation based on the language breakdowns that were occurring. As Gan articulates:

> … within the lower-scoring group, a picture emerges of peer participants actively assisting each other through inviting, prompting, and co-construction. It thus seems that among these lower-scoring participants,

critically exploring each other's ideas appeared to be of lower priority than maintaining a supportive and friendly discourse generally characterized by help and encouragement.

(Gan, 2010, p. 598)

Thus, Gan suggests that in order for students to be able to fully engage with a task, they need to master all of the knowledge and skills associated with it. He proposes that in classrooms, students' group work may be enhanced through teachers' provision of feedback throughout all stages of the oral assessment, and also by mixing grouping of students to include both higher- and lower-proficiency learners so that the former can learn from the latter. Gan also suggests that the structure of the task might contribute to the quality of students' discussions, based on the observation that the lower-scoring group's work was inhibited by the provision of a list of questions for students to respond to during the task. ∎

In this section, we reviewed the ways in which grouping in oral assessment influences group members' performance on oral tasks. We considered students' psychological and cognitive traits as factors contributing to the effect of grouping in oral assessment. These psychological and cognitive traits are not just individual attributes. Research shows that different cultural groups present different personality traits (Ockey, 2009); consequently, grouping members from different cultural backgrounds for oral assessment can influence the members' performance on the test. Such differences in performance are indicative of the influences of students' cultural background at the macrosystem level. All of these observations suggest that assessment does not take place in isolation, but interacts with multiple external and contextual factors. Furthermore, when we assess students' oral proficiency using tasks eliciting meaningful interactions among peers, it inevitably involves confounding factors that might compromise its construct validity—that is, its ability to measure what it is intended to measure, as discussed in Chapter 1.

Assessment Should Consider the Influence of Parents' Beliefs about Assessment

As students get older, and gain experiences with schooling, they develop distinct learning goals which, in turn, foster different orientations to academic tasks. During adolescence, these orientations become even more pronounced (Dweck, 1986). Both parents and teachers play a significant role in the development of students' goal orientations. According to Dweck, there are three main goal orientations:

- mastery: students tend to enjoy challenging tasks to enhance their skills and competence
- performance–prove: students prefer to demonstrate their competence to others seeking positive responses from them
- performance–avoid: students avoid challenging tasks because they fear the demonstration of incompetence and negative judgments from others.

Underlying these goal orientations are two distinct views of ability (Dweck & Leggett, 1988). Students and teachers who hold the incremental view consider ability as a malleable attribute, that is, it can be improved given effort. In contrast, those who hold the entity view see it as a fixed (innate) attribute, that is, it cannot be changed. The goal-orientation theory posits that the incremental view leads to a mastery goal orientation whereas the entity view fosters the two performance goal orientations.

What distinguishes these different views and orientations is the role of effort that students make in learning. I am sure you are familiar with various excuses students make for the failure of or low performance on tasks. For some students, putting forth effort means that they are not smart. Therefore, they are unlikely to say that they failed although they tried really hard. Instead, they may say that they fell asleep while preparing for the test.

Understanding students' goal orientations in academic settings offers a critical insight into their attitudes and beliefs about assessment tasks. It is equally important to recognize students' perceptions about the goals that their teachers and parents emphasize to engage students in academic tasks. Let us explore these concepts in more depth through Activity 4.2.

Activity 4.2

Table 4.2 illustrates statements from two questionnaires developed by Jang et al. (2013) to understand students' goal orientations to language tasks. The first questionnaire is for students; items from 1–22 concern three distinct goal orientation types we reviewed above: mastery; performance–prove; performance–avoid; items from 23–8 refer to students' perceptions about their parents' goal orientations; and items from 29–34 seek students' perceptions about their teachers' goal orientations. The second questionnaire instrument is intended for their parents to complete.

	Not at all true	Somewhat true	Very true
1 I feel successful on a task if I at least do well compared to other students doing the same task.			
2 I avoid asking questions that might make me look stupid.			
3 It's important to me that I learn a lot in tasks I do.			
4 It's important to me that I don't look stupid on tasks.			
5 Challenging tasks give me a chance to learn more.			
6 I try to look like I can do tasks even when I don't really understand.			
7 It's important to me that other students think I am good at the tasks we do.			
8 I like to show other students that the tasks we do are easy for me.			
9 It's important to me that my teacher doesn't think that I know less than others doing the task.			
10 When doing tasks I really try to keep others from thinking I'm not smart.			
11 It's important to me that others tell me I am good at the tasks I do.			
12 When doing tasks I want to learn a lot of new skills.			
13 I avoid tasks where other students might think I'm not smart.			
14 I prefer tasks that make me learn new things.			
15 When doing tasks I avoid looking like I have trouble doing the task			
16 It's important to me that I really understand the tasks I do.			
17 When doing tasks I want to learn as much as I can.			
18 It's important to me that I look smart compared to others doing the task.			

	Not at all true	Somewhat true	Very true
19 I like to show other students that I'm good at the tasks we do.			
20 It's important to me that I improve the skills that I use in tasks I do.			
21 I think if students work hard enough, they will get smart.			
22 If students work too hard, they are not that smart.			
23 My parents would like it if I could show that I'm better at class work than other students in my class.			
24 My parents tell me that it is important that I don't look stupid in class.			
25 My parents want my work to be challenging for me.			
26 My parents say that showing others that I am not bad at class work should be my goal.			
27 My parents want me to understand concepts, not just do the work.			
28 My parents don't like it when I make mistakes in my class work.			
29 My teacher lets us know which students get the highest scores on a test.			
30 My teacher says that showing others that we are not bad at class work should be our goal.			
31 My teacher points out those students who get good grades as an example to all of us.			
32 My teacher gives us time to really explore and understand new ideas.			
33 My teacher thinks mistakes are okay as long as we are learning.			
34 My teacher tells us that it is important that we don't look stupid in class.			

Table 4.2 Students' goal orientation questionnaire

If you are currently teaching, I invite you to conduct an inquiry into your students' goal orientations using the first questionnaire in Table 4.2. If circumstances permit, you can send home the parent questionnaire (Table 4.3) via your students. Think about how students' goal orientations are related to their language background and academic achievement level. Are their goal orientations in line with their teachers'? To what extent do you think your students' goal orientations are similar to their parents'?

	Not at all true	Somewhat true	Very true
1 I want my child to understand his/her class work, not just memorize how to do it.			
2 I have different ideas about what my child should learn in school than the teacher does.			
3 I want to see how my child's schoolwork relates to things outside of school.			
4 I would like my child to show others that they are good at class work.			
5 I want my child to understand concepts, not just do the work.			
6 I think that it is very important that my child gets the right answers in class.			
7 I want my child's schoolwork to be challenging for them.			
8 I would be pleased if my child could show that class work was easy for him/her.			
9 I don't like it when my child makes mistakes in his/her class work.			
10 It is important to me that my child gets good marks on his/her report card.			
11 I would like my child to do challenging class work, even if he/she makes mistakes.			

Table 4.3 Parent goal orientation questionnaire

How did your students respond to the questionnaire? Was it helpful in understanding their goal orientations? Was there a relationship between their goal orientations and their language proficiency or their academic achievement level? Spotlight Study 4.2 below provides some answers to these questions.

Spotlight Study 4.2

Jang et al. (2013) studied 44 students in Grade 6 from a private elementary school in Ontario; the study offers some insights into the relationship between students' goal orientations to academic language tasks and their parents' and teacher's goals. Among the 44 students, 57 percent heard and spoke only English at home; 34 percent spoke both English and L1; and 7 percent spoke only L1. Approximately 75 percent of the students were born in Canada, and about 33 percent of the parents were born in Canada.

The study results suggest that immigrant students tend to show a higher performance orientation than their domestic counterparts. Further, the analysis of students' perceptions of their parents' orientations shows some interesting results. Compared to their domestic counterparts, immigrant students tend to perceive their parents as more performance-oriented than mastery-oriented.

How do students' goal orientations correlate with their language achievement? The study reports that students' goal orientations did not show statistically significant correlations with their reading achievement. However, students' perception of their parents' and teacher's goal orientations did show significant correlations with their achievement levels. Specifically, when students perceived their parents as more mastery-oriented, they tended to show higher reading achievement. In contrast, when students thought their parents are more performance-oriented, they presented a lower reading achievement level. In addition, lower-achieving students tended to perceive their teachers as more performance-oriented as well. ■

These findings highlight the importance of contextual influence on students' language learning. Surprisingly, rather than students' own goal orientations, their perceived goal orientations of their parents and teachers show stronger associations with their achievement in reading. When students are exposed to mastery-oriented learning environments at home and school, they tend to show higher achievement levels. What complicates this matter is that parents holding different cultural values appear to have different beliefs about their role in their children's schooling. For example, Asian parents tend to hold the belief that there should be a clear division between schools and parents in taking responsibility for educating students (Lam, Ho, & Wong, 2002). This contrasts strongly with Western parents' viewpoint about the relationship between school and home. Chen & Uttal (1988) report that only 19 percent of American mothers (compared to 66 percent of Chinese mothers) believed that teachers are more important than parents in influencing children's academic performance. As this finding holds important implications for promoting students' positive experience with assessment tasks, we now turn our attention to the roles of parents and teachers under the influence of large-scale tests.

What are teachers' and parents' roles in assessment? As we discussed in Chapter 1, a test is frequently used as a way to spearhead educational curriculum reforms and meet the accountability demands (Jang & Ryan, 2003). A test itself cannot change how teachers teach and students learn; it is the educational agents at the micro- and macro-system levels that play a key role in generating positive washback effects on teaching and learning (Bailey, 1999; Messick, 1996). Needless to say, teachers have a direct influence on students' learning in school. The classroom assessment atmosphere is shaped largely by teachers' beliefs about assessment in general and attitude to the assessment policy mandated externally.

Parents' belief systems about tests also contribute to adolescents' classroom learning and assessment experience. You will recall that the ecological assessment system in Figure 4.1 also recognizes parents as important agents. However, research on the extent to which parents have an impact on their children's learning and assessment tends to focus on influences through their socio-economic and educational backgrounds. Little is known about how parents' beliefs about the test influence their children's perceptions of it.

In fact, parents are often left out of important assessment and learning decisions made at their adolescents' school. Ideally, when new assessment policies are introduced to school systems, important stakeholders (including test users) should be informed about the purpose of the test and key changes. However, as Scott (2007) shows, parents have insufficient understanding about what the test is intended to assess and how to interpret test information. There is much room for improving the current test score reporting practice, as it fails to provide useful information for parents in understanding their children's learning progress (James, 2000).

A study by Cheng, Andrews, & Yu (2010) draws our attention to the importance of engaging parents in the testing practice. Cheng et al. examined students' and their parents' perceptions about the new school-based assessment (SBA) introduced to the Hong Kong Certificate of Education Examinations (HKCEE) in English, which is the high-school exit examination. Students aged 16–17 take the HKCEE at the end of Secondary 5, which is the fifth level of seven-level secondary education. The test's SBA component in English assesses students' oral proficiency. Since its first introduction to the senior secondary school system in 2005, the SBA has made significant changes to teaching and learning. It allowed teachers to evaluate their own students' performance on individual presentations or group interactions, and teachers' evaluation to be counted toward the students' high-stakes test scores. Cheng et al. reported that when parents are more educated and spend more time with their children, they provided more support for their children's participation in SBA. Additionally, when parents knew more about SBA, they provided more support for their children in SBA. Another interesting finding from the study is that when the parents perceived tests to be motivational for their children's learning, their children tended to have a similar attitude towards the test.

In this section, we reviewed students' goal orientations and the relationship of the orientations with their reading achievement. We further examined students' perceptions about the goal orientations of their parents and teachers. Surprisingly, students' own goal orientations do not show a statistically significant relationship with their reading achievement. It is their parents' goal orientations that better predict students' reading achievement level. We also discussed the finding that students' goal orientations reflect their cultural background, because there is a clear difference between immigrant and domestic students; immigrant students tended to be more performance-oriented, and they perceived their parents to be also more performance-oriented.

We further discussed the role of parents in shaping their child's orientations to academic tasks and attitude to assessment. The Cheng et al. study confirms the significant influence of parents on their children's attitudes to the newly introduced assessment system. All of these observations emphasize the importance of recognizing parents as important agents for students' learning.

Teachers' Assessment Competence is Key to High-Quality Assessment Practice

Most current standards-based achievement assessments assume that all teachers, not just those designated as language specialists or ESL teachers, should be involved in identifying the needs and instructional strategies necessary to support students' language and learning needs in their classrooms, and that all teachers will eventually be involved in documenting and tracking students' language progression. Though teachers' assessment competence is crucial for learners regardless of their ages, it is more vital for adolescent ELLs because they have less time to catch up to their proficient peers. Therefore, teachers' ability to diagnose students' language needs and to provide them with language support in secondary classrooms is key to high-quality assessment practice leading to appropriate instructional practice. How do teachers develop the capacity to recognize and differentiate strengths and areas for improvement for each student? Meet a teacher and her ELL student in Grade 11 in Classroom Snapshot 4.3.

Classroom Snapshot 4.3

The following interaction between a teacher and a student in Grade 11 illustrates a one-on-one conference to discuss the student's essay on Internet safety that she had been working on in class in previous weeks. Pay attention to how the teacher interacts with the student during the conference.

T: Whenever we're writing our introduction, I always bug you guys to make sure you include two things; do you remember what they are?

S: A quote or a surprise.

T: Exactly, two different hooks to draw the reader in, right? So you just gave me two different examples, they could be a quote, they might be a surprising fact, do you remember some of the other things we sometimes include?

S: A little short story.

T: Yeah, an anecdote or a little short story that you can relate to.

…

T: So can you tell me where your two hooks are … what two you used?

S: Um.

T: I can already see them. Which means that you've done a super job, right? That they just pop right out at me!

S: I used a quote.

T: Yes, you did.

S: And I gave a surprising fact.

T: Yeah you gave us an interesting fact, that he's been a really popular host of a long-running CBC TV show.

(Jang et al., 2011, p. 87) ■

During this conference, the teacher was seeking to elicit information about the student's ability to develop and organize content in her writing. She asked the student to highlight where in her text she had used a specific writing strategy. After they had identified all of the strategy uses, they discussed the effectiveness of the student's choices and discussed ways in which the student could improve these strategies in her writing. In an interview following this teacher–student conference, the teacher commented that this activity, alongside other information that she had collected, enabled her to make a judgment about the student's proficiency level and helped her to share this information with the student to facilitate the selection of future learning goals.

The teacher conference in Classroom Snapshot 4.3 illustrates how ongoing assessment can be used for formative purposes. However, there are many more purposes for which assessment is used in classrooms, and we briefly reviewed some of them in Chapter 1. Jang et al. (2011) surveyed 40 teachers working in both elementary and secondary schools in Ontario to understand their uses of assessment in classrooms. Table 4.4 presents a summary of the teachers' responses to the survey. They were asked to give their responses to each statement using a 5-point scale with 1 indicating 'Almost never,' 5 indicating 'Almost always' and 3 'Sometimes'.

Reflecting on my assessment practice:	N	M	SD
I use assessment results when I prepare student report cards.	40	4.70	.56
Assessment helps me identify students' learning needs.	39	4.67	.58
I use assessment results when I plan lessons.	39	4.23	.81
Rubrics are an important part of my assessment practices.	38	3.71	1.09
Standardized assessments such as DRA, CASI/ PM Benchmark provide useful information about my students.	40	3.28	1.11
Students need to understand how their performance compares to others'.	38	2.66	1.10
I try to evaluate how much students know before instruction.	40	4.27	.72
I discuss students' work with them individually after they finish their work.	40	3.85	.83
I give whole class feedback after students finish their work.	38	3.66	1.15
I discuss students' needs with other teachers.	39	3.97	.74
I tell students in advance how their work will be evaluated.	38	4.16	.89
I try to provide descriptive feedback to students without assigning numerical marks/letter grades.	39	4.05	.72
I assign numerical marks/letter grades to students without descriptive feedback.	40	1.75	.78
I provide descriptive feedback alongside numerical marks/letter grades to students.	39	3.59	.99

Table 4.4 Teachers' reflections on the uses of assessment

The mean values (M) in Table 4.4 represent the average of the teachers' responses on the Likert questions. Relatively larger standard deviations (SD) indicate that teachers' responses to some statements vary to a greater extent than to other statements. For example, 40 teachers responded to the statement that read: 'I use assessment results when I prepare student report cards.' The average of these teachers' responses was 4.70 on the 5-point scale, which indicates that teachers almost always use assessment for this purpose, and its relatively small standard deviation suggests that there is not much variation in teachers' responses. The other three primary uses of assessment are:

1 to identify students' learning needs
2 to know how much students know before instruction
3 to plan a lesson.

Using assessments to compare the relative performance of students is the least frequently used purpose of assessment. Remember how students' perceptions about their teachers' goal orientations influence students' achievement level? I suggest you try to answer the questionnaire in Table 4.4 and compare your responses with the teachers' responses and those of other teachers in your school. Understanding and reflecting upon your beliefs will aid you in advancing your students' learning.

How do you think that teachers from different cultural settings would respond to questions concerning the uses of assessment? In Spotlight Study 4.3 we will read about the beliefs and values concerning assessment from teachers in Australia and Hong Kong. Note that regardless of their geographical differences, all of the teachers in these different school contexts are increasingly involved in assessment activities for both pedagogical and accountability purposes. Before reading Spotlight Study 4.3 take a moment to reflect on the question: To what extent do you think teachers' assessment activities differ from country to country?

Spotlight Study 4.3

Davison (2004) states that the use of criterion-referenced assessments (you will recall our discussion of CRT in Chapter 3) in schools has arisen in response to a desire for greater reliability in teacher-based assessments. She alerts us to three limitations of the use of CRT from the perspective of teacher-based assessment:

1 teachers interpret assessment criteria differently depending on their personal backgrounds, previous experiences, expectations, and preferences regarding the relative importance of the identified criteria, and their ideological orientation

2   there is an assumption that teacher-based assessment requires minimal professional judgment and interpretation and that it is a technical activity
3   there is an assumption that teachers willingly accept external standards as the basis for their classroom assessments.

Working with ESL secondary Cantonese-speaking students, 12 teachers in Australian and Hong Kong schools assessed their students' written arguments, using assessment criteria. Based on various methods including questionnaires, think-aloud protocols, and interviews, Davison investigated teachers' assessment beliefs, attitudes, and practices. Not surprisingly, the study results show a great deal of variation within and between the contexts. Although all the Melbourne teachers chose the assessment criteria developed for summative school-based assessment and the standardized reporting approach with equal weight assigned to all criteria, they struggled between their professional judgment and 'gut reactions' (p. 314). In contrast, the Hong Kong teachers showed much more variation in terms of assessment processes and the use of assessment criteria for making their judgments. Davison attributes variations among the Hong Kong teachers to the lack of common assessment criteria for evaluating students' written work in secondary schools in Hong Kong and teachers' reliance on norm-referenced testing.

Another notable difference between these two contexts is teachers' beliefs about the social impact of the assessment on students. Whereas the Melbourne teachers maintained that 'it is the fate of the individual and their life chances that are paramount in teachers' thoughts' (p. 321), the Hong Kong teachers expressed concerns about respect and face by stating that their judgment would not be respected and authorized by the outside including their own students if their assessment is not explicitly linked to the external test. The Hong Kong teachers' concerns about the lack of respect for their assessment judgments reflect their negative beliefs about assessment. One Hong Kong teacher states:

> We don't mark … Any marking we do is pretty negligible … It's quite sad that should be the case. I believe we waste a lot of our time marking when we should be giving back to their process writing or getting them to write journals or all sorts of other things. 'So, my faith in the system is pretty low. And therefore, my faith in how I mark and the devotion I put into marking is very low, and therefore I am very frequently pretty superficial in the way I mark because I don't believe it's going to make the slightest bit of difference. I am sorry that it should be the case. I really wish it was going to improve the students' writing, but it isn't the case.'

(Davison, 2004 p. 323)

Based on the comparative analyses of two very different assessment contexts, Davison developed the typologies of teachers' assessment beliefs, attitudes, and practices. Table 4.5 summarizes the types of teachers' assessment beliefs and implications for validity for school-based assessments.

Type	View of assessment	Implications
Assessor as technician	Assessment is bound by criteria and is treated as a mechanical procedure	Inconsistencies in assessment not a concern
Assessor as interpreter of the law	Assessment is bound by criteria, and judgments are confined to them regardless of external factors or opinions	Inconsistencies are a threat to reliability
Assessor as the principled yet pragmatic professional	Assessment is bound by criteria but takes into account individual student and task	Inconsistencies are to be expected, and not necessarily resolved with ease; requires more teacher communication and dialogue
Assessor as the arbiter of community values	Assessment is community referenced; it is personalized and impressionistic	Inconsistencies are inevitable and a threat to validity
Assessor as God	Assessment is community bound; it is highly personalized and intuitive	Seemingly unaffected by inconsistencies

Table 4.5 Typology of teacher beliefs about assessment ▪

What type of assessor are you? Are you a teacher who is bound by defined criteria or do you and your colleagues develop your own criteria? Do you think that these different types of teachers use assessment for different purposes? The typologies should not be considered as mutually exclusive; rather, they represent multiple beliefs systems that teachers may have. Considering that teachers use assessment for various purposes including summative reporting to providing descriptive feedback, as shown in the Ontario teachers' survey results above, it is likely that teachers hold multiple belief systems depending on the context of assessment use.

In this section, we have discussed teachers' attitudes and beliefs about assessment in various contexts. Teachers often find it confusing when they are expected to play strikingly different roles in assessment. This expectation may be particularly challenging for novice teachers or teachers with limited experience with assessment due to the macrosystem-level cultural norms and traditions. Building and strengthening teachers' assessment competencies is key to success in fulfilling the potential of assessment.

How then can teachers develop the capacity to use assessment in a valid and reliable way while dealing with the demands associated with assessment? When teachers develop the ability to evaluate the quality of assessment tasks, they can use integrated, multi-step tasks that effectively prompt students to use cognitively more complex skills, drawing from their linguistic reservoir. For example, one of the most common assessment tasks used in secondary classrooms is to require students to read a text and complete a written piece about it on their own. Upon completion of the written work, students are asked to perform or share their writing and reflect on it through a conversation with others in a small group or with the teacher (Jang et al., 2011).

I suggest that teachers use a variety of language assessment tasks to provide learners with several opportunities to display their competencies. Gathering a diverse range of student work samples can provide teachers with the confidence to make valid and reliable judgments about what students can do and what they need to improve. Teachers can further develop their diagnostic assessment competence by implementing various instructional strategies to scaffold and accommodate students' performance on assessment tasks. Teachers may use brainstorming activities, jot-notes, multiple drafts of written work, or graphic organizers to provide scaffolding to help students to demonstrate what they can do.

Ample opportunities to observe and gather evidence from students' linguistic performance, using integrated, multi-step language tasks, will provide teachers with both holistic and nuanced understandings of individual students' language proficiency development.

Assessment Should be Culturally Responsive and Fair

Test fairness concerns the extent to which decisions and uses made on the basis of students' test performance are justifiable. We have already discussed test fairness in Chapter 3 extensively. However, there are two main reasons why test fairness is of particular concern when we assess adolescents. One reason has to do with the adolescents' developmental characteristics. Adolescents begin to develop heightened self-consciousness and individual identities. In doing so, they also come to recognize external factors that influence their identity construction either positively or negatively. In particular, adolescent language learners develop heightened awareness of the cultural values and socio-economic contexts in which they live. In addition they form strong moral opinions about what happens in a larger social setting. As a result, they develop a strong yet not always reasonable, sense of morality and fairness.

Secondly, although large-scale tests for educational accountability and policy changes are widely used for all students across all grade levels in K–12 schools, the test stakes for adolescents are much more significant (Scott, 2007). This is evidenced by research showing the trend towards an increase in ELLs' dropout rates just prior to mandatory high-stake exams (Fairbairn & Fox, 2009; Madaus & Clarke, 2001; Watt & Roessingh, 2001). In the name of social integration and equal opportunities for all, the test-based accountability systems around the world prefer to apply a set of common criteria for making such high-stake decisions for all students, regardless of their backgrounds (Leung & Lewkowicz, 2008). How do adolescent ELLs perceive the use of large-scale tests? The following activity offers us an opportunity to think about the cultural sensitivity of high-stakes tests for adolescents.

Activity 4.3

Below is a reading passage with multiple-choice questions (Norton & Stein, 1995). This text was a part of the English proficiency test used to identify black applicants with limited English proficiency to a South African university. Read the passage first, and then answer the reading comprehension questions that follow the text. While reading the passage, think about these questions:

1   What do you think about the content of the passage in terms of its cultural sensitivity?
2   What do you think about the reading comprehension questions?
3   If you were to administer this reading test, how do you think your students would respond to it?

Monkeys on Rampage

A troop of about 80 monkeys, enraged after a mother monkey and her baby were caught in a trap, went on the rampage at a Durban home at the weekend attacking two policemen who were forced to flee and call for help. A 14-year-old boy also had to run for his life and reached the safety of a home split seconds before a full-grown monkey hurled itself against the door. The troop also attacked a house, banging windows and doors. Mrs. Kittie Lambrechts, 59, of Firdale Road, Sea View, told reporters how the monkeys' behaviour was sparked off by events on Saturday. She said her family had been pestered by monkeys for over a year.

"They come nearly every day, and they steal all the fruit from our fruit trees before it's ripe enough to pick," she complained. "We didn't know what to do, so we wrote a letter to the Durban Corporation. They said that it would be unsafe to use guns in the neighborhood, and that we should not poison the monkeys because sometimes dogs and cats eat the poison; rather, we should set traps. On Saturday we bought a trap and put it in our garden. Shortly afterwards, the monkeys arrived and a mother and her baby were caught in the trap. The whole troop went into a raging fury and attacked us. Edwin Schultz, a young visitor from the Transvaal, had to run for his life and slammed the door closed just before a full-grown monkey could get hold of him. It jumped against the door. The troop attacked our home and hit against the doors and windows. It was terrifying."

Mrs. Lambrechts telephoned the police and Const N M Moodely and Const E Coetzer of the Bellair police station went to investigate. But when they arrived, the troop turned on them and they had to run for cover as well. "The men ran to their van and called for help while monkeys surrounded them and jumped against the vehicle," Mrs. Lambrechts said. Police armed with shotguns arrived on the scene and four monkeys were shot dead. The troop then fled into the bushes, apparently because their leader had been among the monkeys shot dead.

(Adapted from *The Star*, July 1986)

1 This newspaper article is about
   a) Edwin Schultz's visit to Durban from the Transvaal.
   b) How Mrs. Lambrechts runs her fruit business;
   c) monkeys that attacked people;
   d) the accidental poisoning of dogs and cats.

2 A 'troop' of monkeys is
   a) Monkeys that live near people;
   b) Any group of monkeys living together;
   c) Any group of animals living together;
   d) Monkeys having the same mother.

3 Why were the monkeys considered pests?
   a) The monkeys were dangerous and attacked people.
   b) The monkeys made a lot of noise and disturbed the family.
   c) The monkeys took unripe fruit from the garden.
   d) The monkeys made a mess in the garden.

4 The Durban Corporation advised Mrs. Lambrechts
   a) To shoot dead the leader of the troop;
   b) To set traps in her garden.
   c) To poison the fruit in her trees.
   d) To telephone the police.

(Norton & Stein, 1995, pp. 52–3)

What do you think about the content of the passage? Do you think the questions adequately measure students' reading ability? You may be surprised at the accounts from black South African high school students who participated in a pilot test. Students' responses to the question, 'What did you think about the passage?' were as follows:

- I was offended by the passage because monkeys have a special significance in our culture ... They are associated with witchcraft.
- Black people are often thought of as monkeys.
- It's about Black people, who are the monkeys "on the rampage" in White people's homes.
- It's about who owns the land—the monkeys think the land belongs to them but the Whites think they own the land. (p. 56)

What do you think about the researcher's (Norton) reaction to the students' responses?

> I was completely taken by surprise at the students' readings of the text as racist. My reading of this text as a simple factual report about monkeys in Durban shot by the police was fundamentally challenged by the students ... Another assumption was challenged as well: my assumption that high school students are relatively naive about the ways in which they might use the different readings of text to their advantage. In this classroom, students were extremely adept at juggling a series of different readings in their heads, which they used appropriately, according to the demands of the social occasion.
>
> (Norton & Stein, 1995 p. 56)

Despite students' negative reactions to the passage, they performed very well on the test. How should we interpret this paradox? This issue is a complex test validity concern, and it highlights that the valid interpretation and fair use of a test are subject to its relevance to a specific socio-cultural context in which the test is used. In the above case, though students' test performance was not compromised by its cultural sensitivity, its consequential validity (Messick, 1989) is questionable.

As we discussed throughout the book, when a test that is inappropriate for language learners is used to make high-stakes decisions, it has far reaching ethical consequences. The same test taken by students from different backgrounds may turn out to measure different constructs. Fox & Cheng (2007) raise this issue based on verbal accounts elicited from 33 focus groups including 22 L1 and 136 ELLs based on their experience with the Ontario Secondary School Literacy Test (OSSLT), one of the Ontario school graduation requirements for all students. One ELL's comment, 'Just give this to me in Chinese and I'd be able to do it in a minute' (Fox & Cheng, 2007, p. 17) answers the researchers' rhetorical question, 'Did we take the same test?'

Whereas all but one of the L1 test-takers expressed satisfaction and relief after the test, the L2 test-takers seemed more rather than less concerned. When taking the test, some L2 test-takers reported that they felt 'sad', 'angry' or 'frustrated'. After taking the test, they seemed to perceive it as more rather than less difficult and did not report that their anxiety lessened while they were in the process of writing the test. Anxiety and perceptions of difficulty are known to impede test performance (Phillips, 1992). Therefore, this finding is a concern.

(Fox & Cheng, 2007 p. 20)

ELLs' accounts of their test-taking experience show that ELLs' limited vocabulary knowledge is a significant barrier (Cameron, 2002). Many of the ELLs noted that in a non-testing situation, they would use dictionaries when they encounter unfamiliar words or expressions during reading for schoolwork. 'I have my dictionary in every class and I always check words to be sure I'm on the right track. I would have been able to do this test much better if I could do it the way I do in class' (Fox & Cheng, 2007 p. 17).

Fox & Cheng's study shows that difficulty with vocabulary affects students' performance not only on reading but also writing tasks. Many ELLs in their focus groups reported that they could not complete writing tests because they could not understand a writing prompt that included unfamiliar words without textual support. Some students did not understand what they were expected to do on the text, indicating their lack of knowledge about test genre. For example, when the writing prompt, 'If you could change one thing in the world, what would you change?,' was provided with two full pages with lines, some ELLs in the focus groups commented that they either had only a few things to write or did not write any because there was nothing to change.

Sixteen year-old Malaysian English language learners report a similar test taking experience (Zainal, 2012). When they took a writing test (which is considered high stakes as the results are used to make decisions for their admittance to higher-level education), they reported that a lack of test instructions misled the students. Though overall the test was appropriate to the curricular level, they felt that the vocabulary used in the test was inappropriate to their linguistic levels.

While the struggle that ELLs experience with vocabulary points to a lack of vocabulary knowledge, it can be also caused by construct-irrelevant sources that make a test favor non-ELLs over ELLs. Test items that use topics and formats that are irrelevant to the construct and familiar to some students but not to others offer differential opportunities for students from different backgrounds to perform on the test. Differential Item Functioning (DIF) is a statistical approach used to detect test items that function differentially across different subgroups when they are at the same ability levels. For example, if ELLs perform poorly on a mathematics problem because of its complex sentence structure or vocabulary, the validity of the inference about these ELLs' mathematics ability is problematic (Abedi, 2008). Another example is when a reading passage requires cultural knowledge that favors some students over others from different cultural backgrounds.

Kim & Jang (2009) confirm that, based on the DIF analysis of students' responses to OSSLT (Ontario Secondary School Literacy Test), test questions that measure vocabulary knowledge exhibit significant and large DIF in favor of non-ELLs. When vocabulary is assessed as part of a reading comprehension test, the test should provide textual cues for students to use to deduce the meaning of unknown vocabulary. When it fails to do so, vocabulary test items are more likely to exhibit DIF against language minority groups. On the other hand, the researchers report that the three grammar questions that favored ELLs all assessed micro-level punctuation knowledge and speculate that ELLs likely received direct grammar instruction in their ESL classrooms. It is also likely that ELLs would practice the test with their ESL teachers, while most non-ELLs would not have any instruction beyond a general information session on the OSSLT.

All of these research examples emphasize that tests developed on the basis of the performance of native English speakers should be used with caution to understand and interpret the performance of ELLs. If standardized tests must be used as graduation exit exams, regardless of students' background, in order to adhere to the societal belief about equal opportunity and equitable treatment (Leung & Lewkowicz, 2008), the tests should not present any construct-irrelevant sources that lead to biased interpretations about subgroups' language competence. Furthermore, some topics used in a test may be culturally sensitive to some ELLs. Considering adolescents' developmental stage, it is crucial to ensure that the language tests they take are responsive to their cultural background and appropriate for their literacy development rate.

Assessment Should Take Advantage of the Benefits of Technology

The integration of technologies into assessment is far overdue. Our students are in the midst of a digital revolution. However, students' use of technologies is primarily limited to activities outside of schools because educational institutions in general have not yet fully embraced the digital revolution. Also, students' access to technologies varies significantly from context to context, depending on students' socio-economic backgrounds.

Most currently available computer-based language assessments are large-scale standardized tests used to measure students' general language proficiency (see TOEFL's iBT or IELTS). Digital media are also widely used in EFL to provide authentic native speakers' language input. Students may take an English listening comprehension test or a dictation test while listening to a CD, cassette-tape player, or watching a video player. It is hard to see these uses as examples of technology integration, because the test is still based on paper and pencil. Nowadays, secondary students are likely to type their essays rather than write on paper. They are fluent in the use of a variety of editing tools (for example, Microsoft Word's spelling and grammar checker, online dictionaries, and thesauruses—all great companions indeed for ELLs!).

One useful approach taken to utilize technologies in assessment is the development of an online test item bank that recycles used test items for teachers. For example, the *TeleNex* test bank is used to support English language teachers' school-based assessment in Hong Kong secondary schools (Coniam, 1995). The items are drawn from public tests used previously, refined and calibrated on the basis of a large number of students' test performance data.

Another example, Denmark's *Evaluation Portal*, provides support materials, including various assessment and evaluation tools for Danish teachers (Shewbridge, Jang, Matthews, & Santiago, 2011). Teachers can use sample test items to prepare students for the final examinations at the end of lower-secondary school, or to establish evaluation criteria for classroom activities. The online portals can thus assist teachers with assessment for formative and summative purposes.

While these supports can be useful technological resources for teachers, they appear to have limited potential for integrating assessment more seamlessly into teaching and learning. A more recent technological resource in language assessment is the development of online automated essay-scoring programs, considered complementary tools for easing the burden on teachers; it takes a considerable amount of time for teachers to mark students' papers by hand and provide detailed feedback—use of these programs also encourages students to revise their work—Chapelle, 2008; Warschauer & Grimes, 2008. In secondary classrooms, teachers' assessment in content courses frequently involves students' writing in a variety of genres. This heavy reliance on writing ability is a significant challenge for adolescent ELLs, regardless of whether they learn English as a second, additional, or foreign language. In addition to their still-developing academic English language proficiency, adolescent ELLs have to deal with heavy curriculum requirements, pressure from high-stakes exams (including graduation exit tests and college entrance exams), and often inconsistent support from content teachers to improve their writing skill—most secondary teachers have insufficient knowledge and the training required for supporting adolescent ELLs' language needs in subject learning.

Teachers could use automated essay-scoring software, such as *My Access!*™ or e-rater® software. These programs come with writing prompts that can be scored by the software. The Educational Testing Service's (ETS) *Criterion*®, for example, is a well-known online automated essay-scoring program. Its e-rater® software is used to score online essays based on the Natural Language Processing (NLP) techniques, analyzing various rates of errors in grammar including usage and mechanics, style, lexical density, organization, and development. A student's essay is analyzed and rated electronically to provide almost instantaneous feedback on the written product. The feedback screen is interactive, allowing learners to scroll over highlighted parts of their text to generate a comment box which offers additional feedback on each micro-feature of the writing. Teachers are also able to insert additional comments for students to view. All of the feedback is available in English or in English and Spanish for language learners who would benefit from the translations.

Another resource is Vantage Learning's *My Access!*™, which uses an artificial intelligence scoring engine called Intellimetric™. It compares semantic, syntactic, and discourse features of a student's essay with features of 300 human-scored sample essays. Each student receives a holistic score, as well as component scores for focus and meaning, organization, content and development, language use and style, mechanics, and convention (Warschauer & Ware, 2006). In addition, teachers can adjust the level and language of feedback. An independent companion resource, *My Editor*, offers more detailed feedback on spelling, grammar, and word usage.

These automated essay-scoring programs are used in large-scale standardized testing contexts where they complement human raters. Research shows that computer-generated and human rater scores are highly correlated with each other, similar to the correlations between human raters alone (Warschauer & Ware, 2006). Although this positive correlation can be considered evidence to support the use of automated essay-scoring programs, it is insufficient to fully justify the appropriateness of their use. We need to consider how teachers and students use the programs in classrooms. Does the use of such programs improve students' writing ability and enhance the quality of writing instruction? Spotlight Study 4.4 provides some classroom-based research answers to these questions.

Spotlight Study 4.4

Warschauer & Grimes (2008) conducted a case study to explore how automated essay-scoring programs (*Criterion*® and *My Access*™) are used in classrooms. Among four participating schools, two used Criterion and two used *My Access*. The study gathered data from interviews with three principals and eight language arts teachers, observations of 30 language arts classes, and a survey completed by seven teachers and 485 students in Grades 6–12. The researchers also gathered 2,400 essays written by students with assistance of the programs.

A majority of teachers and students highly valued the programs and reported that they helped motivate students to write more and to write creatively. The programs freed up teachers' time by engaging students in writing and revising activities. Most teachers asked students to use the programs for feedback on early drafts. Teachers still graded final drafts for scoring and feedback.

Despite all these positive accounts of the programs, the researchers saw little evidence of their frequent use. The explanation given was that teachers had to deal with the pressure of preparing students for upcoming state tests, covering heavy curriculum materials that emphasized reading over writing. Another reason given for limited use was that the programs offered insufficient writing prompts.

The researchers also reported little evidence that students used the programs for iterative revisions. Among those who resubmitted their essays, the revisions made were mostly to mechanics (spelling, word choice, and grammar) rather than content and organization—these revisions were mainly made to raise their scores. The researchers pointed out, 'this limited revision is consistent with more general practices in US public schools, in which student rewriting invariably focuses on a quick correction of errors pointed out by the teacher or peer'.

(Warschauer & Grimes, 2008 p. 29)

The study concludes that the usefulness of automated essay-scoring programs is mediated by various social and contextual factors including student and teacher beliefs and past teaching experiences. In addition, the implementation of the programs is driven by the need to meet the state standards (raising students' test scores on the five-paragraph essay), and is challenged by diverse student populations and varying teacher beliefs and experiences. ▨

Secondary classroom realities are influenced and greatly constrained by external testing pressure, which is beyond teachers' and students' control. This pressure appears to compromise potential benefits from feedback on multiple drafts of their work during process-oriented writing practices (Ferris, 2003) and result in a great deal of variation among teachers with the use of online automated essay scoring programs, as Warschauer and Ware note:

Overall, though, Attali's finding that relatively few revisions are carried out has been confirmed by our own observations. This reflects the general classroom environment in the era of standards high-stakes testing, with teachers feeling pressured to cover as much material as possible. Little time is thus left for multiple revisions of a single essay, especially when the standardized tests that teachers are preparing their students for all involve tightly timed essays, thus obviating the need for much revision.

(Warschauer & Ware, 2006, p. 16)

It is possible that these formative assessment tools designed to aid teachers and guide students' writing practice can in fact be used as a tool to 'teach to the test,' a serious negative washback effect, common worldwide. This test washback effect is also found in students' tendency to focus on outcome-based learning, as expressed in holistic scores. In addition, one may wonder if descriptive feedback is comprehensible for students and concrete enough for them to take action.

In this section, we discussed the use of automated essay-scoring programs for assessing adolescent learners' writing skills. Research confirms that *Criterion*® and other online writing assessment systems that support teachers in their instruction of students' writing are not meant to replace teachers. Though students who have the economic means to access a computer and the Internet tend to use the programs more frequently, research evidence converges on the importance of teachers' beliefs about and attitudes to process-oriented writing and assessment. Adolescent learners who need the greatest support for their academic language and literacy development can benefit from the use of the programs with their teachers' guidance.

This allows teachers and students to spend more time on content and organization, through process-oriented writing assessment practice, and allows students to handle mechanical errors more easily, with the assistance of the automated programs. In summary, automated scoring programs are not intended to replace teachers but to complement teachers' work (Hamp-Lyons, 2007). This point is particularly important to remember because the automated programs we reviewed above may be limited in assessing the full range of writing and speaking skills (Xi, 2010).

Summary

In this chapter, we discussed the roles of various agents in assessing adolescent learners, focusing on the following principles:

- Portfolio assessment should promote the culture of learner autonomy and assessment for learning.
- Assessment of adolescent learners' oral language proficiency should consider the dynamic interactions among peers.
- Assessment should take into account parents' values and beliefs and involve them in the assessment.
- Teachers' assessment competence is key to high-quality assessment practice.
- Assessment of adolescent ELLs should be culturally responsive and fair.
- Assessment of adolescent ELLs should take advantage of the complementary benefits offered by technology.
- Figure 4.4 summarizes the key principles we discussed in this chapter by mapping them onto the ecological assessment system.

Situating assessment activities in the broad ecological system allows us to appreciate the interactive relationships among various agents from the most immediate to most distant environments. I hope this mapping encourages you to think about various contextual factors that influence students' experience with and performance on assessment tasks. As I noted earlier, the ecological assessment framework can also be useful and relevant for understanding young learner assessment. Assessment does not take place in a vacuum. We cannot assess students' language proficiency without taking into account contextual influence in order to make meaningful inferences about what students are able to do and then to take the necessary action for future learning.

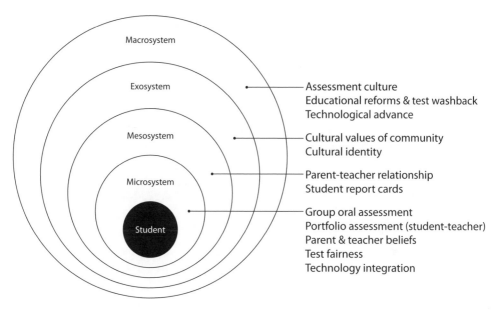

Figure 4.4 Mapping out assessment principles in the ecological assessment system

5

Language Assessment: What We Know Now

Preview

The central theme of this book is that the quality of language assessment depends on its beneficial uses and value for teaching and learning. It is an integral means to pedagogical ends. If assessment is costly in terms of instructional time and resources but is of little use, its validity is questionable. I put forward my argument that all assessments have stakes implications; to regard classroom assessment as lower-stake than large-scale external assessment would be to misrepresent classroom realities. Teachers' judgments and classroom uses of assessments have profound effects on the lives and opportunities of students. Students' first-hand classroom experience of teachers' assessments shapes their sense of fairness and social justice. Many drops indeed make a flood.

Activity 5.1 Review your opinions

In Activity 1.1 (page 10), you indicated how strongly you agreed with some statements about language assessment. Before you continue reading this chapter, go back and complete the questionnaire again. Compare the responses you gave then to those you would give now. Have your views about assessment been changed or confirmed by what you've read in the preceding chapters?

Reflecting on Ideas about Assessment: Learning from Research

We set out on our assessment journey by surveying various uses of assessment in and outside of classrooms in Chapter 1. In Chapter 2 we dealt with the question of 'what to assess,' by exploring some key features of school-aged learners' language proficiency development. We closely examined some principles for guiding 'how to assess' young language learners (Chapter 3) and adolescent learners (Chapter 4). Our discussions were challenged, provoked, and informed by a wealth of research, which examined issues arising from the uses of different assessments in various assessment contexts.

To sum up, let us now return to the opinions you responded to in Chapter 1 to review some key ideas you have encountered in reading this book.

1 Students develop language skills at a fairly even rate among oral, reading, and writing skills

This statement reflects the traditional unitary view of language proficiency that we discussed in Chapter 2. One may argue that language skills are highly correlated with each other, making it difficult to tease them apart, and that this high correlation supports the unitary view. Indeed, this evidence has been used to support the unitary view of language proficiency and, more importantly, to justify single test scores as indicators of students' overall language ability.

However, the unitary view can be disconfirmed for two main reasons. First, research evidence points to L2 students' non-uniform language development in multiple language skills. As we discussed in Chapter 2, a more current view is that L2 students' language proficiency is characterized by multiple components of linguistic and cognitive competences. This multi-componential view of language proficiency helps us pay attention to students' unique language profiles that show their progress in linguistic knowledge and functional skills.

A second reason for debunking the statement is related to the old familiar question: 'Which came first, the chicken or the egg?' Most construct validation research is post hoc; that is, it happens after the test has been developed and uses students' test performance data. As a result, the test results may simply reflect the test developers' intended construct definition, that is, how the test developers defined language ability in the first place. Then, strong correlations among language skills from the test are considered evidence to support the traditional construct validity (whether or not the test measures what it is intended to measure), but not as direct evidence to characterize how language develops.

2 Students' oral fluency is a good indicator of their academic language proficiency

Students' oral fluency is not a sufficient indicator of their language abilities. In Chapter 2, we discussed academic language proficiency in terms of grammar, vocabulary, and discourse knowledge across three interactive modes: oral, reading, and writing. Simply assessing students' oral language fluency does not provide a complete picture of what learners can do, and the areas in which they need additional support.

For example, some immigrant children may come from cultures where L2 varieties are spoken. They may sound fluent but may not have been formally taught academic language in L2. It is not uncommon for US or Canadian-born ELLs to enter school with oral language fluency, but without mastery of the additional language skills needed for success in schools (Jang et al., 2013).

At the same time, the importance of oral language fluency should not be ignored. Students' oral language proficiency is critical for the literacy development necessary for successful academic learning. Researchers concur that it allows students to actively participate in academic content learning (Genesee et al., 2005; Nurss & Hough, 1992; Snow, Cancino, Gonzalez, & Shriberg, 1987). Language learners should be given ample opportunities to use language for communicating with peers and teachers in socially acceptable ways. Teachers' assessment should focus on gaining comprehensive understandings of students' language profiles that include their progress in both oral and literacy skill development. Oral narration assessments that we reviewed in Spotlight Study 2.1 can be useful for promoting oral language proficiency of both young and adolescent language learners.

3 Students are not capable of assessing their own ability

Students have had a limited role in assessment practice partly because so many educators believe this statement to be true. Research confirms that students' self-assessment can accurately represent their ability, and more importantly that enhanced self-assessment ability helps students gain control over their learning process. To this end, students' self-assessment is increasingly used in K–12 schools. Despite its popularity, teachers often show their disappointment in students when they are reluctant to assess their own work and devalue their self-assessments because they think they are of little use. The ability to self-assess one's own learning is not automatically acquired; in fact, it requires higher-order thinking skills, such as critical thinking and reflective skills, all of which need to be cultivated. Teachers need to provide guidance to help their students develop the skills needed to make consistently accurate interpretations of their own learning. This additional support increases teachers' workload in fact, challenging the notion some teachers have that self-assessment lowers teachers' workload or that it undermines teachers' authority (Sadler, 1989)!

In order for teachers to accept self-assessment as an effective and powerful tool in the classroom, they may need to experience a philosophical shift, requiring a conceptual change in their beliefs about assessment, and an acceptance of a shared responsibility for assessment. The ability to self-assess can have a positive impact on students' control of their learning; this is particularly important in contexts where serious stakes tests are involved. Unfortunately, in these situations students have become conditioned to believe that the quantity and quality of their learning are indicated solely by marks—high school students typically ask, 'Does this count toward my final grade?'

Some teachers wonder whether students' self-assessment should be given a weight in summative marks. Ontario, Canada's new assessment policy (Growing Success, 2010) explicitly states that assessment is the teacher's responsibility and should not include the judgment of the student or of his or her peers. Although this policy statement may invite debate with regard to the 'ownership' of assessment, it also reminds us to think about the purpose of student self-assessment, which is not to reduce teachers' workload, but to increase students' self-esteem and motivation to learn.

For young language learners, especially those in transition from learning to read to reading to learn and experiencing 'the fourth-grade slump,' teacher-guided self-assessment may raise students' awareness of changing perceptions on learning beliefs and attitudes. Research shows that students in Grades 4 and higher tend to evaluate their reading ability much lower than it is (McKenna & Kear, 1990), reflecting the challenges children face with increasingly abstract and lexically-dense academic materials in schools. Students' self-assessment of their own learning progress as well as their orientations to learning can provide teachers with useful information on how to raise students' awareness.

For adolescent learners, self-assessment is even more pivotal. As adolescents develop a sense of individual self outside of their families for the first time, teachers need to foster opportunities for them to play a more active role in assessment. Self-assessment provides opportunities for personal reflection and autonomy. Peer assessment fosters adolescents' willingness to work closely with their peers; however, this same desire may make it difficult to assess peers' essays or presentations. Teachers need to demonstrate the formative use of assessment by giving descriptive feedback oriented to problem-solving strategies. Clearly, giving marks to peers is a not an effective form of assessment for adolescents, in light of the significance of peer pressure among adolescents.

4 Teachers' assessments are too subjective

While subjectivity in teacher assessment is of great concern (Brown & Hudson, 1998), it reflects conflicting views. One has to do with a common belief that teachers' assessment is inherently biased because of their opinions, feelings, and beliefs. Another pervasive view is that teachers' assessment is not objective enough to provide reliable information for measuring and comparing students' achievements across schools. As a consequence, a need is seen to use external standardized tests to hold education and teachers accountable for students' academic achievements.

Another view is that subjectivity in teachers' assessment in classrooms has to do with their assessment methods. However, using the same criteria that are used for large-scale standardized tests for classroom-based teacher assessments is problematic (Leung & Lewkowicz, 2008; Shohamy, Inbar-Lourie, & Poehner, 2008). In fact, there is no such thing as absolutely objective assessment, because all assessment involves people's value-laden judgments, from development to use. As the *Monkey* passage in Chapter 4 illustrated, multiple-choice tests that are regarded as objective could include topics that are potentially biased against a subgroup of students.

Sometimes the argument is put forth that teachers' assessment of their students is too subjective because of their intimate knowledge of their students. However, consider doctors' diagnoses of their patients: ideally, they are familiar with their patients' backgrounds and history. The situation is similar in both cases, yet familiarity is considered positive in the medical context, and negative in the educational one. Teachers are qualified professionals who have the most knowledge about students.

One may question then, are they adequately trained to gather, interpret, and use data (i.e. assessment activities)? Unfortunately, as we saw in Chapter 4, not all teachers are afforded adequate professional development opportunities. Torrance & Pryor (1998) report that although teachers are familiar with assessment methods, many lack a clear assessment framework that guides the implementation of assessment for teaching and learning (Shohamy, Inbar-Lourie, & Poehner, 2008). There is no doubt that strengthening teachers' assessment competence is critical for enhancing current assessment practices (Edelenbos & Kubanek-German, 2004). Teachers should be able to provide evidence to support their judgments in assessment by making assessment criteria transparent and consistent, so that students know how their work is evaluated. Teachers should then communicate the assessment criteria to their students in concrete terms so that they can use the criteria as benchmarks for self-assessing their learning progress.

5 Students should know how their marks compare with their peers

6 Frequent testing is an effective way to motivate students to study harder

These two statements reflect the die-hard assumption rooted in Skinnerian behaviorism that testing motivates students to perform better, teachers to teach better, and the public to pay attention to the quality of schools. Have you met any teachers who believe that publicly posting student rankings based on their test results will boost them to study harder? However, during my school years, a few of my teachers actually did post the entire class's ranking on the wall! What is your reaction to policy makers who believe that publishing school-level annual test results online will make teachers teach better? In these instances, testing is only a means used to determine rewards and sanctions, and its original role is ignored. If a test holds a significant consequence for students, there is no doubt that it will motivate students to study harder—but to study only what is tested. This is not a desirable way to motivate students. Research has confirmed that testing has negative consequences when it holds seriously high stakes over students. It should be further noted that not all students are motivated by the tests-based rewards and punishments (Clarke, Abrams, & Madaus, 2001), as evidenced by increased dropout rates for particular demographic groups of high school students.

School-aged language learners go through cognitive, social, and emotional development while learning an additional language. How their teachers use assessment in the classroom may have both positive and negative effects on their development. It is important to ensure that young school-aged learners have positive experiences with assessment in all the areas they develop. Teachers need to avoid comparing among students based on their assessment results, giving marks without feedback, or limiting the types of feedback they give to evaluative and summative.

It is possible that students, especially older language learners, may come from a testing-driven culture. They may have already internalized a strong performance orientation. These learners may view assessment as a threat to self-esteem and show test anxiety, thus handicapping their learning by avoiding challenging tasks. Frequent testing will reinforce the fear of failure for these students. It is necessary for teachers to help students view assessment as a way to cognitively engage themselves with learning tasks. Assessment with descriptive feedback will help students understand that ability can be enhanced through effort and that failure and mistakes are part of the competence-building process (Hoska, 1993).

7 *Students care only about marks. They rarely pay attention to feedback*

Do students care only about marks? Perhaps so, if the marks are the only information provided for them and if they have effects on students' lives and opportunities. When numerical marks are used for young learners, they see assessment as a means to prove their ability to others. As discussed above, summative numerical marks can have a positive effect on motivating students to study harder, but the effect tends to be short-term, and results in distracting young learners from tasks. Do students care about their teachers' feedback? Absolutely! Not all students have experienced the beneficial role of descriptive feedback that emphasizes both the strengths and areas needing improvement in their language learning.

Alternatively, teachers can use assessment to provide descriptive information about progress toward a set of goals. As we discussed in Chapter 1, descriptive feedback focusing on cognitive processes and strategies can help reorient students to focus on tasks rather than outcomes. For young learners, scaffolding descriptive feedback should focus on both strengths and areas needing improvement, to ensure that they do not become overwhelmed with what they cannot do. This practice is especially important for young learners who show a performance-oriented attitude.

For adolescent learners, feedback should be used to help them self-regulate their own learning through critical reflection and planning for future learning. Compared to young language learners, adolescents have acquired cognitive and metacognitive maturity that allow them to appreciate detailed diagnostic feedback on specific areas that they need to improve and use it for planning future learning.

Teachers should take the time to reflect on their oral feedback practices during classroom interactions. One way of doing this is to audio- or video-tape your regular interactions with students in the classroom and see how your classroom discourse is structured. Check to see if your oral interactions with students follow the common classroom discourse pattern called the Initiation-Response-Evaluation (IRE) communication pattern (Cazden, 2001). This IRE communication pattern tends to be given without sufficient wait time and to emphasize evaluative feedback. Try rehearsing oral feedback that avoids evaluative feedback on students' responses and gives sufficient wait-time to nurture students' deep thinking.

8 Formative and summative assessments are different types of tests, so they should not be mixed

We earlier discussed various purposes of language assessment used in K–12 schools. Among them, formative and summative purposes are most frequently mentioned and are most often used as the basis for distinguishing among assessments. Formative and summative assessments are not different kinds of assessment. They are different *uses* of assessment. The formative use of assessment is to provide students with feedback at various stages of the learning process and to provide teachers with evidence for evaluating the effectiveness of teaching. The summative use of assessment is mainly to certify the level of achievement and inform subsequent decisions which will have serious consequences for students, teachers, or schools. Often the formative use of assessment is said to have low-stakes. However, both formative and summative assessments are important for students, and even the formative use of assessment can have far-reaching, long-term consequences. Instead of distinguishing formative from summative assessment in terms of the degree of importance, it may be useful to think about whether or not assessment-based decisions are 'renewable.' Can students set their learning goals based on the assessment results and later change the goals? If yes, the assessment is being used formatively; if no, it is being used summatively.

The formative and summative uses of assessment are not as well distinguished as we might think. Timing (the point in the instruction when the assessment is used) and interval (time lapse between assessment use) of assessment are sometime used to distinguish between them in classrooms. In general, assessment for summative use is less frequent (for example, at the end of an instructional term) while assessment for formative use occurs on an on-going basis throughout the instructional period. Distinguishing formative from summative assessment in classrooms may not be useful because of the continuity of teaching and learning across instructional terms. All classroom assessments should provide formative information for teachers and students about what students have done (prior learning), what they can do now (current level), and what they can do with support (proximal level).

A summative use of assessment can be found in large-scale testing practices used for determining the effectiveness of teachers, schools, and systems, on the basis of students' performance on external tests. They are also used to adjust programs, allocate resources to programs, and report students' annual progress. The tests typically measure students' achievement levels with reference to a set of pre-established standards. Can these external summative tests also serve the formative purposes? Current standards-based assessments, such as the No Child Left Behind Act in the USA highlight both purposes by providing feedback for educators to take remedial actions to improve education. Nevertheless, the summative use of tests for accountability purposes is causing tensions because the summative use outweighs the formative one.

9 Standards-based assessment allows teachers to assess students' academic achievement relative to curricular goals

Standards-based assessment has become a prominent assessment approach in many developed countries. Standards are used as benchmarks to judge the extent to which student have achieved curricular expectations. Content standards are used to specify the content of assessment, and performance standards are used for reporting students' achievements in the proficiency levels. There are two distinct uses of standards in assessment. One is the accountability purposes in which a set of 'standardized' tests are used in alignment with the standards; another is for classroom assessment in which teachers use standards (in the form of rubrics) to evaluate students' performance on tasks (for example, portfolios, essays, oral presentations). We also saw some cases where classroom-based teacher assessments and external tests are jointly used to assess students' achievement (see Spotlight Studies 3.4 and 4.3).

Research confirms that specific descriptions of learning expectations included in the standards increase transparency in the process of assessment and strengthen the link between expected knowledge and student performance (McKay & Brindley, 2007). Detailed accounts of students' performance levels can be formative for student learning and this can be considered evidence of mixing the formative with the summative use of assessment (see point 8 above). Talking with parents and students about what they need to do to be successful at school is important for ensuring that students receive support from their parents. Students moving from place to place are assured of consistent programming and evaluation. As such, having a common curriculum and common assessment standards gives stakeholders a common language to discuss and to compare learning goals and achievement levels.

Despite these advantages, standards-based assessment faces various issues, including an increase in teacher workload and a narrowing of the curriculum to discrete skills. Teachers often feel overwhelmed by what they perceive as an obligation to teach to a long list of expectations specified in the curriculum. They feel pressure from being held accountable for their students' achievement, as measured against the standards. Teachers and low-achieving students are therefore often caught in the conundrum of repeated underachievement and/or failure to meet the standard.

Because standards-based assessments tend to put more emphasis on teachers' judgments for assessing students' performance on tasks, the transparency of standards and consistency in using them are crucial for ensuring that information from assessment represents what students know and can do. Teacher moderation activities can be used to help teachers build a consensus on how to interpret and use standards. Building consensus through assessment moderation activities among teachers, as discussed in Chapters 3 and 4, offers a great professional learning opportunity.

10 Introducing a new test is an effective way to leverage curriculum change

Testing has become a means to get the fastest 'bang for the buck' from informing educational changes to directing curricular reform, and guiding policies and systemic changes. In Chapter 1, we reviewed the use of national English tests in EFL contexts for reforming the curriculum (Cheng, Watanabe, & Curtis, 2004). The test-based reform initiatives reflect policy makers' belief that they will have a positive washback effect on teaching and learning (Alderson &Wall, 1993).

Research on the effect of using tests to guide curricular changes is inconclusive. Changing the curriculum, while maintaining high-stakes tests in EFL contexts, creates a tension and resistance from teachers because they are caught between the need to teach the new curriculum and the need to prepare students to write the test (Sasaki, 2008). As we saw from the use of the NMET in Chinese EFL contexts, introducing new test items that measure productive skills resulted in making the curriculum mirror the test content and delivery. Students' unequal opportunity to learn productive skills raised concerns about the social and ethical consequences of testing in society. As Wall & Alderson (1993) noted, the new exam system is only one of many factors that influence the success or failure of the curricular reforms. Evaluation of the effect of tests-driven curricular reforms on teaching and learning requires a contextual understanding of the dynamic relationship between curriculum, instruction, and assessment (Frederiksen & Collins, 1989; Jang & Ryan, 2003).

11 Most teachers know how to assess students' language proficiency in other subject-matter classes

Teachers should know how to assess language proficiency across the curriculum but unfortunately, many new teachers enter the profession without having had the opportunity to develop professional knowledge about how to assess students, especially students who are learning additional languages or have exceptionalities. For many teachers, assessment is an add-on rather than an integral component of teaching and student learning. Although teachers have basic knowledge about assessment in general, they face increasing challenges in assessing language learners' academic language proficiency and their subject-specific achievements. Research shows that teachers' prior knowledge and beliefs about assessment shape their assessment practices (Davison, 2004).

Of course, teachers' current assessment practices are greatly influenced by national testing policies and culture. Therefore, developing teachers' diagnostic assessment competence is not an individual teacher's responsibility. Professional development activities should be tailored specifically to address the real difficulties that teachers encounter when they assess their students in classrooms. Teachers should be given professional development opportunities to work collaboratively with those who struggle with the same problems within their own schools or districts (Elmore, 2002). Teachers' assessment competence is key to strengthening professionalization, which will enhance the quality of teachers' judgments in classroom assessments; teachers' assessment should not be based on their 'gut feelings.' Assessment information should be gathered systematically through a principled approach—teachers should be able to provide concrete evidence that justifies their judgments and helps students understand their learning progress and achievements.

12 Providing accommodations for some students is unfair to other students

13 Teachers should treat all students equally by using the same assessment methods for everyone

Obviously, all students should be given fair opportunities to demonstrate what they know and can do, and provision of fair opportunities may include offering students a range of supports. The two complementary statements (12 and 13) do not allow for the fact that the provision of extra supports for students with exceptionalities does not compromise equity. For example, teachers may facilitate students' access to test materials by adjusting test administration procedures without changing the content of the test (referred to as test accommodation, Abedi, Hofstetter, & Lord, 2004). Test accommodations do not alter learning expectations or the content of the test. Teachers can allow language learners to demonstrate their learning in a different mode (for example, orally instead of writing, giving them extra time, or permitting them to use bilingual dictionaries). On the other hand, test modifications are changes to the content of the test or to learning expectations. In order to allow test results to be comparable among the students test modifications are not permitted in large-scale testing situations.

In secondary classrooms, teachers often hear from their students and even parents that it is not fair to offer accommodations to some students but not others. Some teachers may wonder if the provision of support in testing situations violates the 'equitable treatment of all students.' These perspectives are problematic. As we discussed in Chapter 3, test accommodations should not affect the performance of students who do not need them. At the same time, students who need support should not be offered an excessive number of test accommodations. Over-supporting students in testing situations may result in inflating their performance, invalidating the test results.

Each accommodation approach requires careful research as it can potentially alter the construct that the test is intended to measure. Research shows varying effects of different types of accommodations on students' performance in tests (Pennock-Roman & Rivera, 2011). Abedi et al. (2004) suggest that reducing the linguistic complexity of a test does not influence non-ELLs but does effectively accommodate ELLs. When teachers assess language learners' academic achievement in subject areas, they should provide appropriate accommodations for students to demonstrate what they know and can do. Teachers should consult with students to determine their needs, and encourage on-going communication on whether the accommodations provided are meeting their students' needs.

14 *Reliability in assessment is the most important factor for high-quality language assessment*

Reliability refers to the consistency with which the same student or group of students would perform on an assessment given the next day or under slightly different conditions. At issue are concerns about possible errors associated with assessment, and as we have discussed, there are many potential sources of error. Some errors are due to uncontrollable random events, and some are systematic. Teachers should try to avoid any systematic error that could potentially influence students' performance on a test. Traditionally, when objectivity was considered the gold standard of testing, reducing the amount of error to increase reliability was mandatory. Historically, indirect tests that use selected-response formats, such as multiple-choice, true/false, and matching tests were preferred over direct tests such as performance assessments because the aforementioned test methods did not require human raters' judgments. It is true that these machine-scorable test methods do not interfere with human raters' judgments, resulting in less error. However, although it is reasonable to assume that more consistent test results will provide more valid information, this does not always happen. For example, a multiple-choice test of students' knowledge about writing conventions will have a higher reliability value than an essay test. However, the validity of the multiple-choice test method is compromised because its results only imply that students have the ability to use the knowledge of conventions in writing an essay, rather than demonstrating that ability (Moss, 1994). We called this a validity and reliability paradox (Brennan, 2001).

In current assessment culture, teachers increasingly wish for more direct assessments of students' proficiency using various performance assessments, hoping to gather more meaningful and useful information from the assessments. As a result, inconsistency in the human scoring of performance assessments has become of great concern. As we discussed in point 4 above, teachers should strive to achieve consistency in their judgments of students' performance on tasks. It is a great idea for teachers to read the essays of all students in the classroom without scoring them. Then they can assign marks (if necessary!) to the essays by applying rubrics consistently. If students participate in district-wide external performance assessments, teachers in the same school can participate in moderation activities in which they judge the samples of students' written products using agreed-upon criteria, and calibrate their judgments by comparing them with the other teachers. Moderation activities offer an excellent professional development opportunity for teachers to develop competence and confidence in assessment.

15 A test is valid as long as it measures what it was intended to measure

This statement represents the view of validity as a test's adherence to the theoretical definitions of the construct. Although current assessment communities still acknowledge the importance of construct validity, they also understand that validity lies in the quality of the interpretation of the assessment and whether it fulfills its purposes meaningfully, appropriately, and usefully.

As discussed in Chapter 1, assessment takes place in a social context that involves multiple stakeholders. As a result, how we interpret and use assessments is inevitably influenced by contextual realities and also likely to be influenced by the expectations that the multiple stakeholders have for the assessment. There is no single best way to evaluate the validity of assessment practices. It should be open to evaluative judgments among those who have stakes in the assessment. The assessment users (teachers, students, and parents), who were not traditionally viewed as agents with the legitimate knowledge required for judging test validity, are now being recognized as key players in assessment validation. Teachers should actively participate in conversations about the validity of language assessment practices in and outside schools and demonstrate their assessment competence through systematic data gathering and documentation.

Conclusion

Developing the academic language proficiency required to meet language demands in schoolwork can be challenging for all students. It is particularly challenging for language learners who must learn challenging academic content while learning the language of instruction. Consequently, assessing their progress in language and academic learning is an important responsibility for all teachers not just school language specialists.

In this book, I emphasized use-oriented assessment for developing the critical knowledge and skills for evaluating school-aged language learners in curriculum-learning contexts. Teachers are at the heart of assessment. It is my hope that the readers of this book have developed both greater competence in assessment and confidence in their understanding of its uses.

Suggestions for Further Reading

There is a considerable body of literature on assessment, some of it focused on pedagogical practice and some on research. Choosing a limited number of items to recommend is not easy, but the ones listed below provide a good foundation in both the history and development of this approach to educating second language learners.

American Educational Research Association, American Psychological Association, & National Council on Measurement in Education. (1999). *Standards for educational and psychological testing*. Washington, DC: American Educational Research Association.

A set of testing standards was jointly developed to promote adequate and ethical use of tests and to serve as guidelines for evaluating the quality of testing practices by three associations: American Educational Research Association (AERA), American Psychological Association (APA), and the National Council on Measurement in Education (NCME). The standards serve both professional test developers and users, by addressing issues related to test construction, evaluation, and documentation, test fairness, and testing applications. This is a great resource for teachers' professional development activities in language and educational assessment in schools and districts.

Bachman, L., **& A. Palmer**. (2010). *Language assessment in practice*. Oxford: Oxford University Press.

This 416-page book is a follow up to the previous edition, *Language testing in practice*, published in 1996. The authors introduce the framework of Assessment Use Argument (AUA) as a guideline for assessment development, use, and validation. They contend that assessment should be evaluated through the justification of assessment use, using practically reasoned argument processes. They offer comprehensive discussions about the theories of language assessment, the application of AUA to specific language assessment examples, and teaching and assessment contexts. The book is an excellent resource for both researchers and practitioners interested in developing assessment competence.

Bailey, K. (1997). *Learning about language assessment: Dilemmas, decisions, and directions.* Heinle & Heinle.

This is one of 13 volumes entitled TeacherSource Series. This book is divided into three sections: teachers' voices, frameworks, and investigations. In the first section, Bailey tells stories from teachers about problems they encountered with assessment. In the following sections, the author discusses how to evaluate assessment methods and she invites the readers to participate in inquiry-based activities designed to evaluate specific assessments. She also discusses the advantages and disadvantages of various assessment methods and argues that teachers need to balance them in particular assessment contexts.

Cheng, L., Y. Watanabe, & A. Curtis. (2004). *Washback in language testing.* Mahwah, NJ: Lawrence Erlbaum Associates.

This edited collection discusses research on test washback in various educational systems. The first section of the book is devoted to the discussions of washback phenomena, and the second section focuses on methodological considerations. Taken together, this collection reports findings from washback studies in a wide range of testing contexts. Some of the studies reported in the book address the effect of the IELT on textbooks and materials, the effects of high-stakes college entrance exams in Asian countries, and the EFL oral matriculation test in Israel. The results reported in the book highlight that the effect of tests depends on specific contexts where teaching and learning take place and that both positive and negative washback effects are observed.

Genesee, F., & J. A. Upshur. (1996). *Classroom-based evaluation in second language education.* New York: Cambridge University Press.

This is a highly practical and accessible resource for teachers who seek specific information about assessment approaches to be used in their classrooms. In the 14 chapters of this book, Genesee & Upshur illustrate assessment procedures in various teaching situations to which different instructional approaches are applied. The authors summarize the approach they have taken in the book as 'practical, classroom based and teacher driven, helpful in making instructional decisions, adaptable to different instructional styles and objectives, and responsible to the needs of different audiences' (p. 8). The book comes with a preview and discussion questions, along with suggested readings for each chapter.

These features make it appropriate for use as a textbook in teacher education programs.

Hattie, **J.**, **& H. Timperley**. (2007). The power of feedback. *Review of Educational Research*, 77(1).

Feedback is one of the most useful and powerful influences that assessment can have on teaching and learning. This article provides a thorough review of research on feedback and identifies parameters that influence the effect of feedback. It offers some suggestions for using feedback to enhance classroom assessment. The authors point out that most current assessments provide little feedback because they tend to measure knowledge requiring recall and more importantly they mainly serve the summative purpose. They call for systematic research that enriches our understanding about how feedback works for students' learning process in the classroom.

McKay, **P.** (2006). *Assessing young language learners*. Cambridge: Cambridge University Press.

This is one of the most comprehensive books written for practitioners about assessing young language learners in EFL/ESL contexts. It was first published in 2006 and the second edition in 2010. The book offers theoretical accounts of young learners' language development, and research on assessments. It covers a wide range of assessment approaches in depth and provides a wealth of examples that illustrate specific assessment practices.

Appendix

Council of Europe self-assessment grid

<table>
<tr><th></th><th></th><th>A1</th><th>A2</th><th>B1</th><th>B2</th><th>C1</th><th>C2</th></tr>
<tr>
<td rowspan="2">UNDERSTANDING</td>
<td>Listening</td>
<td>I can recognise familiar words and very basic phrases concerning myself, my family and immediate concrete surroundings when people speak slowly and clearly.</td>
<td>I can understand phrases and the highest frequency vocabulary related to areas of most immediate personal relevance (e.g. very basic personal and family information, shopping, local area, employment). I can catch the main point in short, clear, simple messages and announcements.</td>
<td>I can understand the main points of clear standard speech on familiar matters regularly encountered in work, school, leisure, etc. I can understand the main point of many radio or TV programmes on current affairs or topics of personal or professional interest when the delivery is relatively slow and clear.</td>
<td>I can understand extended speech and lectures and follow even complex lines of argument provided the topic is reasonably familiar. I can understand most TV news and current affairs programmes. I can understand the majority of films in standard dialect.</td>
<td>I can understand extended speech even when it is not clearly structured and when relationships are only implied and not signalled explicitly. I can understand television programmes and films without too much effort.</td>
<td>I have no difficulty in understanding any kind of spoken language, whether live or broadcast, even when delivered at fast native speed, provided I have some time to get familiar with the accent.</td>
</tr>
<tr>
<td>Reading</td>
<td>I can understand familiar names, words and very simple sentences, for example on notices and posters or in catalogues.</td>
<td>I can read very short, simple texts. I can find specific, predictable information in simple everyday material such as advertisements, prospectuses, menus and timetables and I can understand short simple personal letters.</td>
<td>I can understand texts that consist mainly of high frequency everyday or job-related language. I can understand the description of events, feelings and wishes in personal letters.</td>
<td>I can read articles and reports concerned with contemporary problems in which the writers adopt particular attitudes or viewpoints. I can understand contemporary literary prose.</td>
<td>I can understand long and complex factual and literary texts, appreciating distinctions of style. I can understand specialised articles and longer technical instructions, even when they do not relate to my field.</td>
<td>I can read with ease virtually all forms of the written language, including abstract, structurally or linguistically complex texts such as manuals, specialised articles and literary works.</td>
</tr>
<tr>
<td rowspan="1">SPEAKING</td>
<td>Spoken Interaction</td>
<td>I can interact in a simple way provided the other person is prepared to repeat or rephrase</td>
<td>I can communicate in simple and routine tasks requiring a simple and direct exchange of</td>
<td>I can deal with most situations likely to arise whilst travelling in an area where the</td>
<td>I can interact with a degree of fluency and spontaneity that makes regular interaction with</td>
<td>I can express myself fluently and spontaneously without much obvious searching</td>
<td>I can take part effortlessly in any conversation or discussion and have a</td>
</tr>
</table>

	A1	A2	B1	B2	C1	C2
(Spoken Interaction, cont.)	things at a slower rate of speech and help me formulate what I'm trying to say. I can ask and answer simple questions in areas of immediate need or on very familiar topics.	information on familiar topics and activities. I can handle very short social exchanges, even though I can't usually understand enough to keep the conversation going myself.	language is spoken. I can enter unprepared into conversation on topics that are familiar, of personal interest or pertinent to everyday life (e.g. family, hobbies, work, travel and current events).	native speakers quite possible. I can take an active part in discussion in familiar contexts, accounting for and sustaining my views.	for expressions. I can use language flexibly and effectively for social and professional purposes. I can formulate ideas and opinions with precision and relate my contribution skilfully to those of other speakers.	good familiarity with idiomatic expressions and colloquialisms. I can express myself fluently and convey finer shades of meaning precisely. If I do have a problem I can backtrack and restructure around the difficulty so smoothly that other people are hardly aware of it.
Spoken Production	I can use simple phrases and sentences to describe where I live and people I know.	I can use a series of phrases and sentences to describe in simple terms my family and other people, living conditions, my educational background and my present or most recent job.	I can connect phrases in a simple way in order to describe experiences and events, my dreams, hopes and ambitions. I can briefly give reasons and explanations for opinions and plans. I can narrate a story or relate the plot of a book or film and describe my reactions.	I can present clear, detailed descriptions on a wide range of subjects related to my field of interest. I can explain a viewpoint on a topical issue giving the advantages and disadvantages of various options.	I can present clear, detailed descriptions of complex subjects integrating sub-themes, developing particular points and rounding off with an appropriate conclusion.	I can present a clear, smoothly-flowing description or argument in a style appropriate to the context and with an effective logical structure which helps the recipient to notice and remember significant points.
Writing	I can write a short, simple postcard, for example sending holiday greetings. I can fill in forms with personal details, for example entering my name, nationality and address on a hotel registration form.	I can write short, simple notes and messages relating to matters in areas of immediate needs. I can write a very simple personal letter, for example thanking someone for something.	I can write simple connected text on topics which are familiar or of personal interest. I can write personal letters describing experiences and impressions.	I can write clear, detailed text on a wide range of subjects related to my interests. I can write an essay or report, passing on information or giving reasons in support of or against a particular point of view. I can write letters highlighting the personal significance of events and experiences.	I can express myself in clear, well-structured text, expressing points of view at some length. I can write about complex subjects in a letter, an essay or a report, underlining what I consider to be the salient issues. I can select style appropriate to the reader in mind.	I can write clear, smoothly-flowing text in an appropriate style. I can write complex letters, reports or articles which present a case with an effective logical structure which helps the recipient to notice and remember significant points. I can write summaries and reviews of professional or literary works.

WRITING

Glossary

academic language proficiency (ALP): the language skills necessary to succeed in academic or school contexts. It is differentiated from social language skills.

accommodations: adjustments made to a test administration procedure to facilitate students' access to test materials without changing the test construct.

acculturation: the process of adapting or modifying one's culture over time as a result of contact with another culture or society.

alternative assessments: performance assessments, as an alternative to traditional tests, that allow students to demonstrate what they can do in authentic situations.

assessment as learning: focuses on fostering students' ability to monitor and reflect on their own progress and learning to achieve goals through peer- and self-assessment.

assessment for learning: identifies a broad category of contemporary assessments practices, including formative, diagnostic, and dynamic assessments used for guiding instruction and enhancing students' learning.

basic interpersonal communication skills (BICS): language skills necessary for interactions with others in social situations.

cloze test: a test in which students have to supply words that have been removed from a text either regularly (every nth word) or selectively (content words only) to measure students' reading comprehension and vocabulary.

cohesive device: linking words or phrases that connect ideas and sentences to increase coherence in a piece of writing. Examples include: *however, in conclusion, additionally, moreover.*

collocation: a common grouping of words in a sentence, often in a specific order. The meaning of the combination is determined by their association (for example, *once upon a time*).

Common European Framework of Reference for languages (CEFR): the European language standards (developed by the Council of Europe) for describing foreign language learners' language proficiency. The CEFR describes language proficiency in terms of six reference levels (A1, A2, B1, B2, C1, C2), which serve as the basis for teaching, learning and assessment.

construct: a latent trait (such as motivation, intelligence, or language ability) that cannot be directly observed. In order to observe and measure it, the construct has to be defined, theorized, and operationalized.

constructed-response test: a test that require students to produce an answer (for example, short answer items or an essay question) as opposed to choosing an answer from a list.

content standards: a set of descriptions of knowledge that students should know and skills they can perform in a specific subject area.

correlation: a statistical measure of the degree of relationship between two variables. The variables may be either positively or negatively correlated. A positive correlation indicates that as the value of one variable increases, then so does the value of the other variable. In contract, a negative correlation is observed if the value of one variable decreases as the other increases.

criterion-referenced tests (CRT): tests used to compare the performance of individual students to a standard or a set of criteria in order to determine the mastery of skills.

diagnostic assessment competence: the ability to diagnose individual students' strengths and areas for improvement and plan for remedial actions for students.

discourse knowledge: discourse refers to any written or oral language that is longer than a sentence and is unified through its meaning or purpose. Discourse knowledge refers to the ability to use and understand discourse to communicate effectively.

dynamic assessment: a diagnostic assessment that assesses learners' developmental potential by identifying the gap between their current ability and their next level of development in Vygotsky's Zone of Proximal Development (ZPD).

European Language Portfolio (ELP): a document based on the CEFR for languages and used by language learners to track, record, and reflect on their language learning experiences and achievements. An ELP comprises three parts: 1a a language passport to document language skills, qualifications, and experiences; 2 a language biography; and 3 a dossier to collect representations of learners' achievements.

exceptionalities: refers to students' cognitive, emotional, communication, behavioral, medical, social, and physically developmental strengths and needs.

expository texts: a genre of oral or written language whose purpose is to inform, explain, describe, or provide instruction (for example, a newspaper article, a YouTube video describing how to change a tire on a car, a laboratory report).

fairness: a broad range of concerns in language assessment about whether a test: 1) is biased against a certain group; 2) provides equitable treatment for everyone being assessed; 3) ensures equality of test outcomes regardless of age, cultural, disability, etc.; and 4) offers an equal opportunity to learn the content that is being assessed.

formative assessment: assessment carried out during classroom instruction and used to inform both teaching and learning. Often used interchangeably with the term 'assessment for learning'.

general language proficiency: consists of a single global language ability (based on the unitary competence hypothesis).

genre: a class or category of composition (for example, art, music, literature) with common characteristics. Examples of writing genres include: poetry, narratives, and expositions.

home language environment: language(s) that is (are) both heard and spoken by students at home. The home language environment can also refer to the genres of printed literature and other textual resources that students are exposed to at home, and the language in which they are written.

language functions: a range of purposes for which students use language to communicate in academic content learning.

L1/first language: native language or mother tongue that someone learns from birth.

L2 or L3: someone's second or third language.

language proficiency: the ability to use language to achieve communicative goals.

mean: the average value of a series of numbers obtained by dividing the sum of the means by the number of numbers in the series.

metacognitive ability: refers to the ability to reflect on own thinking, monitor cognitive processes, and evaluate learning.

modalities: any channel of language communication, such as reading, writing, speaking, and listening.

multi-componential view: the view of language ability as consisting of multiple competences (for example, grammatical, sociolinguistic, and strategic competence).

modifications: changes made to a test to remove barriers to student access to test materials.

multimodal language learning: language learning through instruction that uses more than one mode of communication (for example, a language tutorial website that uses videos alongside written text).

narrative: a literary genre that involves storytelling.

No Child Left Behind Act (2001): an American federal policy which requires all states to develop and administer state-wide tests to all students to ensure adequate academic achievement progress in particular content areas.

norm-referenced tests (NRT): tests used to compare the performance of individual students to a larger norm group of students.

observable language behaviors (OLB): descriptions of unique language behaviors that teachers can observe and evaluate using a set of proficiency descriptors.

performance assessments: assessments based on authentic activities that mirror real-life tasks.

performance standards: a set of benchmarks against which students must demonstrate proficiency at a specific level on a continuum.

portfolio assessment: a method of assessment in which students present a collection of their work to demonstrate their learning process and outcome.

proficiency-level descriptors (PLD): descriptions of knowledge and skills that students are expected to master at each proficiency level on a continuum.

qualitative research: an inquiry approach used to describe the phenomenon of interest based on direct contact and prolonged engagement with people in real-world settings.

raw score: the sum of the points that a student earned on a test. It is an original score that has not been converted to a standardized score.

reading disability: reading skills difficulties that show in single word reading, decoding sounds of words, reading sight words, insufficient phonological processing, and text comprehension.

reliability: the degree to which a test result is consistent and stable over time.

scaffolding: instructional strategies to support students' learning by breaking down complex tasks into multiple steps or smaller chunks, or demonstrating successful problem-solving strategies.

scaled score: a score on a common scale that is created through the transformation of a raw score.

selected-response test: a test in which students choose a correct answer from a list of provided options (for example, matching items or multiple choice and true/false questions).

semantic cues: the hints or prompts that help learners understand the meaning of words.

stakeholders: the people who are interested in any aspect of an assessment, including those who are involved in test operations, are served by the test, and use the test results.

standard deviation: the amount of the dispersion of scores from the mean. The more spread apart the scores, the higher the standard deviation.

standards-based assessment: assessment aligned with pre-established standards and used to evaluate level of achievement against the standards. Content standards specify the knowledge and skills that students should know and can do; performance standards determine which level of proficiency students demonstrate.

standardized tests: the tests that have the same questions, format, instructions, scoring, and reporting procedures for all test takers.

Steps to English Proficiency (STEP): a descriptor-based language assessment framework developed by the Ontario Ministry of Education to allow teachers to assess and track the English language development of English language learners in Ontario schools.

strategic competence: one aspect of communication competence that language users use to compensate for their lack of language (for example, grammar or vocabulary) by using other verbal- and non-verbal forms of language in order to communicate effectively.

summative assessment: an assessment designed to summarize students' overall achievement levels at a particular time.

syntactic cues: the use of sentence structure to help one understand the meaning of words.

systematic errors of measurement: the amount of error caused by non-random predictable events.

teacher moderation: collaborative assessment of samples of students' work among a group of teachers in order to gain a shared understanding of evaluation criteria and evidence for justifying teachers' judgments in assessment.

test bias: a systematic difference in scores between subgroups of students from different backgrounds, caused by linguistic or cultural factors that favor one group over another.

think-aloud: a teaching and research method whereby students verbalize their thoughts while completing a task or soon after completing the task.

trait: a distinguishing characteristic of one's personal nature.

unitary view (of language ability): the belief that language ability consists of a single global (general) trait.

validity evidence: evidence for justifying the claim about the extent to which a test provides appropriate and useful information about what a student can do. Different types of validity evidence include construct, content, and criterion validity (consisting of concurrent and predictive validity), and consequential validity.

validity: value-laden arguments about the extent to which interpretations and use of test scores are theoretically and empirically justifiable.

vertical scale: the scale used to track growth in achievement across grades.

washback: the positive and negative effects of testing on teaching and learning in the classroom.

References

Abedi, J. (2004). The No Child Left Behind Act and English language learners: Assessment and accountability issues. *Educational Researcher*, 33, 4–14.

Abedi, J. (2008). Measuring students' level of English proficiency: Educational significance and assessment requirements. *Educational Assessment*, 13, 193–214.

Abedi, J., C. H. Hofstetter, & C. Lord. (2004). Assessment accommodations for English language learners: Implications for policy-based empirical research. *Review of Educational Research*, 74(1), 1–28.

Alderson, J. C., C. Clapham, & D. Wall, (1995). *Language test construction and evaluation*. Cambridge: Cambridge University Press.

Alderson, J. C., & D. Wall, (1993). Does washback exist? *Applied Linguistics*, 14(2), 115–29.

American Educational Research Association, American Psychological Association, & National Council on Measurement in Education. (1999). *Standards for educational and psychological testing*. Washington, DC: American Educational Research Association.

American Federation of Teachers (1999). *Making standards matter*. Washington, DC: American Federation of Teachers.

Andrews, S. (1994). The washback effect of examinations: Its impact upon curriculum innovation in English language teaching. *Curriculum Forum*, 4(1), 44–58.

Andrews, S. (2004). Washback and curriculum innovation. In L. Cheng, Y. Watanabe, & A. Curtis (Eds.), *Context and method in washback research: The influence of language testing on teaching and learning* (pp. 37–50). Mahwah, NJ: Lawrence Erlbaum.

Anglin, J. M. (1993). Vocabulary development: A morphological analysis. *Monographs of the Society for Research in Child Development*, 58(10), Serial No. 238, 1–165.

Anstrom, K. (1997). *Academic achievement for secondary language minority students: Standards, measures and promising practices*. Retrieved from http://www.ncela.gwu.edu/files/rcd/BE021079/Academic_Achievement.pdf

Arter, J. A., & V. Spandel. (1992). Using portfolios of student work in instruction and assessment. *Educational Measurement: Issues and Practice*, 11(1), 36–44.

Assessment Reform Group (2002). *Assessment for learning: 10 principles*. Retrieved from: http://www.assessment-reform-group.org/CIE3.PDF

August, D. A., M., Calderon, & M. Carlo. (2002). Transfer of skills from Spanish to English: A study of young learners. Report for practitioners, parents and policy makers. Washington, DC: Center for Applied Linguistics.

August, D., & T. Shanahan. (Eds.). (2006). *Developing reading and writing in second language learners*. Report of the national literacy panel on language-minority children and youth. Mahwah, NJ: Lawrence Erlbaum Associates.

Bachman, L. F. (1990). *Fundamental considerations in language testing.* Oxford: Oxford University Press.

Bachman, L. F. (2005). Building and supporting a case for test use. *Language Assessment Quarterly,* 2(1), 1–34.

Bachman, L. F., & A. S. Palmer. (1996). *Language testing in practice.* Oxford: Oxford University Press.

Bachman, L. F., & A. S. Palmer. (2010). *Language assessment in practice: Developing language assessments and justifying their use in the real world.* Oxford: Oxford University Press.

Bailey, A. L. (2005). Cambridge Young Learners English (YLE) Tests. *Language Testing,* 22(2), 242–52.

Bailey, A. L. (Ed.). (2007). *The language demands of school: Putting academic English to the* test. New Haven, CT: Yale University Press.

Bailey, A. L., & F. A. Butler. (2003). *An evidentiary framework for operationalizing academic language for broad application to K–12 education: A design document* (CSE Tech. Rep. No. 611). Los Angeles: University of California, National Center for Research on Evaluation, Standards, and Student Testing (CRESST).

Bailey, A. L., , F. A., Butler, C. LaFramenta, & C. Ong. (2001). *Towards the characterization of academic language in upper elementary classrooms* (Final Deliverable to ERI/OBEMLA, Contract No. R305B960002). Los Angeles: University of California, National Center for Research on Evaluation, Standards, and Student Testing (CRESST).

Bailey, K. M. (1998). *Learning about language assessment: Dilemmas, decisions, and directions.* Pacific Grove, CA: Heinle & Heinle Publishers.

Bailey, K. M. (1999). *Washback in language testing. TOEFL Monograph Series,* Ms. 15. Princeton, NJ: Educational Testing Service.

Barootchi, N., & M. H. Keshavarz. (2002). Assessment of achievement through portfolios and teacher-made tests. *Educational Research,* 44(3), 279–88.

Barringer, C., & B. Gholson. (1979). Effects of type and combination of feedback upon conceptual learning by children: Implications for research in academic learning. *Review of Educational Research,* 49(3), 459–78.

Beck, I. L., & M. G. McKeown. (2001). Text talk: Capturing the benefits of read-aloud experiences for young children. *The Reading Teacher,* 55(1), 10–20.

Bennett, R. (2011). Formative assessment: a critical review. *Assessment in Education,* 18(1), 5– 25.

Berry, J. W., U., Kim, T. Minde, & D. Mok. (1987). Comparative studies of acculturative stress. *International Migration Review,* 21, 491–511.

Bialystok, E. (2001). *Bilingualism in development: Language, literacy and cognition.* Cambridge: Cambridge University Press.

Bialystok, E. (2002). Acquisition of literacy in bilingual children: A framework for research. *Language Learning,* 52(1), 159–99.

Bialystok, E., G. Luk, & E. Kwan. (2005). Bilingualism, biliteracy, and learning to read: Interactions among languages and writing systems. *Scientific Studies of Reading,* 9, 43–61.

Black-Allen, J. (2011). *Validity and fairness in accommodations, special provisions, and participation decisions on the Ontario Secondary School Literacy Test.* Unpublished Master's thesis. University of Toronto, Toronto, ON, CA.

Black, P., C. Harrison, C. Lee, B. Marshall, & D. Wiliam. (2003). *Assessment for learning: Putting it into practice.* Buckingham: Open University Press.

Blanche, P., & B. Merino. (1989). Self-assessment of foreign language skills: implications for teachers and researchers. *Language Learning,* 39, 313–40.

Black, P., & D. Wiliam. (1998). Assessment and classroom learning. *Assessment in Education,* 5, 7–74.

Bloom, B. S. (1969). Some theoretical issues relating to educational evaluation. In R. W. Tyler (Ed.), *Educational evaluation: new roles, new means: the 63rd yearbook of the National Society for the Study of Education (part II)* (Vol. 69(2), pp. 26–50). Chicago, IL: University of Chicago Press.

Bonk, W. J., & G. J. Ockey. (2003). A Many-Facet Rasch analysis of the second language group oral discussion task. *Language Testing* 20(1), 89–110.

Brennan, R. L. (2001). An essay on the history and future of reliability from the perspective of replications. *Educational Measurement,* 38, 295–317.

Brindley, G. (1998). Describing language development? Rating scales and second language acquisition. In L. F. Bachman & A. D. Cohen (Eds.), *Interfaces between SLA and language testing research* (pp. 112–14). Cambridge: Cambridge University Press.

Brindley, G. (2001). Outcomes-based assessment in practice: some examples and emerging insights. *Language Testing,* 18(4), 393–407.

Bronfenbrenner, U. (1992). Ecological systems theory. In V. Ross (Ed.), *Six theories of child development: Revised formulations and current issues* (pp. 187–249). London: Jessica Kingsley Publishers.

Brown, J. D., & T. Hudson. (1998). The alternatives in language assessment. *TESOL Quarterly* 32, 653–75.

Bunch, G. (2011). Testing English language learners under No Child Left Behind. *Language Testing,* 28(3), 323–341.

Butler, Y. G., & J. Lee. (2006). On-task versus off-task self-assessment among Korean elementary school students studying English. *The Modern Language Journal* 90(4), 506–18.

Butler, Y. G., & J. Lee. (2010). The effects of self-assessment among young learners of English. *Language Testing,* 27(1), 5–32.

Butler, F. A., & R. Stevens. (1997). *Accommodation strategies for English language learners on large-scale assessments: Student characteristics and other considerations* (CSE Tech. Rep. No. 448). Los Angeles: University of California, National Center for Research on Evaluation, Standards, and Student Testing.

Butler, F. A., & R. Stevens. (2001). Standardized assessment of the content knowledge of English language learners K–12: current trends and old dilemmas. *Language Testing,* 18(4), 409–27.

Byrnes, H. (2002). Toward academic-level foreign language abilities: Reconsidering foundational assumptions, exploring pedagogical options. In B. L. Leaver & B. Shekhtman (Eds.), *Developing professional-level language proficiency* (pp. 34–58). Cambridge: Cambridge University Press.

Cameron, L. (2001). *Teaching languages to young learners.* Cambridge: Cambridge University Press.

Cameron, L. (2002). Measuring vocabulary size in English as an additional language. *Language Teaching Research,* 6(2), 145–73.

Canale, M., & M. Swain. (1980). Theoretical bases of communicative approaches to second language teaching and testing. *Applied Linguistics, 1*(1), 1–47.

Case, R., & K. M. Obenchain. (2006). How to assess language in the social studies classroom. *Social Studies, 97*(1), 41–8.

Cazden, C. B. (2nd. Ed). (2001). Classroom discourse: *The language of teaching and learning.* Portsmouth, NH: Heinemann.

Centre for Information on Language Teaching and Research, Council of Europe (2001). *My languages portfolio.* CILT.

Chalhoub-Deville, M. (2003). Second language interaction: Current perspectives and future trends. *Language Testing, 20*(4), 369–83.

Chall, J. S., V. A. Jacobs, & L. Baldwin. (1990). *The reading crisis: Why poor children fall behind.* Cambridge, MA: Harvard University Press.

Chapelle, C. A. (2008). Utilizing technology in language assessment. In E. Shohamy (Ed.), *Encyclopedia of language education* (2nd Ed., pp. 123–34). Heidelberg, Germany: Springer.

Chen, C., & D. H. Uttal. (1988). Cultural values, parents' beliefs, and children's achievement in the United States and China. *Human Development, 31,* 351–58.

Cheng, L., D., Klinger, & Y. Zheng. (2009). Examining students after-school literacy activities and their literacy performance on the Ontario Secondary School Literacy Test. *Canadian Journal of Education, 32*(1), 118–48.

Cheng, L., & L. Qi. (2006). Description and examination of the National Matriculation English Test. *Language Assessment Quarterly, 3*(1), 53–70.

Cheng, L., S., Andrews, & Y. Yu. (2010). Impact and consequences of school-based assessment (SBA): Students and parents' views of SBA in Hong Kong. *Language Testing, 28*(2), 221–49.

Cheng, L., Y. Watanabe, & A. Curtis. (Eds.). (2004). *Washback in language testing: Research contexts and methods.* Mahwah, New Jersey: Lawrence Erlbaum Associates, Publishers.

Chik, A., & S. Besser, (2011). International language test taking among young learners: A Hong Kong case study. *Language Assessment Quarterly, 8,* 73–91.

Christie, F. (2012). *Language education throughout the school years: A functional perspective.* West Sussex, UK: Wiley-Blackwell.

Chun, C., & E. E. Jang. (2012). Dialogic encounters with early readers through mediated think-alouds. *Language and Literacy, 14*(3), 63–82.

Clarke, M., L. Abrams, & G. Madaus. (2001). The effects of and implications of high-stakes achievement tests for adolescence. In T. C. Urdan & F. Pajares (Eds.), *Adolescence and education: General issues in the education of adolescents* (pp. 201–29). Greenwich, CT: Information Age.

Clarke, S. (1998). *Targeting assessment in the primary classroom.* Bristol: Hodder & Stoughton.

Coelho, E. (2003). *Adding English: A guide to teaching in multilingual classrooms.* Toronto: Pippin.

Cohen, E. G. (1994). Restructuring the classroom: Conditions for productive small groups. *Review of Educational Research, 64,* 1–35.

Collier, V. P. (1987). Age and rate of acquisition of second language for academic purposes. *TESOL Quarterly, 21,* 617–41.

Coniam, D. (1995). Towards a common ability scale for Hong Kong English secondary-school forms. *Language Testing, 12*(2), 184–95.

Council of Europe. (2001). *Common European Framework of Reference for Languages: Learning, teaching, assessment.* Cambridge: Cambridge University Press.

Coxhead, A. (2006). *Essentials of teaching academic vocabulary.* Boston: Houghton Mifflin.

Cronbach, L. J. (1988). Five perspectives on validity argument. In H. Wainer & H. Braun (Eds.), *Test validity* (pp. 3–17). Hillsdale, NJ: Lawrence Erlbaum.

Cumming, A. (2009). Language assessment in education: Tests, curricula, and teaching. *Annual Review of Applied Linguistics, 29*, 90–100.

Cummins, J. (1979). Cognitive/academic language proficiency, linguistic interdependence, the optimum age question and some other matters. *Working Papers on Bilingualism, 19*, 121–9.

Cummins, J. (1981). Age on arrival and immigrant second language learning in Canada. A reassessment. *Applied Linguistics, 2*, 132–49.

Cummins, J. (1983). Language proficiency and academic achievement. In J.W. Oller (Ed.), *Issues in language testing research* (pp. 108–30). Rowley, MA: Newbury House.

Cummins, J. (1984). *Bilingualism and special education: Issues in assessment and pedagogy.* Clevedon, UK: Multilingual Matters.

Cummins, J. (1996). *Negotiating identities: Education for empowerment in a diverse society.* Ontario, CA: California Association for Bilingual Education.

Cummins, J. (2001). *Negotiating identities: Education for empowerment in a diverse society* (2nd ed.). Los Angeles: California Association for Bilingual Education.

Cummins, J., & E. Yee-Fun Man. (2007). Academic language: What is it and how do we acquire it? In J. Cummins & C. Davison (Eds.), *International handbook of English language teaching* (Vol. 2, pp. 797–810). New York: Springer.

Cummins, J., E. E. Jang, S. Stille, M.,Wagner, J. Byrd Clark, & M. Trahey. (2009). *Steps to English Proficiency (STEP): Validation study.* Final research report presented to the Ministry of Education. Modern Language Centre, OISE, Toronto, ON.

Cummins, J. & M. Swain. (1986). *Bilingualism in education: Aspects of theory, research and practice.* London: Longman.

Darling-Hammond, L. (1994). Performance-based assessment and educational equity. *Harvard Educational Review, 64*, 5–30.

Dann, R. (2002). *Promoting assessment as learning: Improving the learning process.* London: Routledge Falmer.

Danzak, R. L. (2011). Defining identities through multiliteracies: ELL teens narrate their immigration experiences as graphic stories. *Journal of Adolescent and Adult Literacy, 55*, 187–96.

Davidson, F., & B. Lynch. (2002). *Testcraft: A teacher's guide to writing and using language test specifications.* New Haven, CT: Yale University Press.

Davison, C. (2004). The contradictory culture of classroom-based assessment: Teacher assessment practices in senior secondary English. *Language Testing, 21*(3), 305–34.

Duff, P. (2001). Language, literacy, content, and (pop) culture: Challenges for ESL students in mainstream courses. *Canadian Modern Language Review, 59*, 103–32.

Dweck, C. S. (1986). Motivational processes affecting learning. *American Psychologist, 41*, 1040–8.

Dweck, C. S., & E. L. Leggett. (1988). A social-cognitive approach to motivation and personality. *Psychological Review*, *95*(2), 256–73.

East, M., & A. Scott. (2011). Assessing the foreign language proficiency of high school students in New Zealand: From the traditional to the innovative. *Language Assessment Quarterly*, *8*, 179–89.

Earl, L., & S. Katz. (2006). *Rethinking classroom assessment with purpose in mind.* Western Northern Canadian Protocol.

Eccles, J. S. (1993). School and family effects on the ontogeny of children's interests, self-perceptions, and activity choices. In R. Dienstbier, & J. E. Jacobs (Eds.), *Developmental perspectives on motivation* (Vol. 40, pp. 145–208). Lincoln: University of Nebraska Press.

Edelenbos, P. & A. Kubanek-German. (2004). Teacher assessment: the concept of "diagnostic competence." *Language Testing*, *21*, 259–83.

Elmore, R. F. (2002). *Bridging the gap between standards and achievement: The imperative for professional development in education.* Washington, DC: Albert Shanker Institute.

Ericsson, K. A., & H. A. Simon. (1993). *Protocol analysis.* Cambridge, MA: The MIT Press.

Ferris, D. R. (2003). Response to student writing: Implications for second language students. Mahwah, NJ: Lawrence Erlbaum Associates.

Field, J. (2011). Cognitive validity. In L. Taylor (Ed.), *Examining speaking.* Cambridge: Cambridge University Press.

Fairbairn, S. B., & J. Fox. (2009). Inclusive achievement testing for linguistically and culturally diverse test takers: Essential considerations for test developers and decision makers. *Educational Measurement: Issues and Practice*, *28*(1), 10–24.

Fox, J., & L. Cheng. (2007). Did we take the same test? Differing accounts of the Ontario Secondary School Literacy Test by first and second language test takers. *Assessment in Education: Principles, Policy & Practice*, *14*(1), 9–26.

Frederiksen, J., & A. Collins. (1989). A systems approach to educational testing. *Educational Researcher*, *18*(9), 27–32.

Fulcher, G. (1996). Does thick description lead to smart tests? A data-based approach to rating scale construction. *Language Testing*, *13*(2), 208–38.

Fulcher, G., & F. Davidson. (2010). Test architecture, test retrofit. *Language Testing*, *26*(1), 123–44.

Gan, Z. (2010). Interaction in group oral assessment: A case of higher- and lower-scoring students. *Language Testing*, *27*(4), 585–602.

Gardner, H. (1983). *Frames of mind.* New York: Basic Book Inc.

Gardner, H., & T. Hatch. (1989). Multiple intelligences go to school: Educational implications of the theory of multiple intelligences. *Educational Researcher*, *18*(8), 4–9.

Gardner, R. C., P. F. Tremblay, & A.-M. Masgoret. (1997). Toward a full model of second language learning: An empirical investigation. *Modern Language Journal*, *81*, 344–62.

Gass, S. M., & A. Mackey. (2000). *Stimulated recall methodology in second language research.* Mahwah, NJ: Lawrence Erlbaum Associates.

Genesee, F., K. Lindholm-Leary, W. Saunders, & D. Christian. (2005). English language learners in U.S. schools: An overview of research findings. *Journal of Education for Students Placed at Risk, 10*(4), 363–85.

Genesee, F., J. Paradis, & M. Crago. (Eds.). (2004). *Dual language development and disorders: A handbook on bilingualism and second language learning.* Baltimore, Maryland: Brookes Publishing.

Genesee, F. & J. A. Upshur. (1996). *Classroom-based evaluation in second language education.* New York: Cambridge University Press.

Geva, E. (2000). Issues in the assessment of reading disabilities in L2 children—beliefs and research evidence. *Dyslexia, 6*, 13–28.

Geva, E. (2006). Learning to read in a second language: Research, implications, and recommendations for services. In R. E. Tremblay, R. G. Barr, & R. D. Peters (Eds.), *Encyclopedia on early childhood development* (pp. 1–12). Montreal, Quebec: Center of Excellence for Early childhood Development. Retrieved 10 July 2–13 from http://www.child-encyclopedia.com/documents/GevaANGxp.pdf

Gibbons, P. (1998). Classroom talk and the learning of new registers in a second language. *Language and Education, 12*(2), 99–118.

Gibbons, P. (2006). *Bridging discourses in the ESL classroom.* New York, NY: Continuum.

Glaser R. (1991). The maturing of the relationship between the science of learning and cognition and educational practice. *Learning and Instruction, 1*, 129–44.

Goodwin, A., A. C. Huggins, M. C. Carlo, et al. (2012). Development and validation of extract the base: an English derivational morphology test for third through fifth grade monolingual students and Spanish speaking English language learners. *Language Testing Journal, 29*(2), 261–85.

Gottardo, A. (2002). Language and reading skills in bilingual Spanish–English speakers. *Topics in Language Disorders, 23*, 42–66.

Graham, S., & D. Perin. (2007). *Writing next: Effective strategies to improve writing of adolescents in middle and high school.* A Report to the Carnegie Corporation of New York.

Green, C., L. Hamnett, & S. Green. (2010). Ontario Ministry of Education. Growing success: Assessment, evaluation, and reporting in Ontario schools. Retrieved 26 August 2011 from http://www.edu.gov.on.ca/eng/policyfunding/growsuccess.pdf

Grosjean, F. (2001). The bilingual's language modes. In J. Nicol (Ed.), *One mind, two languages: Bilingual language processing* (pp. 1–22). Oxford: Blackwell.

Guilford, J. P. (1946). New standards for test evaluation. *Educational and Psychological Measurement, 6*, 427–39.

Gunderson, L. (2007). Where have all the immigrants gone? *Contact, 33*(2), 118–128. Retrieved February 7, 2012, from http://www.teslontario.org/uploads/publications/researchsymposium/ResearchSymposium2007.pdf

Guthrie, J. T. (2001, March). *Contexts for engagement and motivation in reading.* Reading Online. http://www.readingonline.org/articles/handbook/guthrie/index.html

Haertel, E. H. (1999). Validity arguments for high-stakes testing: In search of the evidence. *Educational Measurement: Issues and Practice, 18*(4), 5–9.

Hamp-Lyons, L. (1991). Scoring procedures for ESL contexts. In Hamp-Lyons, L. (Ed.). *Assessing second language writing in academic contexts* (pp. 241–76). Norwood NJ: Ablex.

Hamp-Lyons, L. (2007). The impact of testing practices on teaching: Ideologies and alternatives. In J. Cummins & C. Davison (Eds.), *International handbook of English language teaching* (pp. 487–504). New York: Springer.

Hamp-Lyons, L., & W. Condon. (2000). *Assessing the portfolio: Issues for research, theory and practice.* Cresskill, NJ: Hampton Press.

Hargreaves, A. (1997). Rethinking educational change: Going deeper and wider in the quest for success. In A. Hargreaves, (Ed.), *Rethinking educational change with heart and mind: 1997 ASCD Yearbook* (pp. 1–26). Alexandria, Virginia: Association for Supervision and Curriculum Development.

Hasselgreen, A. (2003). *Bergen 'Can Do' project.* Strasbourg: Council of Europe. Retrieved from: http://blog.educastur.es/portfolio/files/2008/04/bergen-can-do-project.pdf

Hasselgreen, A. (2005). Assessing the language of young learners. *Language Testing,* 22(3), 337–354.

Hattie, J., & H. Timperley. (2007). The power of feedback. *Review of Educational Research,* 77(1), 81–112.

He, L. & Y. Dai. (2006). A corpus-based investigation into the validity of the CET-SET group discussion. *Language Testing,* 23(3), 370–401.

Heilmann, J., J. Miller, & A. Nockerts. (2010). Sensitivity of narrative organization measures using narrative retells produced by young school-age children. *Language Testing,* 27(4), 603–626.

Hoska, D. M. (1993). Motivating learners through CBI feedback: Developing a positive learner perspective. In Dempsey, V., & G. C. Sales (Eds.), *Interactive instruction and feedback* (pp. 105–32). Englewood Cliffs, NJ: Educational Technology Publications.

Hudson, T., & B. Lynch. (1984). A criterion-referenced measurement approach to ESL achievement testing. *Language Testing,* 1(2), 171–210.

Hume, K. (2008). *Start where they are: Differentiating for success with the young adolescent.* Toronto: Pearson.

James, M. (2000). Measured lives: The rise of assessment as the engine of change in English schools. *The Curriculum Journal,* 11(3), 343–64.

Jang, E. E. (2002). *In search of folk fairness in language testing.* Unpublished Master's thesis, University of Illinois at Urbana-Champaign.

Jang, E. E. (2004). Voices from teachers at a failing school. Panel presentation to session on "*Engaging with accountability.*" American Evaluation Association Conference, Atlanta, GA.

Jang, E. E. (2005). *A validity narrative: Effects of reading skills diagnosis on teaching and learning in the context of NG-TOEFL.* Unpublished PhD dissertation, Urbana: University of Illinois at Urbana-Champaign.

Jang, E. E. (2009). Using think-aloud protocols to understand elementary school students' cognitive strategy use in literacy and numeracy tasks. In C. Rolheiser (Ed.), *Partnerships for professional learning: Literacy and numeracy initiatives* (pp. 34–42). Toronto, ON: OISE Initial Teacher Education Program.

Jang, E. E. (2010a). Implications of assessing school-aged L2 students in Ontario. Paper presented at Canadian Association of Language Assessment Symposium, Montreal, Ontario.

Jang, E. E. (2010b). Thinking on think-alouds. *American Educational Research Association Division D Newsletter,* 19(2), 9.

Jang, E. E., J. Cummins, M. Wagner, S. Stille, M. Dunlop, & J. Starkey. (2011). *2011 Field Research on Steps to English Proficiency*. Final research report presented to the Ministry of Education. Modern Language Centre, OISE, Toronto, ON: Authors.

Jang, E. E., M. Dunlop, G. Park, & E. Vander Boom. (2013). Centrality of cognitively diagnostic feedback in language learning classrooms. Paper presented at the Centre for Educational Research on Languages and Literacies Colloquium, University of Toronto, Canada.

Jang, E. E., M. Dunlop, M. Wagner, Y. Kim, & Z. Gu. (2013). Elementary school ELLs' reading skill profiles using cognitive diagnosis modeling: Roles of length of residence and home language environment. *Language Learning, 63*(3), 400–36.

Jang, E. E., & K. Ryan. (2003). Bridging gaps among curriculum, teaching and learning, and assessment [Review of the book *Large-scale assessment: Dimensions, dilemmas, and policy*]. *Journal of Curriculum Studies, 35*(4), 499–512.

Jessner, U. (2008). Multi-competence approaches to second-language proficiency development in multilingual education. In J. Cummins & N. H. Hornberger (Eds.), *Encyclopedia of language and education* (2nd ed.), Vol. 5: Bilingual Education, (pp.1–13). Springer.

Jiménez, R. M., & M. Terrazas Gallego. (2008). The receptive vocabulary of English foreign language young learners. *Journal of English Studies, 5*, 173–91.

Kariya, T. (2002). Kyouiku kaikaku no gensou [Disillusion of educational reforms]. Tokyo: Chikumashobou.

Kenyon, D. M., D. MacGregor, D. Li, & H. G. Cook. (2011). Issues in vertical scaling of a K–12 English language proficiency test. *Language Testing, 28*(3), 383–400.

Kiely, R., & P. Rea-Dickens. (2005). *Program evaluation in language education*. New York: Palgrave Macmillan.

Kim, Y.-H., & E. E. Jang. (2009). Differential functioning of reading subskills on the OSSLT for L1 and ELL students: A multidimensionality model-based DBF/DIF approach. *Language Learning, 59*(4), 825–65.

Kletzien, S., & M. Bednar. (1990). Dynamic assessment for at-risk readers. *Journal of Reading, 33*(7), 528–33.

Kunnan, A. J. (2005). Language assessment from a wider context. In E. Hinkel (Ed.), *Handbook of research in second language learning* (pp. 779–94). Mahwah, NJ: LEA.

Lam, C.-C., E. S. C. Ho, & N.-Y. Wong. (2002). Parents' beliefs and practices in education in Confucian heritage cultures: The Hong Kong case. *Journal of Southeast Asian Education, 3*(1), 99–114.

Lantolf, J. P., & M. E. Poehner. (2004). Dynamic assessment: Bringing the past into the future. *Journal of Applied Linguistics, 1*, 49–74.

Lazaraton, A. (2002). *A qualitative approach to the validation of oral language tests*. Cambridge: Cambridge University Press.

Leung, C. (2009). Book review: Penny McKay (2006) Assessing young language learners. *Language Testing, 26*(1), 145–49.

Leung, C., & J. Lewkowicz. (2008). Assessing second/additional language of diverse populations. In E Shohamy & N. H. Hornberger (Eds.), *Encyclopedia of language and education* (pp. 301–17, 2nd ed.), Vol. 7: *Language testing and assessment*. New York: Springer Science/Business Media.

Linn, R. (2000). Assessments and accountability. *Educational Researcher, 29*(2), 4–16.

Linn, R. L., E. L. Baker, & S. B. Dunbar. (1991). Complex performance-based assessment: Expectations and validation criteria. *Educational Researcher*, 20(8), 15–21.

Liski, E., & S. Puntanen. (1983). A study of statistical foundations of group conversation tests in spoken English. *Language Learning*, 33, 225–46.

Little, D. (2002). The European Language Portfolio: structure, origins, implementation and challenges. *Language Teaching*, 35, 182–89.

Little, D. (2005). The Common European Framework of Reference and the English Language Portfolio: Involving learners and their judgements in the assessment process. *Language Testing*, 22(3), 321–36.

Lipka, O., L. S. Siegel, & R. Vukovic. (2005). The literacy skills of English language learners in Canada. *Learning Disabilities Research and Practice*, 20(1), 39–49.

Llosa, L. (2001).The impact of high-stakes testing on minority students. In M. Kornhaber & G. Orfield (Eds.), *Raising standards or raising barriers: Inequality and high-stakes testing in public education* (pp. 85–106). New York: Century Foundation.

Llosa, L. (2008). Building and supporting a validity argument for a standards-based classroom assessment of English proficiency based on teacher judgments. *Educational Measurement: Issues and Practice*, 27(3), 32–42.

Llosa, L. (2007). Validating a standards-based classroom assessment of English proficiency: A multitrait-multimethod approach. *Language Testing*, 24(4), 489–515.

Llosa, L. (2011). Standards-based classroom assessments of English proficiency: A review of issues, current developments, and future directions for research. *Language Testing*, 28(3), 367–82.

Lynch, B., & P. Shaw. (2005). Portfolios, power, and ethics. *TESOL Quarterly*, 39(2), 263–97.

Madaus, G. F. (1994). A technological and historical consideration of equity issues associated with proposals to change the nation's testing policy. *Harvard Educational Review*, 64(1), 76–95.

Madaus, G., & M. Clarke. (2001). The impact of high-stakes testing on minority students. In M. Kornhaber & G. Orfield (Eds.), *Raising standards or raising barriers: Inequality and high stakes testing in public education* (pp. 85–106). New York: Century Foundation.

Markstrom-Adams, C. (1992). A consideration of intervening factors in adolescent identity formation. In G.R. Adams, R. Montemayor, & T. Gullotta (Eds.), *Advances in adolescent development: Vol. 4. Adolescent identity formation* (pp. 173–92). Newbury Park, CA: Sage.

McGloin, M. (2011). *An achievement gap revealed: A mixed method research investigation of Canadian-born English language learners*. Master's dissertation. University of Toronto theses database at http://hdl.handle.net/1807/30098, ON.

McKay, P. (2006). *Assessing young language learners*. Cambridge: Cambridge University Press.

McKay, P. (2000). On ESL standards for school-age learners, *Language Testing*, 17, 185–214.

McKay, P., & G. Brindley. (2007). Educational reform and ESL assessment in Australia: New roles and new tensions. *Language Assessment Quarterly*, 4(1), 69–84.

McKay, P., C. Hudson, & M. Sapuppo. (1994). *The NLLA ESL Bandscales. ESL development: Language and literacy in schools: Vol 2.* Canberra: National Languages and Literacy Institute of Australia.

McKay, P., & A. Scarino. (1991). *The ESL framework of stages.* Melbourne: Curriculum Corporation.

McKenna, M. C., & D. J. Kear. (1990). Measuring attitude towards reading: A new tool for teachers. *The Reading Teacher, 43,* 626–39.

McNamara, T. & C. Roever. (2006). *Language testing: The social dimension.* Malden, MA & Oxford: Blackwell.

Meltzer, J., & E. T. Hamann. (2005). *Meeting the literacy development needs of adolescent English language learners through content-area learning, Part two: Focus on classroom teaching and learning strategies.* The Education Alliance.

Messick, S. (1989). Validity. In R. L. Linn (Ed.), *Educational Measurement* (3rd ed., pp. 13–104). New York: Macmillan.

Messick, S. (1994). The interplay of evidence and consequences washback in the validation of performance assessments. *Educational Researcher, 23*(2), 13–23.

Messick, S. (1996). Validity and washback in language testing. *Language Testing, 13,* 241–256.

Messick, S. (1998). *Consequences of test interpretation and use: The fusion of validity and values in psychological assessment.* ETS Research Report-98–48. Educational Testing Service.

Miller, G. A. (1999). On knowing a word. *Annual Review of Psychology, 50,* 1–19.

Moss, P. A. (1994). Can there be validity without reliability? *Educational Researcher, 23*(2), 5–12.

Moss, P. A. (2004). The meaning and consequences of 'reliability'. *Journal of Educational and Behavioral Statistics, 29*(2), 245–49.

Nagy, W., & R. Anderson. (1984). The number of words in printed school English. *Reading Research Quarterly, 19,* 304–30.

Nation, I. S. P. (1993). Measuring readiness for simplified material: A test of the first 1,000 words of English. In M. L. Tickoo (Ed.), *Simplification: Theory and application.* RELC Anthology Series 31, 193–203.

Nation, I. S. P. (2001). *Learning vocabulary in another language.* Cambridge: Cambridge University Press.

National Institute of Child Health and Human Development. (2000). Report of the National Reading Panel. Teaching children to read: An evidence-based assessment of the scientific research literature on reading and its implications for reading instruction: Reports of the subgroups (NIH Publication No. 00–4754). Washington, DC: US Government Printing Office.

National Research Council (2001). *Knowing what students know: The science and design of educational assessment.* Washington, DC: National Academy Press.

Neugebauer, S. R. (2008). Editor's review of double the work and the language demands of school. *Harvard Education Review, 78*(1), 252–64.

Nichols, P. D., J. L. Meyers, & K. S. Burling. (2009). A framework for evaluating and planning assessments intended to improve student achievement. *Educational Measurement: Issues and Practice, 28*(3), 14–23.

Nicholls, J. (1984). Conceptions of ability and achievement motivation. In R. Ames & C. Ames (Eds.), *Research on motivation in education: Student motivation* (Vol. 1, pp. 39–73). New York: Academic Press.

Norton, B., & P. Stein. (1995). Why the "Monkeys Passage" bombed: Tests, genres, and teaching. *Harvard Educational Review*, 65(1), 50–65.

Nurss, J. R., & R. A. Hough. (1992). Reading and the ESL student. In S. J. Samuels & A.E. Farstrup (Eds.), *What research has to say about reading instruction* (pp. 277–313). Newark, DE: International Reading Association.

Ockey, G. J. (2009). The effects of group members' personalities on a test taker's L2 group oral discussion test scores. *Language Testing*, 26(2), 161–86.

Oller, J. W. (1976). Evidence for a general language proficiency factor. *Die Neueren Sprachen*, 76, 165–74.

O'Loughlin, K. (2001) The equivalence of direct and semi-direct speaking tests, Studies in Language Testing Volume 13. Cambridge, Cambridge University Press.

O'Malley, J. M., & L. Valdez Pierce. (1996). *Authentic assessment for English language learners: Practical approaches for teachers*. New York: Addison-Wesley.

Ortiz, A. A., & S. B. García. (1989). Profile of Language Dominance and Proficiency. Retrieved from http://www.k12.wa.us/SPECIALED/pubdocs/culturally_linguistically_diverse/profile_language_dominance_proficiency.pdf

Ortiz, A. A. & J. R. Yates. (2001). A framework for serving English language learners with disabilities. *Journal of Special Education Leadership 14*(2), 72–80.

Oscarson, M. (1989). Self-assessment of language proficiency: Rationale and applications. *Language Testing*, 6(1), 1–13.

O'Sullivan, B. (2011). Language Testing. In J. Simpson (Ed). *Routledge Handbook of Applied Linguistics*. Oxford: Routledge.

Paradis, J., E. Nicoladis, M. Crago, & F. Genesee. (2011). Bilingual children's acquisition of past tense: A usage-based approach. *Journal of Child Language*, 38, 554–578.

Paris, S. G., & R. S. Newman. (1990). Developmental aspects of self-regulated learning. *Educational Psychologist*, 25, 87–102.

Paris, S. G. & A. Paris. (2001) Classroom applications of research on self-regulated learning. *Educational Psychologist*, 36(2), 89–101.

Pennock-Roman, M. & C. Rivera. (2011). Mean effects of test accommodations for ELLs and non ELLs: A meta-analysis of experimental studies. *Educational Measurement: Issues and Practice*, 30(3), 10–28.

Perclová, R. (2006). *The implementation of European Language Portfolio pedagogy in Czech primary and lower-secondary schools: beliefs and attitudes of pilot teachers and learners*. Unpublished dissertation. University of Joensuu.

Pinter, A. (2006). *Teaching young language learners*. Oxford: Oxford University Press.

Popham, J. W. (1999). Where large-scale assessment is heading and why it shouldn't. *Educational Measurement: Issues and Practice*, 18(3), 13–17.

Phillips, E. M. (1999). The effects of language anxiety on students' oral test performance and attitudes. *The Modern Language Journal*, 76(1), 14–26.

Qi, L. (2003). *The intended washback of the National Matriculation English Test in China: Intentions and reality*. Unpublished PhD dissertation. Hong Kong: The City University of Hong Kong.

RAND Reading Study Group (2002). *Reading for understanding: Toward an R &D program in reading comprehension.* Report prepared for the Office of Educational Research and Improvement. Santa Monica: RAND.

Rea-Dickens, P. (2004). Understanding teachers as agents of assessment. *Language Testing, 21,* 249–58.

Read, J. (2004). Research in teaching vocabulary. *Annual Review of Applied Linguistics, 24,* 146–61.

Ross, S. J. (1998). Self-assessment in second language testing: A meta-analysis and experiment with analysis of experiential factors. *Language Testing, 15*(1), 1–20.

Rowe, M. B. (1974). Wait time and rewards as instructional variables, their influence on language, logic and fate control: Parts I and II. *Journal of Research in Science Teaching, 11,* 81–94, 291–308.

Sadler, D. R. (1989). Formative assessment and the design of instructional systems. *Instructional Science, 18*(2), 119–44.

Sasaki, M. (2008). The 150-year history of English language assessment in Japanese education. *Language Testing, 25*(1), 63–83.

Saunders, W. M., & C. Goldenberg. (2010). Research to guide English Language Development instruction. In D. Dolson, & L. Burnham-Massey (Eds.), *Improving education for English Learners: Research-based approaches* (pp. 21–81). Sacramento, CA: CDE Press.

Scarcella, R. (2003). *Academic English: A conceptual framework.* The University of California Linguistic Minority Research Institute.

Schleppegrell, M., & C. O'Hallaron. (2011). Teaching academic language in L2 secondary settings. *Annual Review of Applied Linguistics, 31,* 3–18.

Schmitt, N., D. Schmitt, & C. Clapham (2001). Developing and exploring the behaviour of two new versions of the vocabulary level test. *Language Testing, 18*(1), 55–88.

Schoonen, R., A. van Gelderen, R. Stoel, J. Hulstijn, K. De Glopper. (2011). Modeling the development of L1 and EFL writing proficiency of secondary-school students. *Language Learning, 61,* 31–79.

Schoonen, R., & M. Verhallen. (2008). The assessment of deep word knowledge in young first and second language learners. *Language Testing, 25*(2), 211–36.

Scott, C. (2007). Stakeholder perceptions of test impact. *Assessment in Education, 14*(1), 27–49.

Scriven, M. (1967). *The methodology of evaluation.* Washington, DC: American Educational Research Association.

Shanahan, T. (2004). Improving reading achievement in high school and middle school: Structures and reforms. In D. Alvermann, & D. S. Strickland (Eds.), *Bridging the achievement gap: Improving literacy for pre-adolescent & adolescent learners grades 4–12* (pp. 43–55). New York: Teachers College Press.

Shepard, L. A. (2000). The role of assessment in a learning culture. *Educational Researcher, 29*(7), 4–14.

Shewbridge, C., E. E. Jang, P. Matthews, & P. Santiago. (2011). *OECD reviews on evaluation and assessment in education: Denmark.* OECD Publishing.

Shohamy, E. (1996). Language testing: Matching assessment procedures with language knowledge. In M. Birenbaum & F. J. R. C. Dochy (Eds.), *Alternatives in assessment of achievements, learning processes, and prior knowledge* (pp. 143–60). Dordrecht, Netherlands: Kluwer Academic.

Shohamy, E. (2001). *The power of tests: A critical perspective of the uses of language tests.* Harlow, UK: Longman.

Shohamy, E., O. Inbar-Lourie, & M. E. Poehner. (2008). Investigating assessment perceptions and practices in the advanced foreign language classroom (Report No. 1108). University Park, PA: Center for Advanced Language Proficiency Education and Research.

Shute, V. J. (2008). Focus on formative feedback. *Review of Educational Research,* 78(1), 153–189.

Sireci, S. G., S. Li, & S. Scarpati. (2003). The effects of test accommodation on test performance: A review of the literature (Center for Educational Assessment Research Rep. No. 485). Amherst: University of Massachusetts.

Smith, M., & J. Wilhelm. (2002). Reading don't fix no Chevys: Literacy in the lives of young men. Portsmouth, NH: Heinemann.

Snow, C. E., H. Cancino, P. Gonzalez, & E. Shriberg. (1987). Second language learners' formal definitions: An oral language correlate of school literacy (Technical Report No. 5). Los Angeles: University of California, Center for Language Education and Research.

Solano-Flores, G. (2008). Who is given tests in what language by whom, when, and where? The need for probabilistic views of language in the testing of English language learners. *Educational Researcher,* 37(4), 189–199.

Stanovich, K. E. (1986). Matthew effects in reading: Some consequences of individual differences in the acquisition of literacy. *Reading Research Quarterly,* 21, 360–407.

Stevens, R. A., F. A. Butler, & M. Castellon-Wellington,.(2000). Academic language and content assessment: Measuring the progress of ELLs (CSE Tech. Rep. No. 552). Los Angeles: University of California, National Center for Research on Evaluation, Standards, and Student Testing (CRESST).

Stiggins, R. J. (1995). Assessment literacy for the 21st century. *The Phi Delta Kappan,* 77(3), 238–45.

Swain, M., & S. Lapkin. (1998). Interaction and second language learning: Two adolescent French immersion students working together. *Modern Language Journal,* 83, 320–37.

Tabors, P., & C. Snow. (1994). English as a second language in preschools. In F. Genesee (Ed.), *Educating second language children: The whole child, the whole curriculum, the whole community* (pp.103–25). New York: Cambridge University Press.

Taylor, L., & N. Saville. (2002). Developing English language tests for young learners. Research Notes, 7, 2–5. Cambridge: Cambridge University Press.

Teachers of English to Speakers of Other Languages (TESOL), Inc. (1997). *ESL standards for pre-K–12 students.* Alexandria, VA: Author.

Torrance, H., & J. Pryor. (1998). *Investigating formative assessment: Teaching, learning and assessment in the classroom.* Buckingham, UK: Open University Press.

United States Department of Education (2001). The No Child Left Behind Act of 2001. Retrieved from http://www2.ed.gov/policy/elsec/leg/esea02/index.html

van Wyk, A. L., & W. Greyling. (2008). Developing reading in a first year academic literacy course. *Stellenbosch Papers in Linguistics*, 38, 205–19.

Vasiljevic, Z., (2010). Dictogloss as an interactive method of teaching listening comprehension to L2 learners. English *Language Teaching*, 3(1), 41–52.

Vygotsky, L. (1986). *Thought and language*. Cambridge, MA: MIT Press.

Wall, D. (1997). Impact and washback in language testing. In C. Clapham & D. Corson (Eds.), *Encyclopedia of language and education: Vol. 7. Language testing and assessment* (pp. 291–302). Dordrecht: Kluwer Academic.

Wall, D., & J. C. Alderson. (1993). Examining washback: The Sri Lankan impact study. *Language Testing*, 10(1), 41–69.

Wajnryb, R. (1990). *Grammar dictation*. Oxford: Oxford University Press.

Warschauer, M., & P. Grimes. (2008). Automated writing assessment in the classroom. *Pedagogies: An International Journal*, 3, 22–36.

Warschauer, M., & P. Ware. (2006). Electronic feedback and second language writing. In K. Hyland & F. Hyland (Eds.) (pp. 105–22), *Feedback and second language writing*. Cambridge: Cambridge University Press.

Wechsler, D. (2009). *Wechsler Individual Achievement Test—Third Edition*. San Antonio, TX: NCS Pearson.

Weigle, S. C. (2002). Assessing writing assessment in the classroom. Cambridge: Cambridge University Press.

Watt, D., & H. Roessingh. (2001). The dynamics of ESL drop-out: Plus ça change... *Canadian Modern Language Review*, 58(2), 203–23.

Weir, C. (2005). *Language testing and validation: an evidence-based approach*. Basingstoke, Palgrave Macmillan.

Woodcock, R. W., K. S. McGrew, & N. Mather. (2001). *Woodcock-Johnson III*. Itasca, IL: Riverside Publishing.

World-Class Instructional Design and Assessment (WIDA). (2012). ACCESS for ELLs®. Retrieved from http://www.wida.us/assessment/access/

Wu, J. (2012). GEPT and English language teaching and testing in Taiwan. *Language Assessment Quarterly*, 9, 11–25.

Xi, X. (2010). Automated scoring and feedback systems: Where are we and where are we heading? *Language Testing*, 27(3), 291–300.

York District School Board (2012). Board improvement work plan for student achievement and well-being. Retrieved from http://www.yrdsb.edu.on.ca/pdfs/w/BoardImprovementPlan.pdf

Zainal, A. J. (2012). Validation of an ESL writing test in a Malaysian secondary school context. *Assessing Writing*, 17, 1–17.

Zimmerman, B. J. (1990). Self-regulated learning and academic achievement: An overview. *Educational Psychologist*, 25, 3–17.

Zwiers, J. (2007). Teacher practices and perspectives for developing academic language. *International Journal of Applied Linguistics*, 17(1), 93–116.

Index